When Your Way Gets Dark

When Your Way Gets Dark

A Rhetoric of the Blues

Jeffrey Carroll

Parlor Press
West Lafayette, Indiana
www.parlorpress.com

Parlor Press LLC, West Lafayette, Indiana 47906

© 2005 by Parlor Press
All rights reserved.
Printed in the United States of America

SAN: 254-8879

Library of Congress Cataloging-in-Publication Data

Carroll, Jeffrey, 1950-
 When your way gets dark : a rhetoric of the blues / Jeffrey Carroll.
  p. cm.
 Includes bibliographical references and index.
 ISBN 1-932559-38-8 (pbk. : alk. paper) -- ISBN 1-932559-39-6 (hardcover : alk. paper) -- ISBN 1-932559-40-X (Adobe ebook) 1. Blues (Music)--History and criticism. I. Title.

ML3521.C37 2005
781.643--dc22
                                2004030507

Printed on acid-free paper.

Cover photograph: © 2003 by Dick Waterman. From *Between Midnight and Day: The Last Unpublished Blues Archive*, Thunder's Mouth Press, 2003. Used by permission.

Parlor Press, LLC is an independent publisher of scholarly and trade titles in print and multimedia formats. This book is also available in cloth, as well as in Adobe eBook format, from Parlor Press on the WWW at http://www.parlorpress.com. For submission information or to find out about Parlor Press publications, write to Parlor Press, 816 Robinson St., West Lafayette, Indiana, 47906, or e-mail editor@parlorpress.com.

To Ruth

Contents

Acknowledgments *ix*
Introduction: Working (into) the Blues *xi*

1 Writing (on) the Blues *3*

2 Reading (for) the Blues *36*

3 Cooking (with) the Blues *71*

Nine Performances of the Blues *73*

    Charlie Patton *73*
    Skip James *80*
    Memphis Minnie *87*
    Little Walter *94*
    Jimi Hendrix *102*
    J.B. Lenoir *109*
    B.B. King *116*
    Muddy Waters *123*
    Eric Clapton *130*

4 Teaching (by) the Blues *137*

Works Cited *167*
Index *173*

Acknowledgments

My parents, Glenn Arthur Carroll and Doris Alva Carroll, helped me love music; I honor their role first in this modest project of mine. My brothers and sisters, all five of them (Audrey, David, Alan, Robyn and Holly), are themselves music-lovers, and I, being the youngest, fell luckily under their influence and the sounds that issued from their rooms and cars and stages; I thank them for such a rich education. My friends have always kept the blues pot boiling, too; I mention Gary Ashbrook especially for his love of the roots music that is so important to the life of America. My colleagues at the University of Hawai'i at Manoa have always supported me and my varied research projects; for this book I especially want to thank Glenn Man and Cristina Bacchilega, department chairs whose unfailing commitment to faculty research swept me up and helped me complete my work. Susan Schultz read an early draft of this book; her comments were typically incisive and helped me immensely in the revision stage. Arnold Edelstein was my mentor in many things, and a colleague whose support was constant and bracing. Thanks also to Thomas Rickert for his early and positive reading of the book; his suggestions were helpful in the revision stages. My editor and publisher, David Blakesley, has brought this book to completion with skill, patience, and a personable mastery of the publishing art and craft.

   I acknowledge finally the blues makers, the blues lovers, men and women of the blues everywhere who speak to one another through the power and beauty of the blues—and to whose danceable conversation I hope this book contributes.

Rhetoric moves the soul with a movement which cannot finally be justified logically.

—*Richard Weaver*

Introduction: Working (into) the Blues

My interest in the rhetoric of the blues began on a cool September night in Chicago in 1994. I had gone with two friends to a club on the north side and found myself seated at a table about ten feet from the stage. We sat on stools and drank beer from bottles and said nothing at all through the thick air of the place that seemed to vibrate like water in a washtub with every heavy, thick pulse of the music. The keyboard player was a young white man who was earnest and looked to his guitarist with a furrowed brow. The sound of his Fender electric bounced off the low ceiling of the club with a high clashing sound that reminded me of stage thunder. The rest of the band was black. The bassist's eyes would go from the keyboard player to the drummer to the leader and then back up to the low ceiling as if he had put some sheet music there and was checking a figure, but his eyes were more in time to the music than with anything else, and occasionally he would bite his lower lip like a boxer coming off his stool to start one more round. The guitarist and drummer were older men, dressed in dark shirts and jeans that looked well-lived in, wrinkled up under the arms and sagging in the knees. The drummer was soft and easy, finding the way the best drummers do to go into and out of a groove and make it sound right, loose, and smart. You never heard him by himself, you only felt him, and the band lived off his beat. The guitarist was a singer as well, who had led off the set with a couple of tunes to warm up the band and club. He played and sang okay, and you knew if he was any better he probably wouldn't have been here waiting for the real show to start, but on his own somewhere else. He pulled his cowboy hat down low and muscled out some familiar licks, sang hard and steady against the crowd that was still coming in the door. Then he introduced the man walking through a plywood door at the side, and the band crushed my attempt to say a few words to my friends by finding a riff to fill in the few moments it took Otis Rush to plug in.

It is conceivable that the word *rhetoric* sprang to mind as, having rotated on my stool, I watched the band working up to this moment. I was a white fan of the black and brown (and white) blues for years, since Muddy Waters played at my college in 1968, but had been for an even longer time an English major who was interested in the broad universe of language and emotion. My love of literature bled comfortably into my love of music, where the poetry of both mingles with its primary matter, which is sound. As with many young people, music with its double-barreled strengths of lyric and melody, to say nothing of explicit rhythms emanating from both these barrels, soon outdistanced literature as the favored medium of unalloyed pleasure in my life. I could work hard to tease all the music out of F. Scott Fitzgerald, in its full flowering a gorgeous performance to be sure, but there was something downright magical to have wash over you from your speakers, in a short five years, the Beatles, Dylan, the Bluesbreakers with Eric Clapton, and then Muddy Waters. And the lesson probably began much earlier, with my father's 78s of Benny Goodman and especially Count Basie. This was a lofty arc indeed, or a serpentine that describes many journeys of my young adulthood, beginning in the exotic, the foreign, the hip and unknown, and working through a sense of discovery, a sense of origin or source. This journey was taken in far more authentic terms by the young white men who went south to find the bluesmen in the early 1960s; my journey until the one that began on the north side of Chicago was purely aesthetic. I didn't care about the lives of the musicians, their ethnic or cultural biases and strengths. For me, enjoying Muddy Waters perform "Blow Wind Blow" in 1968 was to sense the highest degree of transparent speech I had ever heard, transparent as to its meanings, its feelings, the inner music of the human voice, the inflections of phrases and sentences, augmented and whipped up and creamed by a band second to none, led by a man whose voice was all honey and thunder. This transparency had something to do with a reaction to the aesthetically difficult poetry of literature, which invariably led me to interpretive gymnastics while, I hoped, leaving undamaged the essential beauty of the language.

Song lyrics tended to be "simpler" or more "vernacular" than published poetry in their usage; pop music has grown a huge general audience based on this principle. The blues was even more of this street feel, back porch feel, with a downhome rhyme scheme that was even simpler, more "transparent" than Tin Pan Alley.

The idea of rhetoric was not too far beyond my apprehension of the blues that night. We sometimes associate rhetoric with pleasure, but not often; rhetoric is more often the term we use to label that which uncovers, covers, or merely embellishes the truth. But certainly there has been for many, and always will be, great pleasure in the sermonic rhetoric of a great preacher, a great politician—or the rhetoric of a great poem or novel or drama that moves us to something more than sadness or happiness—moves us, or persuades us, to know, to believe, to act.

The performance of music became for me—after listening hours on end to the radio, and to my growing collection of records—a complete *environment* of language, in which its finest moments were those that jumped forward and grabbed your attention, and which I knew that I understood totally, with every part of my self. This sense of wholeness was, perhaps illusory—given the folly of a youth's sense of mastery—and was, certainly, pleasure, although it could be of parts joyful or sad, nostalgic or doom-filled.

The term *rhetoric*, I will show in a later chapter, has many meanings and senses, but at this point in my study of the blues, I mean rhetoric to suggest a language-use that is consciously constructed, and which aims at an understood audience whose expectations are primarily affective, and whose understanding of this rhetoric is contextualized culturally. Rhetoric arises in particular moments, in performances both real and virtual, and can echo down the years for new users, new audiences. Rhetoric allows for the testimony of the oral and the erased, the hidden song, the subversive gathering, the innocent dance. It can exist without the machinery—what F. Scott Fitzgerald called the "inner mechanics"—of the literary world. And it can still provide for the expression and needs of a culture's *soul*, which the blues was for African-American culture—what Angela Davis calls "experience as emotionally configured by an individual psyche" (112). Rhetoric is that old and new illumination of this configuration, I argue in this study; rhetoric can take the blues back—or borrow it—from its still nascent position within the canon of American literary study and reinvigorate the blues as rhetoric, as *public* address that melds the power of music with the emotional, social, and political needs of the audience in a language that comprises representations of black and white cultures in America.

This complete environment of language was appealing to a part of me (since I was a post-adolescent, and never changing in at least this one way) that wanted "the lost word," the need—as I read and wrote and listened and spoke—for a truly *linguistic* essence, a reality that would be present only insofar as we knew it *through* words. How better to make that transparent reality thick and delicious than through the complex workings of a song, and then—by the miracle of electricity, lights, auditoriums, clubs, and student unions—the power of the performance, the ritual by which people gather for this evocation of sound, word, rhythm, movement, and response?

I understand rhetoric as a tool for the examination of blues to be the ways language has meaning, force, and beauty in the complex of conditions and contexts surrounding performances of the blues. I argue for rhetoric's use in our understanding the blues—and add an opening apology, to which I hope I will not have to return to again. This apology is directed to all those writers, thinkers, scholars, and hipsters to whom I have silently hurled curses over the years for their *missing the point*. As many do, I eat up work on the blues, on rock, on jazz, voracious in my appetite to understand, to enjoy at least vicariously yet another run-through of the Chess years, or the Robert Johnson legend, Coltrane's last flights, or even the classical elements of the Beatles' middle period. But I have always felt faintly misdirected for going so deeply into the literature on the music, suspecting that the lost word I seem to be searching for won't be revealed at that remove. Perhaps I have been looking for clues, or for a comfortable, interpreted road map to the source. It is one thing to read Robert Palmer's *Deep Blues* for its foundational excellence and clear sense of affection for the music—but it is another thing altogether to listen to the hours of music referred to in this book. Indeed, it is not another "thing"—it is another universe, another reality. Puzzling out the lyrics on Charlie Patton's acetates isn't nearly as much fun as reading Stephen Calt and Gayle Wardlow's description of his performance tricks, yet listening to Patton has no substitute. To write a book about rhetoric and the blues is a somewhat suspect undertaking, then, if the intellectual and the visceral must be so jarringly brought together. As Elvis Costello so tellingly put it, to write about music is like dancing about architecture. He didn't need to supply anyone an explanation

Introduction   xv

My own intentions in this book seem to replicate much of what I have scorned over the years for missing the point. And, if a glance at my sources is sufficient, my sin will be greater than most. I drag a host of interpretive tools to the work that has little or no obvious relevance to, for example, Leroy Carr or anyone else singing "How Long How Long Blues." Part of my task will be to show the usefulness of these tools in understanding the blues, but my compounding the error of our Western analytical ways will have to be excused by readers who hope, as I do, that there are still other ways to know and feel the power and the beauty of the blues. It is my contention that the tools of rhetorical analysis have not been brought to bear on the blues in such a way as to increase our understanding—and our love—of the blues. I will got out on a limb with my baggage and see if the weight will hold. It is surely not the blues that will break. Beethoven, Mozart, and Stravinsky are still standing under the weight of published studies that have no music themselves. The Beatles still endure an industry of analyses. It is no surprise that Patton, Johnson, and Waters sing endlessly in our airspaces without the aid of interpreters.

Yet it is the nature of our linguistic universe that we must talk about all this.

So *rhetoric*. Not only is its sense a negative one for many, but a related term seems to seek to bring everything around us into its gloomy maw: it has become fashionable in recent years to see *rhetoricality* as the primary truth (or disruption of truth) of our times. Rhetoricality is a kind of extension of rhetoric's basis in argument to all matters, but an argument for which there is no recourse to resolve. We argue that everything is words and the clever arrangement of words—or arguments—for the purpose of gaining advantage, of getting things done, of exerting power over someone or something that will, then, have less power, or will have its power dominated by others. "Views"—or serious, ideological positions—compete with each other; we find, often, no final or foundational truths to hold down or hold up our conversations, "language that is infected by partisan agendas and desires"(Fish 474). Our lives, according to this view, become competitions in wit, deceit or, at best, *possibilities* (not even Aristotelian probabilities or *eikota*) of truth. We scrap and argue; the best wins—with "best" meaning "most rhetorically effective," with no necessary reference to the truth, or goodness, necessarily intended. It is a sophist's best nightmare.

There is something fascinating about this view, even for the blues around which this book will try to circle. It concerns the politics of language-use, which will also come into play in my analysis to come. A rhetoricality of our world suggests that there is no source of truth or meanings to our language acts other than those which impinge *specifically* on the act—for example, the reasons for speaker A grabbing listener A and telling him that person B is a crook and should not be trusted. (Speaker A wants your vote so he can get a job.) The implications of such a rhetoricality in our lives can be both attractive and appalling because they free up power to *create* powerful *stories* (Person B, it will be shown through testimony provided by Speaker A, beats his wife)—for each of us to argue as if we do indeed have a strong, if private or individual, pact with the truth. At the same time, however, such a freedom to persuade destroys the underlying comfort that, somewhere out there, there is a clear and good source-point of resolution, of an ending to argument and a certainty of meaning and significance. In conventional rhetorical terms, this is the difference between an Aristotelian rhetoric of the heuristic and a Ciceronian rhetoric of controversy: solve a problem, or give voice to diverse points of view. It may come as no surprise that I wish to use both kinds of rhetoric, Aristotelian in arguing strongly for a new, effective story of the blues—unifying many stories about it—while arguing, like Cicero, for the beauty of the blues being in its sense of cultural communality, of voices thrown back at voices, the mingling of voices in endless musical conversation.

For the blues, rhetoricality suggests a political freedom of expression, an appropriation of forms, figures, and arguments without regard to source or original meaning, a free evolution of the blues (and blues criticism) without the constraint of prior ideological positions. The mostly covert politics of the blues, now overtaken and made far more explicit by rap music, was that makers and listeners *made it their own;* by doing so bluesmakers and audiences were casting into new forms the relatively stable Western poetic lyric, its authority and ownership, its prior patrilinearity to the great Western poets. (David Evans's *Big Road Blues* in fact describes this free exchange, play, and appropriation of lyrics, motifs, and music among the bluesmen who shared one song over many years and miles of performance.) Similarly, rhetoricality suggests for the blues its appropriation *by* other musical forms, other interests, many of which seem purely commercial or economic, so that we are faced with so-called "blues-based" performers (blues-rock, for example) who are as difficult to accept as *making* the blues as many poets have with accepting rap artists or song lyricists as poets. The blurring of genres and their attendant modes of understanding and evaluation is not the only concern. We are faced—if we accept the blues as "just language," as I did when young and callow and most interested in the electricity of the performance—with cutting the blues off from its experiential ground, turning it loose in a textualized place of primitivist poetry and virtuoso musicians, so that the cultural heart of the music is unheard and unknown. What remains of the blues—if it is *only* a feeling in words, or *only* a protest in volume—is somehow only pentatonic, cool with shades, guitar-based, and ultimately sterile.

I recognize that the rhetoricality of our times is indeed reflected in its cultural products—their market-based ephemerality, their disinterest in the local or the narrowly contextual. The blues, spread thinly now across a mostly-white audience of affluence, is not an exception. I will, however, attempt to show how an attention to rhetoric today does not necessarily suggest that we must cut ourselves loose from the histories of our bluesmakers, from the *experiential truths* of its audiences. Rhetoric is the conscious use of words, sound, movement to create a meaning, or force, or beauty by which we communicate with one another through and within a shared or given moment. The truth about participants in this shared moment can still be sought.

I suspect if you confronted Otis Rush with the term rhetoric he might give you that faraway look, the half-smile with which he greets his audience. He would probably rub his fingers against his thumb and wish he were just playing and singing for you. When he plugged in that September night the faraway look was there, and the half-smile. The eyes were invisible under the shadow of his white cowboy hat, and as the sounds came effortlessly from his white Fender Stratocaster, left-handed, strung upside down, it seemed to me that here was a man of words and music, for whom the word artist was an honorific, certainly, but to whom the word "rhetorician" might never be self-applied. Yet contained in the term "bluesman," however, is all the power of the rhetorician. And bluesman/rhetorician Otis Rush admits to this tendency:

> Let me tell you [. . .] being a blues musician is one of the hardest things you could ever want to do. But it's sweet, too, if you make it. I've been up a little bit; I've

been down. And I think I suffered more because I quit. I have a gift and I chose not to use it for awhile. And it felt like God give me a whuppin,' you know. "I gave you this and you're just hangin' around in pool rooms?" (qtd. in Drozdowski, "Rush" 68)

Rush speaks of the gift, and of the choice, of pain and sweetness, of God and pool rooms. He begins, "Let me tell you"; he has the awareness of the performer for his audience even in a relaxed moment. His discourse, briefly, embraces much of the power of the blues—its scope and depth. I hope to bring his experience of the blues to my understanding of the blues in this book.

There are scholars of the blues for which the use of "artist" to describe the performer would have been a difficult stretch; their adherence to a primitivist label precluded the kind of conscious shaping that our understanding of art generally requires. Other critics err perhaps too much on the other side—and see classic poetry in every line of Robert Johnson's largely derivative lyrics. Others see the bluesman as a working entertainer, a craftsman aiming to make a living by making people want to dance and sing. Indeed, some believe that the blues became the blues as we know it when it became an economic reality, a job, a thing to do for money. It only became art when it came under the view of critics, commentators, and political or cultural polemicists who would use aesthetics as a tool for understanding the form only as part of a larger rhetorical project—LeRoi Jones's *Blues People* is an example of this polemic as part of a rhetorical project to claim jazz as a political art. It is rarely the interest of the performer himself to say whether or not the product of that performance is or is not art. It is certainly *work;* perhaps we are safe in standing on that ground for now. Certainly it was work that Otis Rush was doing that night. He may have been entertaining us, but he was working himself, working his band, working the blues so that it throbbed and stabbed out onto North Belmont until midnight.

To have a rhetoric of the blues you need a few basic elements, which may sound similar to a familiar "art of the blues" but which have important differences as well. We associate rhetoric today with discourse (i.e. communication that goes on within an obvious, time-specific context, with a specific purpose, directed at a specific audience that is itself adept, or familiar, with the subject of that communication). Un-

Introduction xix

like a classic text that is reprinted and read anywhere, anytime, a performance of the blues—like oral rhetoric, or a church sermon—is usually confined to a clearly delimited context; the rhetorical situation, in other words, is a rich triangle of performer, song, and audience, caught within a circle of contextual clues like the club, backyard, or concert hall. *Recordings* of the blues are complicating factors—they make the context a conceptual and highly plastic one, given the million different encounters such a recording may produce, and textualize the blues as a book does the poem—but it is the goal of this study to try to *reinvent,* or reimagine, to "subjectivize," the rhetorical moment that surrounds the blues performance, and to enlarge that moment, through research and analysis (a more objective task that may balance the affective element), into cultural contexts in which we can understand the meanings of the blues.

Besides the discursive nature of blues rhetoric, I will argue for the importance of the blues performer's *ethos*: his role, character, and reputation in the community where he performs, his life on the stage—in short, the way he or she "moves" (or, literally, in classical terms as *movere,* the art of producing one's emotions in others so that *pathos* is a term of *relation,* not separation, of artist and audience) the blues into the life of its audience by offering it as their common bond. For every stoic stage presence like Otis Rush, there is the intense, furious pulse of an acoustic artist like Son House or the nearly nonstop clowning of a Howlin' Wolf or Guitar Slim. The *ethos*—the essential character, the vices and virtues—of these performers, evinced in performance, is a critical, and highly varied, part of blues rhetoric.

The audience or hearer is a necessary element of this rhetorical analysis. In the blues it is an historical fact that the audience has undergone a radical change from the blues' early history, from pre-1930 to its (from our perspective) middle period (1930 to 1960) to its later and contemporary periods, roughly from the folk blues revival of the early 1960s to the present. Discussions of the blues audience necessarily trace this evolution, or what I believe is better described as an *accretion* of audience, in which the commercialization of the blues pushed its reach beyond original contexts into those of concert halls and living rooms. Race and class considerations are obvious in looking at the blues audience; the effects of that audience on the rhetoric of the blues—and the blues critic—are profound. This work of criticism can construct, dialogically, a reading of the blues performance even as it speaks miles and years away from that performance. The result, as with any dialog, is a kind of compromise of two truths: the source, never fully recoverable but supposedly historical, and the response, always an invention, yet convincing for its subjective qualifications.

Finally, there is the text itself, the signal, the poem and the harp, the fingerpicking and the deep comeback of the bass, the brushes and the black keys: those elements of the blues that we can extract from the performance and call its grammar and its style, its arrangement. It is what we can hear on a recording, or hear at the club. It is the substance of the blues because it both denies and enables differences of time and place and knowledge. It is, in another way, a technological gift (albeit with a downside) in part responsible for the survival of the blues. This study will try not only to judge the aesthetic successes of the text (whether, for example, something elicits a response of "beauty" or "truth") but will try also to gauge how well these textual elements serve the greater whole of the rhetorical act of the blues performance. What does the blues want? What does it want us to do? Dance? Laugh? Cry? Protest?

An Aristotelian harmony of the parts, for example, is just as relevant to the blues as it is to a political speech. The apparent simplicity of the blues structure, for example—its twelve bars, I-IV-V chording, flatted notes, and AAB rhyme scheme, its turnarounds—has endless variations played upon it. In doing textual analysis, we can ask ourselves why Charlie Patton affected several vocal styles within—*and for*—one song and why, in response to those rhetorical choices (or affectations), Son House would become so irritated. This kind of analysis is the most common done on the blues, but I hope that my rhetorical perspective on the uptake, or success, of these musical texts contributes productively to our understanding of the blues.

The importance of this understanding is another issue that I want to address. The blues is a matter of survival and response, of a holler against injustice, an often-comic sidestepping of the darkness that came with every day to the singers of and listeners to the blues. This argument is social in nature, addressed to the American nation, within which cultures of unequal power jostle for fairness, economic freedom, and respect for its million individual voices. Blues has correctly been seen as a child of African-American culture, giving rise to (or being raised a sibling to, depending on historian) jazz, rhythm and blues, even rock 'n' roll. It has, then, at the very least, a kind of progenitorial role in American culture, and we should be interested in helping it maintain that important role. But this act of mere preservation is too stuffy for me, too locked in history, caught up in old 78s and museum tours.

The old blues is as much a *living* blues if we can see the continuum of the blues performance as a cultural phenomenon, a part of America's genealogical awareness of its short history, its easy recovery through its own technology, through the current life of the blues as a somewhat puzzling pact—in fact, a complex dialog—between black performers and white audiences, white interpreters and black masters, aesthetic prejudices and new theories, political change and new artforms. The blues charts a strange and wonderful course through this part of the century, digging into a new millennium like a beast with two faces, one very old and dignified, the other young and yet unlined and perhaps uncertain of its own character.

A part of this uncertainty, I believe, is the uncertainty of its role here and now. Its *purpose* is now unclear, and it is also an aim of this study to try to delineate what I believe the importance of the blues to be in our time. The argument is exacerbated by the blues' own failure with much of the African-American culture of today, its being "outside," curtained behind the enormous pop machine of our visual culture, in which even relatively healthy segments of the musical life of America, like soul, rhythm and blues, and jazz struggle to be heard amid the tremendously noisy, ceaseless dial-flipping and button-pushing of the American listener.

The final chapter of this study tries to put this struggle to be heard into a framework of education. It concerns the teaching of the blues—not as an art to be performed but one in which we can in fact become part of the performance. I will argue that the educational institutions of America, at any level, should recover the blues as it recovers the literature of America and the cultures of America. The recovery of much lost, or "ethnic," literature in our past has been ongoing now for a quarter-century. In fact, the blues revival of the early 1960s was an early avatar of this spirit. But I will argue for an introduction of the blues into our schools not for its picturesque qualities, its quaint framing of a serious cultural response to hardship—but for its representative rhetoric of what Ralph Ellison calls its "poetry and ritual" in showing what is comic and what is tragic about the American experience. The blues should stand next to DuBois, Hughes, Hurston, Baldwin, and Morrison. Ellington, Armstrong, and Basie should be there as well, Davis and Parker and Coltrane and Monk. The syllabus of American culture is enormous, yet the blues speaks for all Americans in the language of the soul. Mance Lipscomb says that "The blues is just a feeling." He is being as modest about the achievements of the blues musician as he always was of himself, but his remark still suggests the question, What is that feeling? How has the blues taken it out of—and moved it back into—our culture, and how can we express that rhetoric for new audiences? This study will tackle these questions.

A few words, gently, about beauty and truth. I take these terms as nearly synonymous for the purposes of this study, deriving their importance to any rhetorical analysis from a Platonic rhetoric, especially the *Phaedrus,* and from two contemporary figures of great importance—Kenneth Burke and Richard Weaver—who explored rhetorics of, respectively, circumstance and definition, and who both married rhetorical issues with those of ethics and community, and who attended to the importance of the subject, or audience, in committing to action (if only sometimes as a *responsive* rhetoric itself). I will wander far from Muddy and Otis and Memphis Minnie to try to pin down what is essentially a subjective response to what our language and language-acts can still aspire to, which is the good—which is, in turn, of parts beautiful and true. These conceptual terms are not in favor these days in either literary or rhetorical analysis; they are often thought sentimental or naive. I plan to stick with them when revealing *my* subjective responses to the blues, but with the important Platonic anchor—or, better yet, kite—that asserts that these values, when tempered by analysis, thought, and research, represent forms or ideals about which we can agree as members of a community of citizens, if not of their sources (God, for Plato), then of their current location in the self-consciousness of the individual and, I believe, the collective consciousness of an American culture.

For Plato, those values have been put into the soul by God, and brought to consciousness through the instruction of wise men. Our ideological apparatus is really quite similar, but God has largely been replaced by *Kultur,* a thousand-headed God found in shopping malls and textbook departments. By the act of translation that music critics must do, I will try to define beauty and truth in the blues as its users have defined or implied these terms in performance. These users have not often made *specific* reference to these terms; therefore, I intend to show the ways context, performer, audience, and text have created a rhetorical blues-complex of beauty and truth. I hope that my discussions of that beauty and truth do not often fall into bickering over taste, a game we all like to play when discussing who is better than who—but which does not serve, finally, the purposes of this study, one of which is to approach the problem of representing the blues in aesthetic terms for study outside the blues' original context.

This problem, which will also bedevil any attempt to evaluate the blues using an *objective* measure (such as the sociological device Charles Keil used in *Urban Blues*), leads often to a rhetorical excess of enthusiasm. It isn't enough to describe how much one loves this performer or that performer, or that performer's skills. The histories of certain performers, their influence and performance techniques, their poetry: these elements will be put alongside rhetorical considerations of the blues-complex, the singular response of one listener, and the critical and theoretical texts of African-American culture.

Otis Rush caught me that night as a lover of the blues in a pleasurable subjectivity that, as I noted, equals for me no other aesthetic response. I was delighted by what I think are his two great skills—his singing vibrato and his guitar vibrato. They are, taken singly, perhaps the best I have ever heard, but to have them in one performer is close to miraculous. But what good is a vibrato—by itself? How have I extracted it from the performance, and why? I can argue that this vibrato is a trope, a rhetorical figure for the rhythmic rise and fall of the human condition, the ceaseless alternation of good and bad, sad and happy, the way day and night follow each other and take us riding through our lives. Rush himself relates guitar vibrato, as B.B. King does, to the human voice, and insists that the guitar is an echo of the voice, not a sufficient replacement. Its insufficiency, then, is its poignancy. We may be able to see how the meaning and power of the blues is contained in these bits and pieces, grammar and syntax, tropes and figures. This study will attempt to deal with the substance of the blues in such a way as to reanimate its living moments.

After many choruses of Don Robey's "As the Years Go Passing By," a song made popular by Albert King, who had died not long before that night, Otis Rush was gone with a shy nod of the head. Walking slowly, he disappeared through that plain plywood door at the side of the stage. He had said nothing to the audience, stopping only once to give a very quiet lecture to a young photographer who was contorting himself unnecessarily at the foot of the stage. At another moment, he lost his band completely and turned to say something to his second guitar, who took a deep breath and tried to ride the band back into the same woods as Rush had found. Otherwise, he played on, his eyes half-closed in the darkness under the brim of his hat, his hands moving effortlessly over the strings, his voice from deep in the throat with that vibrato taking each held note and caressing it. While walking back to the car, Belmont Avenue still full of people out there looking for Saturday night, I asked the rhetorical question in my mind. What did that all mean? How can I feel that music so much?

These and other questions have been asked many times, and have provoked answers of many kinds, each according to theory, whether formal or not, conscious or not. I hope to investigate those theories in this study by reviewing, in Chapter 1, the rhetorical positions of the most significant writing and writers on the blues—to see how the canonical figures of Lomax, Charters, Oliver, Palmer, Ferris, Keil, Evans, and others have approached their own theoretical conversations with the blues. I will also look at those African American writers who have written on or in the blues—LeRoi Jones, Ralph Ellison, Larry Neal, Albert Murray, Charles Shaar Murray, Jon Spencer—and seek to find rhetorics there that may serve to resolve or exacerbate the question of race, culture, and the blues.

In Chapter 2, I present a survey cluster of rhetorical and literary theories that I believe can, when applied to the blues, illuminate their place in our social, political, and cultural traditions, and can give us ways to understand the rhetorical power of the blues as it existed seventy-five years ago, and as it can exist today and tomorrow. These theories are, using general categorical labels, classical rhetoric from Plato to Aristotle to Cicero and Quintilian, and to contemporary figures like Burke and Weaver who would maintain a rhetorical tradition for our times; the reception aesthetic, or what I call response or "subjective rhetorics" of Rosenblatt, Iser, Holland, Rabinowitz and others; a dialogical rhetoric, and discourse analyses, of Mikhail Bakhtin; and the postcolonial rhetorics of Bhabha, Fanon, Brathwaite, Fee, Griffiths, and others. I synthesize these theories into an instrument of rhetorical analysis, aimed at the phenomenon of the blues: individuals, contexts, texts, audiences.

Chapter 3 of this study is a series of nine extended readings of blues musicians and their music. I analyze performances, and certain accounts of performances, in order to reach an understanding of each performer's rhetoric (i.e. his or her way with the blues or, to paraphrase Dylan Thomas: the force through which the blue fuse drives the music). These nine musicians have been chosen for their familiarity to the general blues audience, for their giving me great pleasure, as well as for their applicability (as I will argue) to my theoretical positions. These musicians are not meant to represent the "best" of the blues; their canonical positions would suggest this but, in fact, I plead a reductive approach simply for the reasons stated.

Chapter 4, described earlier, suggests ways the blues can become a part of the literary canon of American educational institutions in such a way as not to extract its vibrancy, its essence or vitality, from the heart of the blues, which is its performance rituals. I turn primarily to Henry Louis Gates Jr.'s "heroic" black rhetoric and Houston Baker, Jr.'s, Samuel Floyd's, and Carol Lee's interpretations of this rhetorical trope of signifying to show how the blues can be considered part of an oral tradition that, when brought into classrooms for study, will inevitably be transformed by context—but which can recover the power of the blues by a reinvention of context, sound, and effect.

The blues, which Son House met "walking just like a man," is still walking down strange paths and through strange doors; this journey I take with the blues is no different. But I hope this study can catch the blues in stride, take its full measure, and see that it keeps on walking.

When Your Way Gets Dark

1

Writing (on) the Blues

> Eloquence.
> Deception.
> Persuasion.
> Just words.
> Cosmetics.
> Cookery.
> A bad smell.
> Communication.

What do these words have in common? They define, for some, the word *rhetoric,* a term in use for some two millennia-and-a-half, rising in ancient Greek culture for civic use, the ways men spoke in public in order to air opinions, to seek truth, and to drive others to action. This public or civic context was the heart of rhetoric's development as a science (some said art) because it was in that context that the everyday business of Greece was discoursed upon, argued about, and refined into act or law or sensibility or philosophy. Until the late nineteenth-century, rhetoric was also routinely studied in the schools, an educational surety along with Latin and Greek, placed there by a continuing Western fixation on the voice as a present synecdoche of the character, which in turn was a key way, or appeal, to the truth. Rhetoric, often made "visible" through the art of oratory or public speech, was, for the school-aged, the materials of an effective speech—no more, no less. For many in the twentieth century, "speech class" was effectively rhetoric without the label: practice in exposing and improving one's abilities to speak and persuade in public forums. Rhetoric was certainly marginalized in our educational system; its power as a method of truth-seeking was supplanted by the study of literature, as if the latter phenomenon, or its body of texts, were more *engaging* for the uncovering of contingent and eternal verities.

But for the ages before ours, in which the printed word was either non-existent or held close to class or discourse centers, the *spoken* word—or its text, the speech—was the linchpin in social and cultural representations and visions. We think naturally of the court, of those in power who held sway over a multitude of citizenry, or a coterie of lawmakers and lesser royalty. We must also think of the church, whose function was not only to preserve the word of God but to disseminate it through as many of His children as possible. Rhetoric was the means to make the sermon eloquent, or the legal argument persuasive; for Augustine it was making the word of God understandable, and attractive, to man. It was the way *logos,* a God-given substance (such as language was regarded before, at least, Locke and Nietzsche) could be shaped in as beautiful a form as possible—not to *overtake* truth but to contain it. This shaping of language could not be seen as any more "deceptive" than the shaping of one's home to please the needs or senses of the inhabitant, unless it were put to evil use by evil men for evil purposes. But language, when used in so critical way as the Greeks insisted it should be—to be the very lifeblood of the state in the carrying out of its political functions—was perhaps ready for the kind of attack that Plato made upon it, and which (for us, taking first steps into a new millennium) can be plainly seen as our inheritance. We equate rhetoric with the lie, as much as with the truth. We remain confused as to its actual constitution: is it ornament, mere style, or is it the art of inquiring into the very essence of things?

We are all welcome, given the tendency to hold opposites in our minds as a part of the postmodern contradictions of life (and which F. Scott Fitzgerald said was the sign of the really first-class mind) to recognize that there is, indeed, good and bad rhetoric. Good rhetoric does not only mean good writing or good speech by any *stylistic* measurement. A Renaissance sense of style, Eupheuistic, loaded with figures and the acrobatic tropes of a Shakespeare, is good for that age and good for that literary universe, good for the audience who wishes to be tickled by inventive language. But the same stylistic choices transported elsewhere are uniformly rejected, say, at a conference on computer science. There, the will for what Barthes called "writing degree zero" is in fact a sign of good rhetoric—a transactional language that opens windows onto referents, seemingly without play, leaps of vision, vocal or personal perspective. Every audience has an expectation of form, so that "when one turns to the production of the enjoyment of a work of art, a formal equipment is already present, and the effects of art are involved in its utilization" (Burke, *Counter-Statement* 141–42). The "wholly conventional" forms of the blues—recognized by many who are not fans of the genre—are not in themselves "good" or "bad," but are, in their smallest units, the grammar of blues rhetoric. Burke reminds us that these units are not in themselves "aesthetic" forms; rather, "[t]hey can be said to have a prior existence in the experiences of the person hearing or reading the work of art" (*Counter-Statement* 143). Reception is assured; particular effects are not.

We always note in discussions of rhetoric, good or bad, specific audiences such as playgoers and scientists. We should remember that rhetoric is easily measured—its success evaluated—by the *kind* of effect or effects it has on its audience. In other words, the rhetoric of a comic performance is measured by the number of laughs, the rhetoric of a politician by the number of votes she gets. One might argue, It isn't the rhetoric—it's the joke that matters. But the joke *is* the rhetoric: without the effect of the joke there would appear to be only gibberish coming out of the comedian's mouth. Effective language constitutes our communication—even in the rhetorical tricks of a raised eyebrow or pointing finger, considered, traditionally, as a part of rhetoric called elocution. Rhetoric, for our argument in this study, is the shaping of both form and content, the unity of which is clarity and eloquence—a quality felt and accepted by the audience as *transporting* the truth of the matter at hand, whether jokes or votes or even sad stories. Meanings are teased out, reflected upon or argued (and here is where the issue of *rhetoricality* is beaten back, where listeners compare and analyze this new rhetoric against all those that they know or can summon to the conversation of the mind)—and the rhetoric of the "text" is finally "good" in that there is a general yea-saying of the audience, or "bad" in that there are "nays" hurled back at the speaker.

Measuring the rhetoric of massively received texts—say, a speech given on television to twenty million listeners—is more difficult than the cozy responses of thirty people in a meeting room; indeed, this difficulty reveals one of the great prejudices of Western cultural criticism, and one relevant to any discussion of the rhetoric of the blues.

First, as I have noted, rhetoric now often means "just words." It is an outgrowth of an anti-intellectualism that is a defining American trait, one that does not only have as its progeny a mediocre educational system (which is nevertheless supported by those who point to a Japanese or Chinese system and inevitably make racial, or racist, remarks about uniformity and collectivity) but a distrust of ideas, ideals, founding concepts, and those abstractions of life that can only be held onto through ideas, ideals, founding concepts, and those abstractions of life which *must be expressed precisely and truly through words*. The old rhetorical strongholds of the royal court and church are weaker today than they have ever been in (at least American) history, in part—I would argue—for their having to rely on essentially rhetorical arguments of truth and virtue woefully expressed through the mouthpieces of the obscure or the distrusted or criminal. Once proud holders of a distinct literacy, these strongholds now trail a world exploding with thousands of special discourses and the extra-dimensional literacies of electronic media.

We have now—it is certainly better than nothing—endless polling of general audiences for their positions on issues posed as questions, the very mode of questioning and responding suggesting a slippery slope toward that relativity, that rhetoricality that makes argument endless and foundational principles hopelessly archaic. The audience is, on the one hand, an undifferentiated mass, simplistically objective, generally posed for maximum effect to be a Peorian, white, male, of no interest to anyone but his family, friends, and politicians; on the other hand, it is endlessly varied and then targeted or *parceled* into elite groupings by college degree or number of automobiles in the garage or favorite hobbies of tennis and golf and video games. These ways of normalizing the American audience have led to a second difficulty with modern rhetoric: it has as its stylistic benchmarks the language of television advertising, which stands today as the most disseminated syntax in the world. This is not the place for an extended excoriation of the television age, but the language of our preachers, politicians, even our stand-up comics seems gauged to the short attention span—and consumerist desires—burned into our culture by television. What we can say about its rhetoric is its syntactical simplicity, its dearth of figural language, its dominant appeal to fear, its *ethos* of toughness, vigilance, and threat. We are left with, until we turn to the deliberately deviant margins of such forms as metal or rap music or concrete poetry, a homogenized speech and rhetoric of accessible coolness and righteous simplicity. Propriety in the defense of mass appeal, still, is all.

The American rhetorician follows in similar form. At first glance we have what seems to be the result of a great change, in that the gender bias of the pronoun *he* and the adjective *white* is denied by such statistical evidence as the numbers of women in Congress and State houses, people of color in the professions, broadcasting, the military, and so on. Those who give speeches, in short, who get our attention using the usual modes of communication available have become much better representative of a multicultural America, at least in quantifiable terms. But that is the hang-up. Quantity, unless it measures households or the number of seats an evangelist can fill, is not a good part of rhetorical analysis; we can count up the number of similes in a text—that sort of thing is interesting if ultimately atomistic and inconclusive. What is the *quality* of these new speakers? Have they offered new argument, new eloquence to the American rhetorical character? I think they have been domesticated (or appropriated, to use a term of postcolonial discourse, or interpellated, to use one of Marxian discourse) by their own choices, so that I don't hear often a *woman* senator from California, or an African-American representative from *Alabama*—I just hear a senator and a representative. Some might say this is *good,* this is the correct outcome of equal-under-the-law, but the homogenized voice is not part of a rhetorical voice except as it seems to reflect a disinterested, normalized audience of conforming minds; rather, the *ethos* of that voice (if we retain classical notions of rhetoric, which I do in this study) must be the product of specific cues, moments, moves, and music, which rely on context or situation. To be simply another voice is to be no voice at all, but a position, a discursive pinprick on an electronic grid of voting positions. Collectivity is one thing—a powerful force in American life—yet the subject at hand, the blues, is about the individual, as Davis notes for us above, and which this study returns to again and again.

American rhetoric, I would argue, *is* "just words" much of the time—and is part and parcel of its massive delivery system, banal in its "impressive" numbers and participatory conceits. I display an elitist stripe, of course, which places any critic of culture somewhat higher, somehow more perceptive, than those he or she views: the critic as crypto-performer, dangling the object of study below him, the audience, in turn, below the object. For now, I will accept that elite stripe in order to bring the blues into this discussion in opposition to the great norm of that rhetoric that seems to surround our everyday lives in ceaseless beats of twenty, thirty, and sixty seconds (or 120 seconds of pop).

The cultural critic is by definition an intellectual—no matter how emotive he may become when describing, for example, the way Memphis Minnie could flash her jewelry, smile, sing, and play her beautiful acoustic blues all at once—because he is *thinking* about the actions of others, and expressing himself in language that is discursive in nature, rhetorical in its effects, and not predominantly expressive or poetic, as is the language he or she is analyzing. This critic—and I conflate the texts of historian, scholars, commentators into this one "critical text" because I believe all these rhetorical positions are argumentative—is in a position to analyze, synthesize, and argue for a version of culture which, in fact, abstracts the bone, sinew, and blood of the texts he or she is working with. This is a "masterful" act. Much as the rhetorician masters the culture of eloquence, the critic does the eloquence of culture. It is by this analyzing of culture that the critic turns to the fundamental Aristotelian topics (or analytical tools) of classifying, defining, comparing, and so forth. It is the critic's usual cross to bear that he must distinguish, for example, the country blues from the classic blues from the urban blues, and then he must assign value, meaning, and power to those newly classified or categorized texts.

We accept these moves. We are familiar with their effects if not their names, and it is sometimes reassuring to get everyone back in order again after a freewheeling time with the blues. Ah, Piedmont over there, Texas there, Memphis right here, and of course the Delta. Don't forget Los Angeles. But what I am most interested in, following these fundamental acts, is the universal rhetorical move of the critic from the bastion of *Kultur* to the dirt-poor path of the blues. This move is a truth of the cultural critic who (for the blues) must show a social and political awareness in characterizing the blues as (usually) a marginalized working man with a dollar in his pocket, women on his mind, and a juke up the road.

Outside the blues, the cultural critic is engaged in the same move, inevitably playing favorites against the house, moving the arguments of canons and favorites, standards and cultural knowledge, to a battlefield of what has been overlooked, outclassed, or bought off. So is the fate of the cultural critic: to wage David's wit against Goliath's mass.

It will always be so, and when we write about the blues, we are replicating this cultural battle of critic against consumer, smart high against intuitive low, urbane North against slow South, sharp city against dull country, artifice against authenticity. The structural principles of the blues critic are in no way different from the critic at large. His rhetoric, too, is not different, and proceeds from these positions of David: the intellectual employing the sorcery of a Western rhetoric in order to save, protect, or champion the threatened texts of others. The perceived threat against the blues (because of its passivity or dignity) will be part of my analysis to follow, but for now let us stick with the rhetoric of the cultural critic who—to summarize—employs an intellectualized rhetoric in dialogical opposition to mass culture for the sake of an expressive or creative form marginalized by that mass culture.

He or she believes in the marginalized text—its soul, its maker, its value to the center, to the margin, to the world. He or she may even "like" the text, though that is certainly giving a part of the game away. What is important is the critic's argument for that attention be directed at that margin. Fair enough. Since most readers of cultural criticism are themselves cultural critics, we are certainly willing to do so; Foucault argued that thus are discourses born and evolved, strengthened and encoded with power, "the thing for which and by which there is struggle, [. . .] the power which is to be seized" (53). I will play the role myself, but only with the clear restriction that this must lead to teaching those who would shudder to be called critics. Since one of my interests is the ideological preserve we call the school, I will try to lead this study to that final context in order that I might make some specific arguments for a change in its ideology. I, too, stand upon the soapbox of the intellectual. And I, too, champion the blues, love it, and grieve for it—yet these admissions are beside the point. In rhetorical terms, my argument has become too personal, stuck in my own feelings rather than attempting to identify or validate those of the audience, of which I am only one member.

I can call the blues a marginalized cultural phenomenon, a product of the middle class, every year evidently pushed father from the public view by such newer musical forms as soul and rap, hip-hop, even rock—yet when I begin to investigate writing about the blues, I discover a preserve of a million words, thousands of authors, dozens of willing journals. Is there anything that America does not talk about? If the blues is dying, are these thousands of voices a linguistic hospice, or is something else at work here, a transgressive industry of rhetoric designed by its users to provide a cultural Other, the apparition of darkness that America has always needed and nurtured in its own forests, alleys, and music halls?

A good going-through of the most comprehensive bibliography of the blues (Hart's *The Blues: A Bibliographical Guide*) reveals the numbers I note above, and a few more. Of the guide's nearly five hundred pages of listings, more than half are biographical, nearly all are written by men, and twenty or so book titles can be identified as having "crossed over" into the view of mass audiences, their periodicals, and reviewers. This winnowing down of an extensive field to an intensive canon is the work of culture, and in the case of the blues this winnowing down replicates the larger literary canon and its formative process. Some differences, however, are there for our taking.

We should remind ourselves that we are not (in this chapter) dealing with the blues itself, but with writing *about* the blues—or, to adopt an old New Critical perspective, *around* the blues but not of it. The blues, one hundred years or so old, less if you begin with recordings, has thousands of titles under its name now, probably tens of thousands, even if we join many under the heading of "derivations" or "variations." Around this cultural pearl is a world of words about it. This reality reminds us of the usual literary study of a canonical text, which retrogresses before accelerating into new territory; in other words, every literary study summarizes past studies, and takes at least a fresh step toward (or around) the object of study. Blues scholarship is no different in this regard, but I find the emphasis on biography intriguing.

An innocent explanation is that we wish to regard the blues as individual expression, much as we do the other texts of our culture, as a singling out of what is particular to each of our life experiences. The blues we write or the blues we choose has, by this line of reasoning, something to say about the life we lead or make. Thus, we are not just curious about the lives of a Charlie Patton or Tommy Johnson; we want to know those lives so that we can better understand the work they did. Biography is, of course, a traditional source of illumination in studying the text, which may contain in the life "connecting links, parallelisms, oblique resemblances" (Wellek and Warren 79).

But why such a preponderance of biographical study? Why fewer than a hundred entries in this same bibliography on African-American history, which I assume, especially given our interest in cultural matrices, was given an exhaustive listing? I think an answer lies again in *ethos,* a concept of character that welds the maker to his or her creation, a *rhetorical tool or measure* by which the maker (and, then, willing audience) is able to judge the power of the created text by the power which seems inherent in the maker. This strong weld of character-to-text is not as present in literary studies (and is almost invisible today, given many postmodern denials of the ethical subject) in part because the text is not performed for audiences by the maker, but by reader-interpreters. More importantly, the literary text has always struggled to become autonomous by virtue of its burden of *universal* application. The blues text, on the other hand, has been wedded to place, time, voice, and feeling so that the shaper of the blues is rightfully seen as the vessel of the blues, shaped, of course, in cultural terms, as will be discussed later.

Compare Aristotle's understanding of *ethos* as the character of a speaker which "may almost be called the most effective means of persuasion he possesses" (qtd. in Vickers 20) with Larry Neal's formulation: "He is appreciated as a meaningful member of the community to the degree to which he expresses the conscious and unconscious spirit of that community" (60). Neal's understanding of the bluesman's role is clearly civic: he is closely in tune with the senses (both surface and hidden) of the community and is valued for that sensitivity. His character, of course, follows from that personal distillation of the community. The biographical means so much to the blues because it is the rhetorical, self-conscious power of the bluesman that we may recognize as emanating not from an artistic mystery, but from the very thinking mind and feeling heart of the community. Writers on the blues recognize this *ethos,* and express it themselves through attention to the lives of the bluesmen and blueswomen. Davis characterizes the power of this *ethos* as self-in-society:

> The new African Americans—women and men alike—came to perceive their individual selves not only as welded together within the community, but as different from and in opposition to one another as well. For working-class women and men, the blues allowed and furnished cultural representations of this new individuality. (45–46)

To "allow and furnish" these representations are the work of both commentators and visionaries.

A second quantifiable observation: the tremendous preponderance of male authors on the blues. Does this only mirror the blues itself, which is still largely a male performance punctuated only briefly by a handful of canonical female figures? Or does this preponderance also find better explanation in the rhetorical nature of the blues?

First, this gender inequality exists in every written mode of discourse in our society except, probably, feminist issues themselves. We could hardly expect writing on the blues to be different. Yet I would argue that the ratio is so extreme that it merits discussion. Literary studies has recently been the site of extended battles over gender, bringing into literary discourse feminist studies, women's studies, feminist literary theory—and, recently, afrafeminist rhetorical theory (Royster 271*ff.*). Writing and publishing about literature is still, by numbers, the work of men, though it is clear to all observers that those numbers have begun to tip in the direction of women writers. Why are these numbers important? The answer is simple: the numbers reveal an American ideology of gender as clearly as do income levels reveal an ideology of race.

Why is the blues so male? We cannot turn to literary theory, even though we are pressing in this study for the blues' apprehension as a full-fledged cultural product. Instead, we need to see that the western tradition of the public speaker, the community voice, the wise elder or wise guy, the politician, the streetcorner bullshitter, the soapbox orator, the door-to-door salesman, the preacher—they are men, virtually all of them, in such numbers as to approximate the maleness of the blues and blues critic. To quote Neal again on the "meanness" of the blues: "To be 'mean' in the lexicon of the blues is to express one's emotional experiences in the most profound, most intense manner possible. It means daring to be, to feel, to see" (57). These ways with one's body and feelings, until recently, were inappropriate in public performance except for those men whose toughness or meanness allowed their raw emotion a stable foundation. It is in the literary or expressive arenas that women have made noticeable changes; until very recently, civic changes in the gender of that public voice were much less audible. Linguistic heroism in the blues is (with several significant exceptions like the great Bessie Smith, Ma Rainey, Louise Bogan, and others) a male phenomenon, leading to (or from) the substance of the blues, its attention to sexuality, brutality, sin, clowning, and preaching about the blues itself. James Brown's "It's a Man's World" is correct as opposed to necessarily fair; the context of American music is still a "man's world" from artist to producer to critic, and the rhetoric of this music is undeniably male—as male as that which Quintilian professed two centuries earlier, as consisting of boy student, male tutors, male teachers, and female "nurses," who, it was hoped, would "speak properly" (1.1.4-5). Not only does this study seem to move horizontally within a mainly working-class context of African American culture, it also leans heavily on its essentially masculine identity.

Writing *about* the blues is a simple displacement of the blues itself into a critical terminology, an analytical framework suited to a culture of linguistic saturation that values a discourse that begins with the blues performer having "a talk with himself about the problem," who then analyzes the situation, and then takes his own advice to remedy it. He "thereby opens up his soul to the world and allows it to see the sadness, the heartache and the joy he has sustained in life [. . .] and if he can get a witness, someone who can testify to the same feelings and experiences, then he has succeeded in revealing the essential essence of human experiences" (Neal 62). The audience is a many-colored creature, of course, much of it conceived years after the performer has disappeared or died. The critic-as-audience often testifies in darkness. This testimony is, however, as rhetorical as the blues itself, in that the maleness of the rejoinder, response, insult, laughter, or logic is a function of the public heart of the blues—its subjective rhetoric looking to "testify" back at the speaker.

Out of this public discourse comes those texts that hang on, echo, rebound. They are canonical for the same reasons that canonical texts exist in any discourse: their value has been judged greatest by those who use the discourse. The membrane that surrounds the canon is semi-permeable, pierced or penetrated with great difficulty. It works two ways as well, so that the canon doesn't only grow and bust its shelves, cupboards, or sacristy, but shrinks by slow exchanges of value and worship.

The canon of the blues is not currently under discussion, but I will present in Chapter 3 one version of a blues canon for rhetorical study. For now, I hope to discover the canon of blues criticism, and what its features are, its strengths and weaknesses, its strategies and outcomes. The purpose of this analysis is not to play favorites or blast others, nor to uncover a plot against free exchange of ideas nor to establish one of my own; rather, I hope this part of my study will show that the blues has a richness and depth of character that allows for several disparate yet equally legitimate approaches to it and, secondly, that the rhetoric of the blues *critic* displays both his understanding of his task and the meaning of the blues itself. In short, the appropriation of the blues is a function of the blues community and occurs in many ways, whether it is shaking it on the dance floor, reading tablature for your own back porch version of Patton's "Pony Blues," or writing about the blues with the sweet voice of J.B. Lenoir coming from your bookshelf speakers.

For Samuel Charters and Paul Oliver the term *appropriation* could have little meaning in 1959, the year Charters published his *The Country Blues* in England, a year before Oliver published his *The Meaning of the Blues*. Together, these two books would signal a double blast of scholarly attention to the blues, attention that has never paused but that has gone through changes, or bifurcations, which this present study wishes to name and explore.

Appropriation is given currency primarily through postcolonial theories of literature and language, and asserts that cultural products of oppressed or recessive cultures are inevitably "appropriated" by the imperial or dominant culture, and put to its own uses, albeit sometimes benevolent or only misguided ones. It is not only ironic but tempting to see that these two authors, one British, were practicing some latter day imperialism when they went to the core of the blues, as both of them did in different ways. Oliver visited the South only after the completion of his book; Charters was a serious tourist, or at best a field researcher who would eventually record bluesmen in the role of producer. But both were foreigners to the blues, not only in region or nation but race; this double remove from the birthplaces of the blues opens the whole tradition of blues criticism to charges of appropriation, or transcultural stealing. I will answer this charge in the next chapter; for now, the distance of these authors from their subjects is, in fact, remarkable for the depth of the work that followed (in both authors' careers as blues critics). There were, of course, dozens of treatments of the blues published prior to 1959; there are the eyewitness or autobiographical accounts, like W. C. Handy's and Jelly Roll Morton's. There are the compilations or transcriptions of primary texts of the blues, like Odum and Johnson's, and Lomax's. There are the creative reworkings of the blues, such as those of Sterling Brown and Langston Hughes. Critical work appeared in musicological and folklore journals as far back as 1930.

These earlier texts are glimmers of what would come, what can be called the first great synthesis of critical or creative attention to the blues. Works of Hughes and Brown and Lomax never tried to surmount disciplinary boundaries, never tried to create for an audience of serious listeners a *totalizing* picture of the blues. I think the blues-as-a-subject found in Charters and Oliver its first "good men: speakers of civic virtue, skill, and emotional commitment to the subject-matter. Charters and Oliver recognized that the blues was a way of looking at the world, the way a great novel does—it was a big world, complex and difficult to unify into a single vision. Yet these two authors attempted this for the first time, and what resulted was a clear starting point for a rhetorical analysis of blues criticism.

As Melville's *Moby-Dick* starts not with "Call me Ishmael" but with the more revealing term "Etymology," it is interesting to note that Charters's *The Country Blues* begins with a dedication to Moses Asch, the globetrotting music collector whose Folkways Records documented and distributed much of the world's folk music to collectors in the 1950s. Charters wonders if what Asch has done is a "creative" endeavor or not, whether the life of the folklorist/music collector is properly called a life of the artist. The identification between Asch and Charters is made clear when Charters says that this documenting of the music creates "a new awareness of both the music around us and the life that has produced it." Charters believes he has done this with the blues (and would continue for many years, including the producing and recording of music by the bluesmen whose lives he documented). In the book's introduction he declares that "the first extended study" of the blues creates the problem of "organizing the material into a coherent pattern" (*Country Blues* 7). Charters is self-conscious about his burden, and explicit about his "overriding sense of responsibility toward the material." He asserts, "It has seemed to me artificial to discuss the music on any other level than that of its relationship with its own audience" but then signals the importance of the recorded weight of the blues and the "capriciousness" of the blues audience.

Taken as an apology for the difficulty of trailblazing a research path into the largely unresearched jungle of the blues, Charters's introduction is understandably agonistic, but we can also taste in this first large view of the blues the white liberal version: the blues as a mysterious, perhaps mystical region that resists clear exposition and must be pieced painfully together by a combination of perspicacious craft and humanistic zeal. Indeed, this rhetorical balance of reason and feeling is made more apparent in the book's opening chapter on the ontological problem of the birth of the blues.

Charters writes, "They sang in the long hot afternoon in the fields and they sang in the lonely quiet of evening" (19). Charters later admits that he considered this a romanticized version of the African-American history because he wished "to force the white society to reconsider some of its racial attitudes, and on the other hand it was a cry for help" (*Bluesmen* vii). The audience as *conceived* is entirely distinct from the audience as perceived. How interesting that Charters's work on the blues was derived in part from the capriciousness of the blues audience, while he worried at the same time that his own audience would be just as capricious. Charters seemed to be working in a rhetorical vacuum out of which he hoped to climb in two directions—toward two very different yet stonily indifferent audiences: the original blues audiences and successive white audiences.

The zeal of trailblazers, of prophets and heralds—Charters's cry for help refers to his hope that others will "journey to find the artists" so that their music will not be lost. He feels that by romanticizing the lives of the bluesmen, their origins in the "wild and unaccountable" music that was documented in slavery times, in appetizing glimpses without genealogy until that first recorded blues could be held in hand—this appeal to the white audience's sentiment of guilt, curiosity, romance manifests itself in Charters's zeal to conjoin his two disparate audiences—black and white—under a social ethic of equality and respect.

Thus, the great bulk of black music-making is derivative, but with a trace of the "wild and unaccountable" which will signal an undomesticated link to Africa—a rope of song and sound by which the origins of the African-American are salvaged from the wreckage of slavery. It is an attractive argument for white audiences of the early 1960s, who long to discover what is authentic within a fairly destroyed culture (as it was seen at the time) in which the blues' first historian cries for help upon hearing the music before it goes out like a candlestub. The mission of Charters is one of savior, and if the rhetoric of the first book does not quite reach that level of messianic fervor (Charters was a poet, and thus knew, I believe, when to say more with less) he was clearly out to show, as he later admitted, that the blues was beautiful and true for what it could show white America about black America.

Charters's journey through the first fifty years of the blues takes him up and away from the "depth and richness of the country blues" (244) to the "thinly derivative" (243) versions of the downhome blues being played in the northern cities. Worse, Charters looks at the urban blues of Muddy Waters and finds too often "endless strings of clichés," "painfully slow blues," songs that are "indistinguishable and undistinguished," for which "a man could impress upon them [. . .] some sort of novelty in the shrill accompaniment or a particularly leering, strutting performance" (*Country Blues* 251). Charter's bias for the self-evident authenticity of the unalloyed *Southern* acoustic performance is obvious; he is unfortunately forgetful of his stated allegiance to the blues audience when he convicts urban artists like Muddy Waters for inciting this same audience to dance as the performers dance, "with wild gyrations that were somewhere between a shake dance, a hula and acrobatic dancing; the fault was that the music itself had become secondary to the din and the dancing" (*Country Blues* 251).

Charters distinguishes between the music and its dynamic echo in the audience, which is the dance. It strikes Charters that this is somehow blasphemous of the music itself, which is, one supposes, the bluesman and his voice and instrument. This latter image, of course, is derived from Charters's initial portrait of the bluesmaker as the homesick African reaching with sorrow into his soul. One can't quibble with that picture as representing perhaps a part of the blues experience, but it was Charters's goal to elevate this image of agony and dignity over the raucous, "happy," and thoroughly vulgar blues of the Muddy Waters experience of the mid-1950s.

Charters finds the fault for this repulsive urban blues in the "rules of the game," changed, of course, by white record producers and companies, whose "rules" dislodged or displaced the authentic country blues for capitalistic gain. Charters's argument is correct as to its factual basis, but his allegiance to the country blues is unfortunately made at the expense of other kinds of blues which, for many audiences, white and black, are essential, not derivative.

When Charters says that Muddy Waters "is not responsible for the rules" (*Country Blues* 253) he is reiterating the strategic apology of the book's opening: what is good in the blues is the black authenticity of the Southern black experience, and what is bad is the whitened duplicity of innocent black performers with their capitalist handlers. This contrast between the Waters's tragedy and the recovery of authenticity is made very clear with Charters's last chapter on Lightnin' Hopkins, whom Charters is credited with "rediscovering," an honor given many young white men who were looking for the blues in the 1950s. After a lyrical narrative of finding Hopkins and following him around, placing him romantically in a lonely place, playing and singing "brilliantly," Charters closes his book with a summation of the proto-bluesman, whom he has recaptured, alive, in the form of Lightnin' Hopkins—a prize taken not by a mean-spirited record producer, but by a sensitive white poet who hopes to save the blues from an encroaching white darkness:

> Lightnin,' in his way, is a magnificent figure. He is one of the last of his kind, a lonely, bitter man who brings to the blues the intensity and pain of the hours in the hot sun, scraping at the earth, singing to make the hours pass. The blues will go on, but the country blues, and the great singers who created from the raw singing of the work songs and the field cries the richness and variety of the country blues, will pass with men like this thin, intense singer from Centerville, Texas. (*Country Blues* 266)

When Paul Oliver disingenuously remarks in the preface to the revised edition of *The Meaning of the Blues* (published in America as *Blues Fell This Morning*), "Throughout these eventful decades blues scholarship has grown, though regrettably, not often among black writers and researchers" (xxi), he is summarizing thirty years of such scholarship on the blues. One look at the author's note to the original 1960 edition, published just a year after Charters, reveals an obvious reason for that lack of attention he notes thirty years later. In the note he thanks, by name or company, about (by my count) fifty sources of great importance to his writing the book, some of these sources thousands of miles away from his base in England. Oliver, like Charters, is aware of his distance from the scene, from the context of the blues, Oliver much more than Charters: Charters had done fieldwork, while Oliver had only listened to records (but would later do fieldwork).

Oliver writes, "I am acutely aware of my remoteness from the environment that nurtured the blues" (ix); he casts himself in the role of historian, yet denies that he can do much more in this trailblazing book than work on "the meaning and content of the blues," which is surely enough for any scholar to devote himself to (*Meaning* ix). In fact, Oliver embeds these discussions of blues songs in extremely well-detailed and -documented histories and cultural contexts. The book still stands as the most comprehensive history of the blues, forty years after its publication. The first and the best—how is this possible? And how can we modify this popular view with a less popular one, that of Ralph Ellison's, who said the book was "sadly misdirected" ("Blues People" 257)?

Coming only a year after Charters, it seems to be a perfect antidote to Charters's romance of the blues. Oliver's is more a reality of the blues. Using the Aristotelian taxonomy of appeals, we might say that Oliver's is clearly logocentric; his logical or rational arguments based on textual evidence are in contrast to Charters's pathetic or ethical appeals. Oliver—no more than any rhetorician—is never purely ensconced in any appeal, but he is interested in the recorded history of the blues, an interest or "service" that Richard Wright notes in his foreword:

> This volume contains three hundred and fifty fragments (a fraction of the material extant) of the blues, and I believe that this is the first time that so many blues, differing in mood, range, theme, and approach, have been gathered together. We thus have here a chance to cast a bird's-eye view upon the meaning and implication of the blues. Certain salient characteristics of the blues present themselves at once. (xiv)

Wright unfortunately goes on to remark that guilt is the "most striking feature of these songs"—an odd, some might say ridiculous, claim that says much more about Wright's state of mind in 1960 than the state of the blues. (His *Savage Holiday,* a horror novel about murder, nudity, and guilt, had been published to an uncaring public five years earlier.) But his enthusiasm for the material of the blues echoes Oliver's own intention to study the texts. Curiously, Oliver writes in his introduction that the history of the form will have to wait, yet the book obviously *is* a history.

Oliver is employing two neat rhetorical tools—one of appeal, the other of invention—at once: *logos,* the appeal to reason based on the unprecedented gathering of recordings, the substance of the blues itself, and *understatement,* a refusal to make claims upon the credibility of the audience that might overextend and thus upset the tone of the earlier appeal. Oliver soon repents on his disclaimer concerning history:

> The blues did not reflect the whole of black life in the United States, and a social study of black problems does not explain the blues. But in order to understand the blues singers it is necessary to explore the background of their themes, and to try to enter their world through them, distant and unapproachable though it may be. (*Meaning* 11)

Oliver chose in *The Meaning of the Blues* to explore these "problems" through a thematic arrangement, again furthering a rhetoric of logic, given Oliver's argument that what we have in material is the music *itself*—and not the impression of "quality" that a casual listening gives us—but a hard analytical study of the words themselves: "[t]o appreciate the music without appreciating the content is to do an injustice to the blues singers and to fail to comprehend the full value of their work" (*Meaning* 10).

Oliver adopts a thematic arrangement because it highlights the words themselves as if they are poetry on the page, indicating a critical stance akin to a literary New Critical reading (a method of reading still current in America and England well into the second half of the twentieth century; see Eagleton 47 *ff.*), in which individual talent, tapping into a tradition of linguistic expression, displays insight and meaning nearly whole upon the page itself. Words are relatively closed in their meaning, with little or no extra-textual reference needed except to describe or define the "stream" or "field" in which all such expressions have risen. Oliver sees the blues lyric as such a text and—unlike Charters—does not feel a need to couch his discussions in the names of each performer or writer. Rather, Oliver works out meanings through theme.

These themes—work, travel, love, lust, magic, gambling, and so on—are painstakingly revealed through careful readings of lyrics and the social histories that ground the lyrics in a convincingly described social field. Oliver's scholarship in the blues has never been questioned (Ellison had problems with its *use,* particularly its use as evidence in

LeRoi Jones's polemical *Blues People*); it provides a foundation for almost all blues criticism that follows. By raising the meaning of the blues to a level of literary and sociological study, Oliver legitimizes the blues as an object of cultural study, which I take to be, in many cases, a conflation of literary and social texts and values, particularly those that can be grounded in matters of race and ethnicity. Whether this legitimization is at the present time a process the blues may want to reverse—a question to be discussed later in this study—blues critics acknowledge that, as Jon Spencer puts it, Oliver "set the tone" for blues scholarship to come (xiii).

It has been, largely, a tone of high seriousness. We can argue (as Spencer does) that Oliver is wrong when he states in his conclusion:

> Though it can be said with truth that the themes of the blues are to a large extent universal ones which have stimulated artists in all fields to create, it cannot be denied that many of the virtues and emotions that have inspired great art are absent. There are shortcomings to the blues. The spiritual values that are to be found in the gospel songs are seldom to be found in the "devil songs" of those who have turned away from the church. Blues are a worldly form of song and its values tend to be worldly also. (*Meaning* 279)

We can also take issue when Oliver challenges a "popular belief" and argues "there is comparatively little humor in the blues" (*Meaning* 278). It is a more popular view today, as Stephen Calt argues when writing of Charlie Patton, that the reason for the blues performance is *partying and dancing*. And it is Spencer's argument in *Blues and Evil* that the blues is a spiritual discourse grounded not in the church grammar but secular vocabularies of sin and salvation. Time has modified our responses to Oliver's book.

Ralph Ellison criticized Oliver's book as "sadly misdirected" in his review of LeRoi Jones's 1963 polemic, *Blues People*. Ellison denies that the blues, as he sees Oliver and Jones defining it, is a separate art, a pure form that can be used as an instrument of social or political change. Oliver's conclusion—that the blues may disappear as African-Americans gain admittance to previously white social environs—contradicts Ellison's understanding of the blues as primarily aesthetic and ritual. Ellison argues that Jones uses Oliver to further Jones's argument that the blues is an *ideological* weapon that has mirrored and enabled social transformations in black culture, a "tremendous burden of sociology" which "is enough to give even the blues the blues" (256); Jones, according to Ellison, "attempts to impose an ideology upon this cultural complexity" and overlooks what Ellison sees as the true meaning of the blues, which is an "imposing" of "values" upon the world ("Blues People" 249); thus I understand Ellison to be arguing for the blues as a rhetorical act, one of beauty and force.

Ellison's rhetoric of dialogical accommodation and collective ritual informs much of my argument to come; his criticism here of Oliver and Jones points out a continuing argument among blues critics, which can be delineated rhetorically using the modal terms of poetic, expressive, and transactional texts. Briefly, the poetic is that text or language that is clearly individualized, often with little or no attention to audience, and refers most clearly to the inner universe of the user's mind, his or her experiential truths. The expressive mode is that text or language that reflects the thoughts and feelings of the user, and is so shaped into language for the purpose of representing those thoughts and feelings in a communicative context; the essay is typically noted for its use of expressive language. A text or language is transactional that seeks to produce a singular effect in the listener, this "transaction" being a passing along of information, opinion, or direction with a clear intention or purpose. Popular understanding of "rhetoric" is usually this third type, especially when we think of rhetoric as public or civic "persuasion."

Our critical founding of the blues can be seen as a competition of these rhetorics; Charters sees the blues as essentially "poetic" in their loneliness, their quiet lyricism, their individual authority that pays little or no attention to listener, media, money, or color. Oliver, while confirming the poetry of the blues, so thoroughly grounds the lyric, the substance of the blues, in social history, in an ideology of suffering and displacement, that the blues is "expressive" for the sake of a race's very continuance in this society, and thus becomes an ideological tool of great importance for those who use it either as artist or audience (as the New Critics argued for poetry as offering a reading of provisional liberality while conserving meaning through eventual resolutions of ambiguity). Oliver's strength, I believe, is his attention to the poetic *and* the transactional while centering his blues criticism in a historiographic reality. Ellison may over-emphasize politics in Oliver because of Jones's use of Oliver for Jones's ideological aims; in short, Ellison may have redirected his fire upon Oliver. I think that Ellison may have overlooked Oliver's better moments as a reader of poetry—but my point is this: our triad of appeals, of *ethos, pathos* and *logos,* and, secondly, our triad of modes—poetic, expressive, and transactional—can begin to help us understand the rhetoric of the blues *critic,* and can begin to illuminate the assumptions that lie behind many of our understandings of the meaning and power of the blues.

With Jones's *Blues People* in 1963, the spectrum of blues criticism was visible at least in outline, from Charters's poetic to Jones's transactional usage through the broad, mostly expressive expressive center of Oliver. *Blues People* still stands as one of only a half-dozen full-length works written by African American critics on the blues, and while in fact appearing to be much more interested in jazz, stakes out a rhetorical position that places blues "in its most moving manifestations" (148) as an obscure yet ideologically powerful music whose function is as "an autonomous music" (147):

> There was no clear way into it, i.e., its production, not its appreciation, except as concomitant with what seems to me to be the peculiar social, cultural, economic, and emotional experience of a black man in America. The idea of a white blues singer seems an even more violent contradiction of terms than the idea of a middle-class blues singer. The materials of blues were not available to the white American, even though some strange circumstance might prompt him to look for them. It was as if these materials were secret and obscure, and blues a kind of ethno-historic rite as basic as blood. (147–48)

This mystical reaction of *blood* to the blues, feeling to *race,* completes for this study a sense of the range of work the first blues critic engaged in. Jones was beginning to set forth a manifesto of cultural independence (even as Ellison was calling him impossibly idealistic in his arguments about the segregational purity of any cultural product as complex as the blues or jazz). Jones's appeal, if we accept his ideological interests, is clearly one of *pathos,* of feelings originating from and directed on behalf of an "ethno-historic" truth which forbids entrance or "sense" to outsiders. The blood ritual of a pre-rational world of feeling and sounds is, ingeniously, turned into a weapon of political transaction in a way familiar to those who lived through the social upheavals of the 1960s, in which passion, love, and anger were wedded to political arguments couched in the language of America's Founding Fathers, as was, for example, the rhetoric of the Black Panthers. Blues, for Jones, loses its aesthetic nature precisely because of its specific origin as a felt response to injustice. In other words, Jones sees the blues as rhetorical in that its purposiveness was politically accusatory, even as its effectiveness was emotional.

Four decades later, blues criticism continues at a pace, if not steady, then perhaps "a blues beat with a jazz feel," surging, according to one critic, at the end of each decade, ebbing with, one supposes, the ebb of a blues *zeitgeist* that meets a fresh ten years with a more rigorous beat. Between Charters and the present have come thousands of texts *about* the blues, perhaps more than blues texts themselves, many of them devoted to the blues of the past, far fewer to current blues. In terms of quantity, the grand syntheses are in a small minority. But we can turn to a number of book-length studies that represent other ways to focus on the blues, other ways to rhetoricize the blues for those who would read while the music is playing.

Charles Keil's *Urban Blues* (1966) was the first flat-out sociological study of the blues to show how the blues functions in an *urbanized* African-American culture. Keil shows great sensitivity toward Jones's *Blues People* because Keil saw the book for what it was: a manifesto of the spirit, black and up North, which needed a coalescent sound around it. Despite what Keil calls sloppy scholarship, especially in its early chapters, Keil attributes Jones's lack of good blues background to the author's middle-class Jersey childhood, and instead chooses to praise the book for its cultural polemic: "Jones is really writing about a complex sort of nativism or, more accurately, a musical revitalization movement" and "gives us the clearest picture to date of the esthetic ideology that molds the musical explorations of America's leading Negro musicians" (43–44). Keil, like Charters, sees these "explorations" in primarily aesthetic terms, in which a musician of mostly lower-class origins plays the role of contemporary mouthpiece for an urbanized black culture, which is not stable but continuing to slide along a continuum of expression that takes, for example, the raw sound out of urban blues and replaces it with the smoother, more sophisticated rhythms and tones of soul music. Keil asks some important questions which the present study seeks to answer as well: "What does the Negro audience expect of a bluesman today, and what does he express for them in his performance?" (2). His problematical fundamentals, to paraphrase, are Negro culture and Negro male, and after arguing that "race" be abandoned as a term, and after writing a new foreword to the book in which he meditates on the changing terms for Negro, we can't help but be left with a sense of discomfort with these fundamentals. Looking back, we can see that the audience for Keil's two major examples, B.B. King and Bobby "Blue" Bland, have gone from black to white in King's case—and to a soul audience in Bland's case—and that Keil's whole orientation toward what was called "Black Studies" in the late 1960s has a taste of aggrandizement, so that multiple appendices calling up psychoanalysis, sociological indices, rigid classificatory schemes, and anthropological and musicological sketches of the blues add little to Keil's original hope to establish *role*.

"Role" for Keil is much like the ethical position I hope to explain in this study, but Keil's role is swathed in too many outfits, a grasping for as many costumes that will fit. His missionary zeal, first placed in a position of solidarity with a fictionalized "autonomous" spirit of the black community, is underscored by his postscript written a quarter-century later in 1991, in which this statement, reasonable enough in our times, would have destroyed much of the argumentative thrust of the original:

> [T]he blues has probably always been about whites learning from blacks, blacks learning from whites—the mutual effort to laugh and sing and cry away the pains of American racism expressed in the metaphors of love gone sour. Because it is the place where the personal and social hurts of both racism and sexism [. . .] flow together and crystalize [sic] in an infinite series of configurations like a kaleidoscope, we can be sure that seekers of truth from both sides of the black/white, male/female divides will be studying the blues for many years to come. (233–34)

This remark is prescient in its understanding of the dialogical relationship of black and white in the blues but tends to remain at the sociological site of discourse that the original book occupies. I don't believe we can argue any longer in terms of this race or that gender having an *exclusive* effect on our understanding of the truths inherent in a discourse of the blues that is nearly a hundred years old. We get to those truths, of course—as Keil argues—through the study of the blues musician, but the process by which the truth is revealed is far more sophisticated—for example, rooted in the performed language of the blues—than Keil would show us by attending a mixed concert of B.B. King's, or measuring actual distances between performers and listeners. Keil is on the verge of breaking through the old labels and exploring the rhetorical function of "role" in our culture, but he never quite gets there (perhaps because of his omnivorous academic interests), and instead returns to hint—in his postscripts—that a purely "African-American" understanding of the living blues is perhaps irrelevant if not impossible. Instead, blues is "a core *metapho*r in process, the center of a worldview that incorporates jazz, literature, aesthetics, philosophy, criticism, and political strategy" (236–37, emphasis added). Not surprisingly, this self-description of Keil's long-term project of twenty-five years sounds very much like contemporary projects of Houston Baker, Jr., Henry Louis Gates, Jr., Angela Davis, David Grazian, and others. The multi-disciplinary approach that Keil attempted then is now much in vogue, and Keil should be seen as an early herald.

What was new is the sense of the blues as a metaphor, a linguistic figure of great complexity—but a figure *only?* Does the blues only get us *somewhere else?* Is it too little in itself, so much in its trope value? Has the blues suffered a vital death, replaced by only its beautiful spirit—but a spirit nonetheless of use in what it points to with its strong dark hand? If we extend to this metaphor the status of great art, then Keil joins Ellison in arguing for the blues as a kind of literature, a full aesthetic text that can have extracted from it virtually everything else we study, whether it is philosophy or politics. Keil, however, does not elaborate on seeing blues as a master key to life.

Four studies appeared in fairly rapid order in the late 1970s and early 1980s to dispel a sense that many felt in the late 1960s and early 1970s that the blues had been appropriated by white rockers for their exclusive economic gain and had been replaced as African-American expression by soul, Motown, even the experimental jazz school of Ornette Coleman, Anthony Braxton, and others. With different approaches and emphases, Albert Murray's *Stomping the Blues* (1976), William Ferris's *Blues from the Delta* (1978), Robert Palmer's *Deep*

Blues (1981), and David Evans's *Big Road Blues* (1982) provide a theoretical backbone for those who would study the blues today, or who would listen to them with some seriousness, or who would browse through the blues with the light touch of a Scrapper Blackwell guitar solo. The rhetorical power of these four books represents a spectrum of discourse on the blues that, if not actually comprehensive, indicates the range of work the blues can inspire or demand.

All but Evans were published by trade publishers, and the Evans reprinted by one. All speak of the blues as a living, growing phenomenon with roots deep in American, African-American, and African cultures. What I find most impressive for my own my convictions about the blues is the way these four books treat the blues as *living performance*, as manifesting itself in the moment and moments of its performative expression. These four studies take the blues back off the record shelves, off the sheet music and transcription, out of the museum and film libraries—and back into the dance halls, jukes, porches, concert halls, and street corners where it belongs, and in which contexts the blues can best be understood as a rhetorical situation.

For Murray, the blues, no matter how sad, is always good for a "good-time situation," and in the following passage presents an almost miraculous paraphrase of the dialogical rhetoric of the carnival that Mikhail Bakhtin first formulated, and that will form a part of my theoretical complex in the next chapter:

> Even when what the instrumentation represents is the all but literal effect of the most miserable moaning and groaning, the most excruciating screaming and howling, the most pathetic sighing, sobbing, and whimpering, blues music is never presented to more enthusiastic response than at the high point of some festive occasion. Nor is it likely to dampen the spirit of merriment in the least. On the contrary, even when such representations are poorly executed they seldom fail to give the atmosphere an added dimension of down-to-earth sensuality. (*Stomping* 45)

Murray is indefatigably upbeat in his synthesis of jazz and blues as a "counteragent" to itself, blues against the blues, jazz against the blues—an artform that must be both earthy and refined, and can be played as a folk art or a concert hall orchestration. Murray believes that

Duke Ellington is the finest exponent of the blues we have had, and finds in him a synthesis "robust and earthy enough but also refined enough with a range comprehensive enough to reflect the subtleties and complexities of contemporary experience [. . .] a very effective counteragent of the blues or any other demons, devils, or dragons" (*Stomping* 214). The high consciousness of the bluesman is obvious here, a craft and art that is brought together and that lives for its audiences in making a sad time less sad and, in fact, fun. Murray's conclusion about the rhetoric of the blues is also enlightening, especially when paired with the black linguistic play of "signifying," in which the language of the land—English—is thrown back upon itself in ironic, playful, angry, understated, overstated ripostes, in which the expression is both torn to shreds and rebuilt. The blues, Murray says, "is a *statement* about confronting the complexities inherent in the human situation and about improvising with (or even gambling with) such possibilities as are also inherent in the obstacles, the disjunctures, and the jeopardy" (*Stomping* 250–51, emphasis added).

William Ferris's *Blues from the Delta* is a close-up version of Murray's wide angle perspective. Ferris works primarily from an ethnographer's position, gathering data in the field, noting his separation from that new context or explored area, and finding in the words of the people the raw material of his conclusions, which are similar to Murray's, though based almost entirely on the observable details of Ferris's own Mississippi:

> When performers explain the blues they often become emotional and are deeply moved by memories associated with their music. [. . .] Bluesmen "talk the blues" with the power and eloquence of their music, for both spoken and sung performances describe the same emotional core. Blues speech comments on the black man's condition and shows how the artist studies his people and voices their experiences. (41)

He then quotes one performer as saying "We have a good time" because "That's all we can do" (41).

Murray and Ferris are uncovering a rhetoric far closer to that of the "public man" than Oliver or Charters did because both see him as a person whose time is now, whose experiences are not couched in the poetry of isolation or the dim past of the classic blues, but whose work is an *ongoing response,* as Neal argues, to the experiences of the every day, the continuing everyday that takes Ferris to a house party and Murray to concerts and dancehalls where the movement is there in front of the writer's eyes, not reduced or represented—but vital and active. And unlike Keil's sociology of relative separation of audience and performer, Ferris finds meaning in the virtual disappearance of this divide, a measure that distinguishes the rhetoric of the blues from other aestheticized language-use: "When the blues singer 'talks' he communicates through his music. By playing well, he talks clearly. Pine Top sings a moving verse, and Jasper replies, 'Now it's talking to me'" (107).

Robert Palmer's *Deep Blues* continues the subjective, though not romanticized, view of the blues that Murray and Ferris argue for—but for Palmer the challenge is partly Murray's: to show a deep history, a big view of the region that most consider the location of the most significant body of blues, and to show the writer interacting with this location, spirit, history while maintaining a distance that Charters, for example, was unable to.

In Palmer's case, the result is the most readable of all blues histories, as rhetorically attractive and convincing as any book on the blues for its spirit of affection and respect (its *ethos* of care and advocacy), its alchemy of the blues in the way Palmer can evoke time and place with words and "talk" so that we can feel the essential components of the blues, for Palmer the "unmatched intensity" (*Deep Blues* 44) of its first performers (its *pathos* of awe derived from the performers), and its foundation of historical research, attention to detail and speech, the grammar of the guitar and harp, and the song line (its *logos* of blues material, its reality independent of the observer). Palmer attempts for the book's close his own definition of the blues, worth quoting (itself part quotation from a jazz musician) for its allegiance to the rhetorical strength that my study argues for the blues:

> A literary and musical form [. . .] a fusion of music and poetry accomplished at a very high emotional temperature [. . .] these are different ways of describing the same thing. A gigantic field of feeling [. . .] that's a way of describing something enduring, something that could be limitless. How much thought (to return to Miss Waddell's Clarksdale English class, May 1943) can be hidden in a few short lines of poet-

ry? How much history can be transmitted by pressure on a guitar string? The thought of generations, the history of every human being who's ever felt the blues come down like showers of rain. (*Deep Blues* 277)

Returning briefly to the interface that I suggested earlier exists between rhetoric and reality(i.e., poetic, expressive, and transactional accounts of the ways language and reality interact), we can see that David Evans's ethnomusicological study, *Big Road Blues,* filled a gap in the work on the blues, the rhetorical "deep end" of the transactional. I call it the deep end because it is perhaps least friendly to the blues fan or avid collector or even blues lover, in that the methodology employed in uncovering the ways blues is made, re-made, and transmitted through time and space is least comfortable to the non-scientist. This transactional rhetoric has no nonsense about it at all, no polite narratives or fiction-like climaxes and resolutions. Yet, in terms of its own rhetoric, it has all of these features; firmly rooted in *logos,* Evans as rhetorician wishes to gather, not create, data, that will by itself show (as self-evidently as Otis Rush saying, "And now a tune Albert King taught me") how the oral tradition works in our culture and, in this time and century, how it cuts across the grain of a print literacy that ties most of us to technology that we sometimes accept as the very substance of our culture, rather than—as it really is—as its carrier. For Evans, the challenge was to go into the field and find out how blues is alive, and how it stays alive. Much like the three authors I discuss above, Evans was a worker in the field, tracking the living breathing blues whose tracks we could all see and hear in the recordings of the artists. Tracks are not the maker and, as Evans criticized Charters for mistaking tradition and variation for derivation, so did he suggest that our understanding of the blues was insufficiently folkloric in orientation. Evans introduced a "fluidity" into our understanding of the blues, so that the usual dichotomies of city/country and pop/folk become part of a continuum. Evans does this through the significant use of the concept of the oral, as speech that moves as everyday instrument of commerce, communication, expression, out of which come recordings as only "spikes" on much wider, more representative bases of human interaction. Evans points to the bluesman's "repertoire" as evidence that the blues was normally only a part of a singer's performative abilities (106 *ff.*). His performance, as Keil noted, was a matter of role-playing, into which his repertoire was brought much as a carpenter brings a belt of tools—or the politician his menu of anecdotes, his figures of speech. Evans's questioning of categories based on recorded data serves to show that location and time, indeed *performance,* is a key factor in our understanding why the blues works, why the blues is still a rhetorically powerful tool for human interaction for the "talk" that Ferris found. To rigidify a living form is to capture it in a such a way as to over-aestheticize its visible features. What Evans did was find the blues talking to itself—a living discourse in a community of the Mississippi Delta, a complex of memory, performance, conversation, and creativity. Inasmuch as performance signals a shift of attention in our understanding the power of the blues from artist-centered studies to context-centered studies, Evans, along with Murray, Ferris, and Palmer, demonstrate a reality for the blues far beyond the mere "texts" of our record collections.

A highly selective study of writing on the blues such as this one will overlook much that is worth more time and study. Oliver's *Screening the Blues,* for example, looks at the transgressive, sexual blues lyric in great detail. Alan Lomax's *The Land Where the Blues Began* is a leisurely, expressive account of the author's fieldwork, much of it pioneering and still relevant to any study of the history of the blues. Collections of lyrics like Sackheim's *The Blues Line* or Oster's *Living Country Blues* are significant for their aesthetic extraction of poetry from the blues.

The blues is, for purposes of categorization, still dominated by *the musician's* life and music. The present study is no different in that dominance; my rhetorical readings of the blues will be organized, in Chapter 3, by musician; indeed, any stroll through collections, whether private or commercial, will reveal an alphabet by last name of musician as artist. Since biography reflects the blues' center as musician-based, I would like to look briefly at the biographical works I think reflect blues critics' interest in the real lives of the music makers.

Charters in *Country Blues* worked mainly through the lives of the musicians, glamorizing them, as he admitted, to engage our interest, or through zeal to recover their spirit before some undefined apocalypse swept all the blues away. Charters continued to work in the biographical vein in works like *The Legacy of the Blues* and *The Bluesmakers;* as early as 1970, and mainly abroad, work was published by John Fahey, Paul Garon, and Bob Groom on seminal figures like Tommy Johnson and Charlie Patton. In America, authors like Peter Guralnick, Charlie Gillett, and Sandra Lieb published articles and books on blues figures.

Big Bill Broonzy's biography was first published in 1955, but did not reach a general audience until its reprinting in 1964.

In 1971 James Rooney's curious pairing of Bill Monroe and Muddy Waters, called *Bossmen,* indicated a willingness in the publishers of blues criticism to see one of its great practitioners stand on his own two feet. The Broonzy biography indicated this as well, but Broonzy was a figure known at least as well to the folk crowd, and who had been advertising himself around Europe as the last of the bluesmen. His biography was a romantic epic designed to validate those who would see the blues as always inhabiting a shadowy world of heartbreak and loss; Paul Oliver's book *Conversations with the Blues,* published a year later, is a much better bellwether for the growing interest in the voices of those who made the blues. The Waters book, alongside the white, grandfatherly, if autocratic, Monroe, demonstrated that the American electric blues, still being brewed by Waters on the road, was of value to a general audience who wanted to hear Waters himself. Rooney's interviews, transcribed more like an oral history, indicate a growing confidence among critics to drop interpretive screens (one might say, screens of standard terminologies, condescension, and a rather crushing benevolence of the imperial-critical voice) and produce on the page more of the text itself, *sans* cultural liaison. This publishing of the spoken, not only the sung, voice of a Waters is tantamount to a liberation of the artist from his "keeper." Oster's, Titon's, and Sackheim's collections of lyrics are early evidence in the blues revival of the 1960s that the blues lyric had power as poetry, and now this extraction of the literary text from its proper context was being balanced somewhat by the emergence of in-depth biography. The life of the bluesman was not a romantic encounter with language (although the Robert Johnson legend did much to keep this version of the life alive, aided by such powerful advocates as his most popular modern interpreter, Eric Clapton, and the imaginative and powerful *Love in Vain,* a screenplay by Alan Greenberg).

The best recent examples of blues biography are Paul and Beth Garon's *Woman with Guitar: Memphis Minnie's Blues* (1992) and Stephen Calt's *I'd Rather Be the Devil: Skip James and the Blues* (1994); Calt makes clear in the James biography his distaste for the ideology he felt was inherent in the blues revival of the early 1960s, in which white blues critics, promoters, and fans placed their favorite black performers in a sort of slave-god position. Calt believes these musicians often responded in kind, in a late but striking appearance of "darkie" shiftlessness:

> One of the reasons James's playing eroded was because the fawning attitudes of white blues fans made it unnecessary for him to put any real care or effort into his musicianship. He could readily count on receiving the same plaudits whether he played capably, or atrociously, performed in earnest, or merely went through the motions. Instead of inspiring him, white appreciation had a corrosive effect on his playing. In this respect, James was no different from virtually all of the blues players who were to become "legends" as they were placed on the white respirator. (327)

Calt's book perfectly complements Charters's pioneering text, *The Country Blues,* for the way Calt closes all the loopholes in the ways we can understand the blues from a distance, as listeners and readers. All of Charters's romantic impulses are deconstructed, or even savaged, by Calt, who recognizes the implicit survivalism in the way James was mythologized by himself, others, and the music business. Calt, in effect, sees the blues "revival" of the 1960s as the bad rhetoric that Plato warned against, speech made for the purposes of only self-interest, masked agendas, a disregard for larger truths, all of which would "discourage the use of their own memory within them" (176–77): *forgetfulness* of the past, not a true recuperation of the blues before it had supposedly gone underground. Lifted out of its real contexts, Calt will not deny that there is great power in a lyric like "Cypress Grove," yet it is his argument that the extraction of poetry from ritual overlooks the utter lack of authentic communication among musician, promoter, and fan. When Calt (and his co-author Wardlow) write in their earlier biography of Charlie Patton, "For its own audience, Mississippi blues functioned purely as party and dance music, and it was to this end that Patton tailors his performing style," Calt and Wardlow are revealing a perceived dissonance between the authentic blues and the blues of Newport and D.C. coffeehouses (Calt and Wardlow 10). I don't believe that Calt is dismissing the bluesman's right to adjust his music to audience; what disturbs Calt in the James biography is a sense of the blues having been reduced to a commodity for white consumption. As "commodity," the blues loses its vitality, becomes a formal object, and thus, torn free, becomes victim to the kind of venal, and rhetorical, sins he accuses James and all the other "respirated" blues legends of.

When Jim O'Neal writes of the same revival time, "If it was a time of rejuvenation for some, it was also a time when many bluesmen had to readjust, regroup, and redefine their approach to cope with changing tastes among blacks and with new listeners among whites," he is expressing an innocent's version of Calt's ideological charge, or one with greater faith in the pact of artist and art (347). Calt's rhetorical skepticism is precisely that of the postmodern literary critic who may see language as a minefield of dissimulation, offering at all times a way to gamble, cheat, and ultimately to destroy one's own right to an authentic *identity,* to which clings an ethical character or "sinew."

More typical of the biographical writing on the blues is Paul and Beth Garon's biography of Memphis Minnie, *Woman With Guitar.* Theoretically sound, using surrealist and feminist perspectives, the text is nevertheless the kind of valentine that we associate with the white critic's view of the bluesmaker. Love, affection, a desire to preserve, protect, and advertise this love is obvious, explicitly stated, and expresses, as I noted above, a rhetoric of warm regard, a tempering of love with analysis, text with eye and ear, in order

> to celebrate and delineate Memphis Minnie's life and songs [. . .] stunning pieces that reveal not only Minnie's magnificence, but the grandeur of the blues as well. [. . .] the blues are at once general, and particular, speaking for millions but in a highly singular, individual voice. This is part of their magic, their art. Listening to Minnie's songs, we will hear her fantasies, her dreams, her desires, but we will hear them as if they were our own. (6)

The Garons' rhetoric of reconciliation acknowledges that Minnie's world is particular and distant, yet sees Minnie's work as the substance or medium by which the distance is erased—or better filled with the sound of the human condition as sung by one of us. Finally, the Garons suggest that this magic is achieved not solely by the artist, but by the audience as partner, whose powers of interpretation (of *reception* and *response,* to use terms discussed in the next chapter) are a part of the blues alchemy, transforming mere sounds and words into our own private lives, something we feel as well as understand.

The biographical approach continues. Besides an earlier important study by Pearson, and ongoing interviews of substantial length in journals like *Living Blues* and *Blues Revue,* and an ambitious feminist approach to the lives of blueswomen by Angela Davis, we have the autobiographies of Mance Lipscomb and David "Honeyboy" Edwards—these latter two of great interest to those who want to hear the musicians themselves in as natural, or oral, a medium as possible. We have now on roomy compact discs the spoken words of musicians like Robert Nighthawk and Robert Pete Williams, and the three-way conversations of John Lee (Sonny Boy I) Williamson, Memphis Slim, and Bill Broonzy. Despite their heavy framing, whether by interviewer, journal, or unseen producer, these living words of the bluesmen suggest to me that the blues is struggling still to stand on its own two feet, even as it walks like a man. The roles we have seen the blues critic take in the past thirty-five years are many; all are to some degree marginal to the object they speak about or for. All seek to find a vocabulary, not of the blues, but of the critic. It is in this search for the language about the blues that a rhetoric of distance is created. Terms like *ethos* and *transactional* try to close that distance, but perhaps they, too, only separate They are just terms, more vocabulary brought into a discussion about a musical form we call the blues. From Samuel Charters's rhetoric of the poetic-as-romance to Calt's rhetoric of the skeptic-as- iconoclast, we have seen that the blues can carry our burden as well as any cultural text, as any art that attracts our love and interest. Rhetoric, in fact, can serve to carry that load while, I hope, deepening its own tradition of inquiry. In the next chapter I introduce a fresh rhetoric—a few more bricks to the load.

2

Reading (for) the Blues

> The blues speak to us simultaneously of the tragic and the comic aspects of the human condition and they express a profound sense of life shared by many Negro Americans precisely because their lives have combined these modes. This has been the heritage of a people who for hundreds of years could not celebrate birth or dignify death and whose need to live despite the dehumanizing pressures of slavery developed an endless capacity for laughing at their painful experiences. This is a group experience shared by many Negroes, and any effective study of the blues would treat them first as poetry and as ritual.
>
> —*Ralph Ellison*

The "literariness" of song lyrics doesn't seem to be in doubt any longer. With the war of the canon that erupted in English departments in the late 1960s, the arrival of debates of relevance, there came to most of the new anthologies, upon which English departments rely to give a survey of the literature variously classified, song lyrics by as diverse a group as Stephen Foster, Cole Porter, and Bob Dylan. Blues-*derived* lyrics could be found especially in the work of Sterling Brown and Langston Hughes, whose roles in the Harlem Renaissance were, in part, the savoring of a dialect. The black vernacular had been until then relegated to novels, classic blues, or minstrel shows when placed in even the most remote "literary" context for general, or white, audiences. The classic blues of Bessie Smith and Ida Cox, for example, were showcases for dialect, but their extraction from context—for their worth as poetry alone, on a page, in the mind of a reader sitting alone with a text—was the work of, most significantly, Hughes and Brown.

This study doesn't wish to linger too long outside of the full context of music and performance except to argue that the *poetry* of the blues is in itself extractable as an object of literary study, but is not sufficient by any measure to indicate the *power* of the blues. As Ellison suggests, it is the poetry plus its ritualistic presentation, its performance under the formal expectations of its audience, that completes the art. The oral tradition in Western contexts is thus always fragmented, or butchered, by our ineluctable usage of the printed word—a severing of performance from content that creates several problems for the blues critic, especially one who sees its many parts interesting and beautiful in themselves.

Besides the poetry itself, there is the wordless music, of course, which is of course much more than a ritualistic vessel to hold the poetry. Ellison's pair of terms is quite unequal in the specificity of its members. A Blind Blake rag, a Blind Willie Johnson vocalized yet nonverbal performance like "Dark Was the Night, Cold Was the Ground," Little Walter's "Juke"—these are powerful blues with a wordless poetry of tone, pitch, rhythm, the elements of music that themselves have grammar, syntax, and style with which to form complex constructions wholly "poetic" or "artistic." Words are left behind. When Albert Collins played "Frosty" he drew on a context of the blues for our hearing it as such; everything was there but . . . mere words. The poetry was in the sassy tone of the Telecaster, the comic speed of the bends, the rocking rhythm of the bass and drums that seem to make the whole performance fall down hill with just enough acceleration to suggest a swinging, reckless, comic undertaking. Conversely, Little Walter's instrumentals, to employ a language of ritual, appropriate that smeared sound of the saxophone obligato (not the clean kind, the messy kind that sounds like it has come echoing down a corridor from a room with a half-closed door) to pull in a jazz feel on top of (or beneath) the deep sound of his harp digging into the blues scale with alternating fury and slow passion. One can be sure that, if played suddenly in the middle of a pop radio station's usual list, nine out of ten listeners would say to themselves something like "I think that's the blues," without one out of ten having ever paid to see a blues musician. One assumes that those nine listeners would be unimpressed, or think the music peculiar and alien. The blues does not have a pop sensibility, and each of us is at least intuitively aware of that sensibility, and its transgressions (which explains, for example, the popularity of Jimi Hendrix's version of the National Anthem, since its referenced appropriation of that sensibility is so to the heart of American culture and its vulnerable targeting by the countercultural rock of the late 1960s and early 1970s).

Similarly, the ritual of the blues is not only the poetry, the music—but its contexts as well, the locations where one will hear it and probably nothing else but blues talk and drinking and blues eating. A club like the old Checkerboard Lounge on the southside of Chicago, or the late Jr. Kimbrough's juke joint south of Holly Springs, Mississippi, or the cottonfield south of Greenville, Mississippi, where the Delta Blues Music Festival is held every September—or the living room that Ferris describes in his house-party chapter in *Blues from the Delta*—these are the places where the blues fills up the spaces. These are deep pockets of the blues, exclusive of any other music. Other contexts of the blues performance are along the interface: clubs with blues nights, festivals, concert halls, arena tours, street corners giving space to the blues, Celtic, folk, and rock music and whatever sounds have been given the name of music by an audience willing to stop a moment and put a dollar bill in the instrument case. Keil and Murray both pay attention to contexts, as do Evans and Ferris, finding a general though fairly slippery divide between a "sit" and "stand" ritual of audience response, the former being the hall blues of a latter-day B.B. King, the latter being the club blues of an emerging Vance Kelly or Shemekia Copeland. The divide is slippery because you can dance to King, or you can sit and just listen to Vance Kelly. And a juke joint has chairs, after all—but the blues critic has been concerned with the nature of the ritual transactions of bluesman and audience; I am as well, but I hope to approach this ritual of poetry, sound, and place with the instruments of rhetoric and rhetorical analysis, a choice that asserts that all of the blues is deliberate communication.

Does this mean that some bluesmen communicate better than others? Yes, but the measure of that success is clearly not an objective one, unless we agree that an objective measure is one that can be agreed upon by a community or collective of judges. We approximate objectivity, perhaps, as we draw upon numbers. A part of us agrees with this measure, since "greatness" is often measured by "presence" in a quantifiable sense. In short, *popularity* is greatness. We find ourselves returning to the dilemma of the critic who finds these arguments of popularity rather distasteful to his or her own measures of greatness by "greater" criteria, such as refinement of expression, allusion to the past, moral content, etc. By these standards of presence, the blues is not great at all. It shrinks to insignificance—blues recordings, according to the International Federation of the Phonographic Industry, account for only 1.5 percent of all sales (Drozdowski, "Blues" 50)—and we are left arguing about a mere molehill of artistic expression that disappears in the shadow of a few well-placed recordings by, for example, pop titans like Britney Spears—to say nothing of current bestselling performers like Eminem.

I think this argument about presence makes clear the importance of context when speaking of what the blues is, what it tells us, how its powers and beauty may be made manifest. It doesn't wash to cite record sales of Bessie Smith any longer, or Leroy Carr's unparalleled popularity among African-American audiences. These arguments are not at all persuasive when placed alongside other statistical arguments that wed even greater numbers and a supposedly higher quality of entertainment, even of communication. Yet they give us at least an inkling of the *potential* for communication in the blues. Thus, we are often confronted with the blues critic's love of the influential figure like Patton or Bessie Smith and the long lost figures like Geeshie Wiley, the everything and nothing of the blues life that carries with it a cultural history and a cultural conundrum: How can some be so great, and some so small?

Historians point out accidents of history, the Depression for one, for knocking back a developing market for the classic blues, pushing the musicians back into more private contexts of performance until the post-World War II period, the electrified instruments, the urban contexts. But between two very "present" bluesmen like Charlie Patton and Son House, how is it that between these two, Patton is the greater in most eyes? House, with the advantages of video, a rediscovery, early and late recordings, and Muddy Waters's blessing as his main influence, is generally regarded as difficult, ultimately respected yet lacking the kind of timelessness or "resonance" that literary as well as blues critics still look for in their greatest figures.

On first glance this would seem to be a needless argument about taste or preference—like picking your favorite King (B.B. Albert, or

Freddie?) or your favorite slide player (Elmore James, Earl Hooker, or Robert Nighthawk?). But behind all of these endless arguments, delicious and vital as they are to the continuance of the blues, is the matter of communication. In other words, what are these musicians, what is the blues, communicating to me—and to us, if it is possible to raise the stakes of our discussion and decide that there is a shared or collective response? And is the substance of this communication open to formulation by others, and how does race or gender affect these formulations? Or is this formulation mine alone? Is the latter—*mine alone*—even possible? Do recordings ease or hinder such a private judgment of the meaning of the blues, its communicative power—its *rhetorical* power as speech performed for the mind, heart, and soul of the listener?

This flurry of questions reminds me of the photographer who messed with Otis Rush at the club that September night. I couldn't hear what Rush said to him, but I imagine it now to be something like, "Just cool it, take your shot, move back a little, and listen to the music. Okay?" The advice is to myself now, since I move next into the first area of the rhetorical blues-complex I promised in the previous chapter.

The communication act is any use of language intended to convey information from speaker to listener. This general definition, as I noted earlier, can be usefully divided among Aristotelian divisions of the political, the forensic, and the ceremonial (8–13); contemporary taxonomies allow for poetic, expressive, and transactional uses of language. These uses, no matter how classical or recently defined, recognize specific relationships between words and reality, and refer to areas on the linguistic continuum that language allows us to draw from in our attempts to represent reality. Genres such as poetry, essays, and scientific reports do not necessarily correspond to these rhetorical or modal labels; poetry (like the protest poems of the Vietnam Era), may contain a high degree of social commentary, historical material, or factual data and, conversely, the historical text (like recent biographies of famous Americans like Benjamin Franklin and Ronald Rreagan) may be constructed with the techniques of fiction and essay.

By denying the necessary usefulness of generic labels such as poetry (and all those inevitable contestations over the suitability of lyrics as poetry), we try instead to move away from their formal properties to their effects in the world as our primary way of judging their value or power or meaning:

> Language is a system of imputation, by which values and percepts are first framed in the mind and are then imputed to things. This is not an irresponsible imputation; it does not imply, say, that no two people can look at the same clock face and report the same time. The qualities or properties have to be in the things, but they are not in the things in the form in which they are framed by the mind. (Weaver, "Language Is Sermonic" 223)

Richard Weaver's neo-Platonism is important to this study's approach to understanding the rhetoric of the blues. In the same essay, Weaver asserts that "rhetoric always comes to us in well-fleshed words, and that is because it must deal with the world, the thickness, stubbornness, and power of it"(207-8)—and reminds us that "rhetoric is cognate with language" (221) and that "[t]he condition essential to see is that every use of speech, oral and written, exhibits an attitude, and an attitude implies an act" (221). "Essential to see" supplies the subjectivity that audience-based criticism was already beginning to display in earnest: to "see a condition" is a rhetorical *synesthesia*—a complex of sensory detail and affective response—that much audience-based criticism has used since Louise Rosenblatt first proposed it in 1937.

Her *Literature As Exploration* is the first serious attempt in American literary criticism to move the reader/viewer/listener subject to the center of the aesthetic experience. Meaning is no longer a guaranteed extraction of the text; instead, the reader derives as much from her own understanding of the world as she does from her understanding of the text:

> The literary work is not primarily a document in the history of language or society. It is not simply a mirror of, or a report on, life. It is not a homily setting forth moral or philosophic or religious precepts. As a work of art, it offers a special kind of experience. It is a mode of living. The poem, the play, the story, is thus an extension, an amplification, of life itself. (278)

The dynamic between these two positions—world and text—creates the aesthetic experience that has a unique foundation in the subject. In other words, no two "readings" done by two individuals of any text will be *exactly* concordant. This assertion was troubling to many critics, as it was to rhetoricians like Richard Weaver, and readers, who doubted that the status of the text could survive this kind of interpretive free-for-all; rather, there would be the status of various readings: all children of some single parent-text that was not so much fixable as it was "felt," like the underground source of a mighty river. The subjectivities of reading ascended, the object of the text receded—yet somehow the rhetoric of the text was preserved—indeed, was augmented by the fresh interest, energy, and contextually-specific power of the *performance* of the text, or the *act* of reading. Reading was no longer thought to be a kind of decoding of arbitrary signs on a page; for every decode there was an encode, so that the power of the text was like an unfolding: outlines giving way to full frames, and frames filled in with the colors of the moment.

Rosenblatt uses dance and music as her best analogies—the ways dancers and musicians use "outlines" or "blueprints" with which to perform text, to make it truly a substantial "in the world" event. By charging the written text with a specific moment of performance, a time in which the "reader" takes the dry and makes it wet, the thin and makes it solid—a sort of double-persuasion occurs: the dancer imagines the notation's dance, turns, and it unfolds in performance for an audience unaware of the notation. The analogy of the dance to reading may not extend for Rosenblatt to performance, since the act of reading is solitary, hidden, and remains, largely, bound up in the mind. But the point is that the subjective response to texts enables the reader herself to unfold a legitimate, moving, deeply important understanding of that initial and clearly *rhetorical* "charge" or text: "Literature fosters the kind of imagination needed in a democracy—the ability to participate in the needs and aspirations of other personalities and to envision the effect of our actions on their lives" (222). In other words, what we might call the "affective alliance" is what brings text, reader, and world together in an extended demonstration of "subjective rhetoric": the text, itself a movement or gesture in time, is recovered and reshaped by the reader, who in turn is the recipient of the reshaping. The reader is changed, the reader changes—and the world, seen anew, is changed. Such is the lightning-quick strike of the greatest art, which occurs without, necessarily, a mass audience, or the formal one of galleries. Such an audience, in fact, may hang out on the south side of Chicago, coming and going, investing such "readings" with the regularity and the commonality of a good poker game.

By extending this performative aspect to literature—making it seem face to face, individualized, in the moment of the reader or listener, not the frozen dryness of the text's unrecoverable moment of creation—Rosenblatt denies that there is anything monolithic about the power of the word over all readers. Instead, she asserts its powers of suggestion, stimulation, and, ultimately, response—a term important to African and African-American theories of aesthetics, as developed most effectively by Henry Louis Gates, Jr., and Samuel Floyd. *Literature As Exploration* can be seen as the beginning of audience-based criticism in American literary theory because what is examined are the responses of a single member—the subject—of that audience. The audience may indeed *share* responses, as Samuel Floyd argues is the heart of the African call-and-response motif; this act is a ritualistic response to (and part of) performance. There is, of course, great power in the shared appreciation of a performance, even the shared demonstrations of clapping, for example, or standing ovations. But we tend to see the reading of the literary work as a solitary event which may or may not, by later comparison, share features with other reading experiences of the same work. For my study, Rosenblatt's analogy of the musician *working from known sources* becomes one understanding of the rhetoric of the blues. Two brief examples will show how the bluesman becomes the interpreter, and performer, of cultural information and lore.

The first is the carefully documented example of *Big Road Blues* made by David Evans. Evans shows how the blues is a shared medium by virtue of its repertoire—in this case "Big Road Blues"—being passed from musician to musician through performance, response, counter-performance, response, and so on. Evans considers this process a "creative tradition" of the blues by which a relatively simple art form is subtly renewed and passed on. But we can also say that the musicians of the Delta were reading each other's performances, gleaning particulars from them, and reinvesting those particulars in their own performances, thus creating the kind of hybrid or dynamic product of "variation" that is at once *creative and repetitious,* thus helping to preserve some forms of expression, while delineating new ones, new ornaments of expression, new rooms of the blues repertoire in which to push forward a tradition that was communal. Kenneth Burke refers to this phenomenon as "conventional form," with both stasis and change present: "It thrives when the audience expects it and also requires the kind of effects which it is best able to produce; but it becomes an obstacle if it remains as categorical expectancy at a time when different effects are aimed at" (*Counter-Statement* 208). Burke goes on to note two other aspects of convention: innovation and exclusion. These aspects are found in blues performance, of course, in the electric harp, for example, and the jug band, respectively.

Most blues listeners today can hardly stand to hear another version of "Sweet Home Chicago," not because the song has any inherently repellent qualities about it, but that its repeated performances have, in many peoples' minds, virtually wrung out all possible variations. In short, the tradition of *constructive* response has been exhausted. This exhaustion explains the blues' need to create new work as well as to rework the old. As great as this vessel of "response" is, it is not great enough to sustain the art form alone. We might suggest that the rhetoric of the blues has one foot on the muddy bank of the river and the other in new water from upstream: there are the expected scales, rhymes, and topics—but there must be a performed eloquence to carry them to the listeners in persuasive ways. Listeners, most simply, must want to get up and dance.

A second brief example of this "reader response" in the blues is the familiar blues jam, common also to jazz, in which a figure is stated by a leader and then passed from soloist to soloist for response, commentary—in short, a reworking that "interprets" the figure first laid down by the leader. In the blues, this "inter-song" response is most common in the urban blues band, in which one might hear a harpist like the late Junior Wells present the figure first—for example, his paradigmatic *Southside Blues Jam*—and let Buddy Guy work it over before Sunnyland Slim takes it further away and then hands it back to Junior Wells. An extreme yet instructive version of the jam can be found on a tribute recording to Stevie Ray Vaughan, called "Six Strings Down," in which a figure is carried through seven or eight "voicings" by musicians as unlike as B.B. King, Dr. John, Robert Cray, and Buddy Guy (again). The jam is especially interesting for its obvious lack of "cutting"—or trying to best the previous players; instead, there is a clear sense of response—some amusing, some contrastive, some deliberately provocative—that establishes a swift, brilliant palette of blues *styles,* of blues *invention* that hints at the fuller rhetorical power of each of these musicians when they do not have to share a stage. The loose jam structure is something like a reading group in literary circles, in which a text is understood to be about something—but the quality of one's expression of that "something" forms the creative core of that response. From these responses, of course, come the kinds of "style" we associate with a Guy or Sunnyland Slim. These styles didn't just arise full-blown from the heads or hands of the musicians; they have evolved over time through the "reading" by these musicians of other musicians, sometimes most dramatically in the moment of performance.

There are two levels, then, of response: a kind of meta-level of which Evans is writing, in which whole communities of musicians construct responses to texts, each of them somewhat different from one another, but clearly related as well; and a micro-level response, in which a single performance can contain a circle of conversation or exploratory response that, together with the first text, forms an impromptu, public "argument" about what this figure means. Such an argument recalls a kind of rhetoric as it may pertain to the blues:

> [C]ontroversia, a dialogue in which practical or philosophical formulations are situated in divergent frames of reference, brought into conflict in debate, and tested for their respective claims of *probabilitas*. *Controversia* requires that both sides of any question be heard, thus creating the conditions necessary for arriving at decisions and negotiating differences in a reasonable way in both politics and philosophy. (Conley 37)

We may conflate politics and philosophy in the blues to mean "getting at the meaning" or "getting at the truth" about the human condition. There is a faith, or hope, involved that, through this *controversia,* differences will be transcended by a unitary moment—no less subjective, but driven by an attitude of negotiation, even *colloquial* conversation.

The argument is a friendly one, and suggests the Bakhtinian, dialogical rhetoric of the blues to be considered below; its friendliness as *reading,* however, is what I wish to stress at this point, because it shows a willingness to be influenced, to see the blues as a text or texts which must be internalized in order to be felt and understood, and must be performed in order to be understood in the fullness of its audience and social or cultural context. It is no wonder that the blues has a complicated relation to gospel music (Humphrey; Spencer). The willingness of the audience to open itself to the music, and to the spirit contained within or upon the music, is what makes the gospel experience so galvanizing. Similarly, the blues is an invited music, in which the rhetoric of the form does not need to break across gaps or skepticism or disinterest: the audience is open to such a degree as to make listeners the ones who "call," and the musicians the one who heed that call and "respond." Such are the larger cycles of the cultural dialog of performer and audience. The blues can be seen as a rhetoric of call-and-response, of equal and different voices in proximal contexts of free expression.

The *feeling subject* is a matter since developed—since Rosenblatt's early work—by critics such as Norman Holland, David Bleich, and to a lesser extent by Wolfgang Iser and Stanley Fish. All are interested in the subject as primary determiner of the aesthetic *experience;* they see the act of reading as important as the reading "material" itself. The performance implications of this perspective are clear. The role of feelings is less clear, but for the purposes of the blues-complex, we are encouraged to see all the "feelings" of the blues as validated by subjective criticism; in other words, subjective criticism suggests that the self of the reader is, by definition, *what it feels,* revealing "perception, affect, associations, relationships, and finally a patterned presentation of all of these in a way that demonstrates how they are organized"; Bleich calls this process a representation of "a combination of the aggregate self-image, and the self-image at the time of the reading" (48)—even if, perhaps, the self is dancing at a blues concert, or moving up between sets for a closer look at the guitarist's fingers. The feelings of the reader—not her analytical powers—are what provoke the act of reading to continue; judgment follows, as in deliberative or forensic rhetoric, for example, but that judgment never is thought to exclude the emotions, or feelings: "The reasons we think are causing our judgments are really only a part of the complete cause for our making them. Ultimately, the separation of conscious judgment from its subjective roots is false and artificial Any such deliberate mental act necessarily involves subjective causes and processes" (Bleich 49). We channel our experiences into an evolution of identity by stacking each experience against any similar experience we have already had. In short, what an experience means is, initially, what it *already means* by prior reference. For example, the sight of a beautiful child will evoke a sense of beauty only in that it *resonates* within us, stirring in us an older memory of a child we have already known whose presence gave us pleasure. Iser, borrowing from psychology, calls this simple process of learning "schema-and-correction"—a way to see everything in terms of the past as we know it:

> The efficacy of a literary text is brought about by the apparent evocation and subsequent negation of the familiar. What at first seemed to be an affirmation of our assumptions leads to our own rejection of them, thus tending to prepare us for a re-orientation. And it is only when we have outstripped our preconceptions and left the shelter of the familiar that we are in a position to gather new experiences. (82)

By this reasoning, no one can tell us that a child is beautiful and expect to be believed except in that person's own encounter with the child, or a song of the blues: such solipsism is hiding at the heart of the aesthetic experience, since there *is* none without the presence of the feeling, thinking, subject itself. Bleich, however, allows for the subjective to become collective, the heart of the social enterprise of mutual understanding (93 *ff.*).

In the blues, feelings are at their most gnomic (to others) when we listen to a recording of Bessie Smith and say, "That is a beautiful version of 'Ain't Nobody's Business If I Do.'" The answer to why that is a beautiful version has yet to be explained, and it is hard to say, using objective musicological measures, what is *beautiful* about the performance. The beauty of the blues is commonly understood to be in the individual *expression* of the blues—both in its performative expression (Bessie feels so bad) and in its responsive expression (I know that feeling—and I feel that feeling):

> The blues in performance creates space for spontaneous response in a manner that is similar to religious testifying. Just as the sermon lacks vitality when no response is forthcoming from the congregation, so the blues performance falls flat without the *anticipated* affirmations of the audience (Davis 55, emphasis added)

The validity of responsive, individual expression is at the heart of the blues world, and the feelings of the subject roll from singer to listener with the ease of a friendly conversation.

Classical rhetoricians are clear about the use of *pathos* to draw feelings from the listener. Among its most lucid definitions is:

> [F]ew indeed are those orators who can sweep the judge with [facts], lead him to adopt that attitude of mind which they desire, and compel him to weep with them or share their anger. And yet it is this emotional power that dominates the court, it is this form of eloquence that is the queen of all. (Quintilian 6.2.3-6)

It is significant that it is *facts* that can induce emotional response—not only of the case, but of life itself, in the contexts of our everyday experiences.

Quintilian also argued that *ethos* was not in itself only a dispassionate tool for persuasion, as if the audience was perusing the vita of the speaker and drawing favorable or unfavorable conclusions based on academic qualifications or impressive references. Instead, Quintilian asserted that *ethos* itself was in part a matter of feelings:

> [T]he force of eloquence is such that it not merely compels the judge to the conclusion toward which the nature of the facts lead him, but awakens emotions which either do not naturally arise from the case or are stronger than the case would suggest. This is known as deinosis, that is to say, language giving additional force to things unjust, cruel or hateful. (7.2.24)

This blending of the emotional with the ethical—the apparently natural eloquence of the speaker—is a highly potent concept, suggesting that character, manifested in language, can itself be the source of *movere*, of the moving of the audience's soul. Imagine, then, that the feelings we associate with the blues—or its importance to rhetoric as a theoretical field—are themselves the product of dialog, or the immediate interaction of speaker and audience, of bluesman and dancer. Before music there are feelings aroused simply by the appearance of the musician—and perhaps before that: the anticipation of the appearance of the musician. The power of the pulpit-and congregation, of position-and-position, is well-known, its rhetoric the subject of countless studies; there is also such inherent power in the blues-complex.

I am thinking of the powers of performance in the moment, in the club or hall. Perhaps there is less legitimacy to such discussions including the lonely art of record-listening. Yet there is still a *recuperative* sense of the feelings of the subject: the blues listener in the home, listening to his recordings, feeling sad, happy, even angry because of the blues he hears. It is one power of the blues that such a response is even possible, given the "outline" of the blues experience that a record indicates. This is rhetoric in a reduced form, yet the feelings are there, even in studio recordings to whose production performers like Patton and Robert Johnson were given train tickets and precious little else.

When bluesmen like Mance Lipscomb say "Blues is just a feeling" the self-deprecation is understood beside the more important force of the remark: the blues doesn't *need* to be anything but a feeling. It has become much more, but at its core is feeling, an *intuited* or *indicated* truth based on the experience of the listener derived, as a subjective rhetoric argues, from the *leading* voice of the bluesman. Feeling is a part of any aesthetic experience, we can say, and in the blues one is always feeling his or her way *through* the text: there is no waiting for crescendi—there is a singular sting to the first note of the first bar that establishes tradition and moment in harmony. Here is the conjoining, perhaps, of the ethical and the pathetic that Quintilian describes: here is the blues again.

The aesthetic power of the blues is the *pathos* generated by an extra-quarter-tone bend on Albert King's Flying V, the speed at which Charlie Patton sings "Hang It on the Wall," or Memphis Minnie's hooting on "Down in the Alley." All refer to *individual* speech, which is also the power of the blues, the *ethos* that Larry Neal finds at the heart of the blues: King's exaggerated inflection of pleading (*and* boasting), Patton's lustful excitement, and Minnie's rustic joy. This rhetoric of the blues-complex is a response of feelings to feelings, generated by speaker and listener in a complex communion of melody, word, and inflection.

To summarize briefly this first part of this blues-complex: subjective rhetoric stresses the individual, who "allows and furnishes" a site for the reception of argument, and who in turn attempts to respond in kind through a blending of tradition and innovation the social and personal testimony of the feeling subject:

> The suggestions of the permanently valid that are offered by the gifted speaker or writer must be confirmed in and through the individual's personal experience. Thus, an interlocutor can suggest truths already discovered by her auditor or she can suggest truths not yet discovered. In the case of the latter, the truths can be accepted as authentic only if and when they are confirmed through the auditor's personal experience, through her own private confirmation in an act of intuition. (Berlin 12–13)

Subjectivity is a condition that exploits and is exploited by the aesthetic experience, the rhetoric of performances done within contexts of strong and expected collectivity of purpose.

Subjective criticism in literary theory focuses on the working of the reading subject as it encounters the aesthetic text, and asserts that the whole psyche of the subject is engaged in this reading. The subject employs memories, feelings, thoughts, and imagination in understanding the text. Indeed, this employment is unavoidable, given the need to recuperate meaning from a text that is only language and not present reality. For the blues, subjective criticism provides a rhetorical understanding of the way expressive performers and audiences understand and respond to one another through creative response and variation, and in so doing create a communal rhetoric of free exchange, an *implied* freedom and equality.

The second of three rhetorics involved in my positing a rhetorical blues-complex is somewhat akin to subjective rhetoric but has much less of a life inside the *aesthetic* text than it does in *everyday speech*. Above, I adjusted subjectivity so it could be understood in the everyday life of the bluesman, his listening and speaking habits, his responding to and making the blues into performance. A second rhetoric springs from a study of both fictional and everyday rhetoric, and will serve as a midpoint on the continuum of rhetoric I am constructing for the blues. (The third part, derived from the political rhetoric of postcolonial discourse, may also pertain to literary and non-literary texts; its origins, however, are necessarily nearly contemporary to this study.) Our second rhetoric is the result of traditional literary study and a linguist's work in speech, and will be discussed as a "completed" rhetoric, fully formulated by its first theoretician, Mikhail Bakhtin, over the course of the first half of the twentieth century.

Bakhtin is a pivotal figure in modern thought about language, and whose broad and sure grasp of several fields, including anthropology, philosophy, aesthetics, literature, and linguistics, suggests to me a figure of particular interest to the blues, both for blues' marginality to dominant speech and ideology and also for its essential characteristic of dialectal speech and recessive thought—a subject for which Bakhtin is famous as the coiner of an overarching, conceptual term of the dialogic. Two important features of the dialogical in Bakhtin's worldview are conditions of speech and communication he calls the *heteroglossic* and the *carnivalesque*. I will discuss these terms at some length, arguing that they bolster the view of the blues as rhetoric; these terms refer to purposeful speech to speech as communication, both in tidbits and in wide panoramas of discourse.

Heteroglossia is a term Bakhtin coined to express the "many tongues" of our speaking. He was interested in a macro- and micro-levels of speech; they are both applicable to our looking at the blues as talk and as art. As talk, *heteroglossia* is most fundamentally divided into official and unofficial speech, or between sanctioned public talk and unsanctioned, private talk. Bakhtin's politics are predictably Marxist, describing a tension or dialectic between competing forces, this tension creating new or synthetic forces which in turn interact as historical momentum. As a linguist, however, Bakhtin was interested in the ways groups had tongues of their own, ways of speaking that could be described as official or unofficial and—operating across all speech—forces that he called "centripetal" and "centrifugal." The first, centripetal, are those conservative forces keeping language stable, centralized, standardized by rule and form. The second, centrifugal, are those forces that push language past its accepted limits and make language fit new situations, new demands. In short, these two forces butt heads, unendingly, as they conserve or liberalize our language:

> Every utterance participates in the 'unitary language' (in its centripetal forces and tendencies) and at the same time partakes of social and historical heteroglossia (the centrifugal, stratifying forces). Such is the fleeting language of a day, of an epoch, a social group, a genre, a school and so forth. It is possible to give a concrete and detailed analysis of any utterance,

once having exposed it as a contradiction-ridden, tension-filled unity of two embattled tendencies in the life of language. (Morris 75)

Applications of an understanding of *heteroglossia* are obvious in the blues. The language of the blues is clearly unofficial, the recessive English that, given any of its labels like dialectal or Black or African-American or vernacular or poetic, is recognizably "outside" the mainstream speech that, as lyrics, becomes the soul of pop music, of rock 'n' roll. The language of the blues is such that many have made careers of deciphering lyrics, of decoding the blues for ears that, even though sympathetic to the blues, yearn to be able to hear the "official" language in the deliberate "code" of the blues lyric (Sackheim; Garon; Titon).

Gates's discussion of Sterling Brown's dialectal poems of the 1930s and Hurston's *Their Eyes Were Watching God* raises the interesting issue of the use of dialect *within* the African-American community itself, its powers as a rhetorical trope for authenticity even as it disrupts the larger project of the African-American artist to join the American canon. Gates sees dialect as "rhetorical structures [. . .] as representations of oral narration, rather than as integral aspects of plot or character development [. . .] verbal rituals [that] signify the sheer play of black language." (194) This issue will be discussed further when postcolonial rhetoric is brought into the discussion. But Gates's argument underscores—as we can apply it to Bakhtin and the blues—the *intentionality* of this dialog between official and unofficial speech, which will serve to underscore the aesthetic of the blues (i.e., of distinct separation from a spoken standard of English not in the *presence* of rhyme, but in the common absence of conventional grammars, vocabulary, syntax from all but the most "literate" blues). When we hear Blind Boy Fuller sing

> Do your water
> out your pitcher,
> mama, let your bowl go dry,
> do your water out your pitcher
> let your bowl go dry?

we are at once in and out of an English that is "official," recognized as, at least, derived from standard English, but "unofficial" in that it deviates from syntactical expectations, to say nothing of inflections present only in its heard version. "Mojo Hiding Woman" takes us down to the micro-level of *heteroglossia*, where we find in a single text indications of both centripetal and centrifugal forces at work. The macro-level exists when we speak of the blues discourse existing on the margin—or at a recessive level, if one prefers vertical metaphors—of a Standard English that the blues typically avoids, but whose transcriptions often approximate.

Garon appropriately criticizes the cleaned-up transcriptions common in lyric publishing for making them look like poetry on the page, as if the reader will be cued by the poetic line to read the lyric as poetry (x-xi; 100). He is correct insofar as the practice sanitizes the blues lyric so that it moves toward the center, *via* a centripetal force that the ideological apparatus we call the publishing industry surely exerts on the American reading public. But Garon overlooks the fact that the blues is so very dependent on the *verbal* performance that *an accurate transcription* is a kind of oxymoron, given the shortcomings of the alphabet and current typesetting practices. There is no easy way to deal with the deviations of the blues language. Sackheim, for example, plays inventively with white space, spacing, line breaks, indentations, as in this excerpt from Robert Johnson's "Milkcow's Calf Blues":

> Te-ell me milkcow
>   what on earth is wrong with you
> Ooooooeeee milkcow
>   what on earth is wrong with you
> Now you have a little new calf
>   oooo-oo and your milk is turning blue. (222)

His approach is at once aurally faithful and typographical creative, and meets, I think, the criteria of the bluesman himself, who finds his language part-"official" and his feelings or thought part "unofficial." There is surely room for compromise; Garon, in his and Beth Garon's biography of Memphis Minnie, retreat to an unornamented, flat, Standard English transcription rather than a "pseudo-dialect" alternative. Underlining the transcription debate was the publication, in 1994, of Mance Lipscomb's oral autobiography, *I Say For Me a Parable,* which overturns the official tongue for a rigid phoneticism which forces the reader to adopt the often strange, sometimes neologistic, world of the Texas songster:

> They kivered him up wit a old blanket. An he was swintled up jest like that, you know. That hot sun was makin him swell up.

> An so when the law come, his people was settin round. Cryin an worryin over the dead man.
> An the old man had his hawss tied to a gary post. The old man what shot im, the overseer. An the law askt him—he knowed he's hawd a hearin—say, "How'd that hapm?" (304)

The "orality" of the Lipscomb text is no more immediate than the lyrics quoted on the liner notes to a compact disc, yet our sensitivity to dialect and standardization, Bakhtin would argue, is our sensitivity to the ways language always reflects real voices in the world—and which is present only for the purpose of its *being spoken back to:*

> [L]anguage, for the individual consciousness, lies on the borderline between oneself and the other. The word in language is half someone else's. It becomes 'one's own' only when the speaker populates it with his own intention, his own accent, when he appropriates the word, adapting it to his own semantic and expressive intention. Prior to this moment of appropriation, the word does not exist in a neutral and impersonal language [. . .] but rather it exists in other people's mouths, in other people's contexts, serving other people's intentions. (Morris 77)

The "halfness" of a blues English will be addressed again when this chapter moves to postcolonial views on dominant language-use by oppressed or minority groups. But as a rhetorical concept, *heteroglossia* allows the blues critic and listener to uncover in the voice, in the words of English that the blues singer uses, the social and cultural forces that so often remain cloudy or out of view when considering the power of the blues, especially when the blues is abstracted as a cultural product, or as flat lyrics on a page. It is one thing to recognize that the voice of a T-Bone Walker is "hip" or "sophisticated," but another to note what is clearly the rhetorical force of an official *enunciation* in Walker's blues singing. It suggests, for example, that his jazz interests were at play, the more economically attractive site of jazz performances exerting itself on his voice. But to call Robert Pete Williams's or Junior Kimbrough's voices as "unschooled" or "primitive" is to fall into impressionistic judgments made with vocabularies that mask ideological biases or, to echo Bakhtin, centripetal forces of "authoritative discourse," "a discourse," Bakhtin asserts, that is "totally affirm[ed]" when we use a term like "unschooled" to describe a style of speech (Morris 79). Bakhtin's rhetoric allows us to see Williams and Kimbrough operating at a distance from the center, largely unassimilated by that "official" speech but nevertheless having much to say to it—and through it.

But Bakhtin warns us against "experimentally objectifying another's discourse" because to settle on that object is to parody *a living being's* very breath (Morris 79). We would do well to remember this, especially when we see the blues performance as an event (even on record), never duplicated, never quite captured except by a diffuse and largely invisible audience, whose responses as subjects to this rhetoric are as many or few as there are listeners.

Bakhtin was also interested in the ways our speech and behavior fall into like-patterns of response across social or even class lines. This interest can be understood by imagining the *heteroglossia* of the marketplace being somewhat less finely heard, and a clearly dialogical *repartee* between sellers and buyers replacing the "many tongues" of the general babble. This repartee of the haves and have-nots is ongoing in the marketplace; Bakhtin, however, was interested in the way this repartee was ritualized in times of celebration. These times of celebration, and of the dialogical rhetoric of the street they encouraged, Bakhtin called the *carnivalesque*.

I want to introduce the term *carnivalesque* to our understanding of the blues, and to see that term as the result of a subversive discourse the blues creates, which is *released into a laughter* that is, to Bakhtin, a "victory over fear [. . .] a simultaneous uncrowning and renewal [. . .] Hell has burst and has poured forth abundance" (Morris 209–10). The reference to Hell is important since the laughter that we hear in the blues, that is made in the blues and around it in performance, is not always the laughter of the angels, but the laughter of the lone man caught in the dark with nothing but darkness gaining over both shoulders. The uncrowning and renewal is the alternation of loss and gain that suggests the ring trope of Floyd's study, or the cyclical trope that we hear in blues like Skip James's "Devil Got My Woman":

> The woman I love
> woman that I love
> the woman I love

> stoled her from my best friend
> But he got lucky
> stoled her back again
> And he got lucky
> stoled her back again (Sackheim 175)

The laughter of the carnival is part of a discourse that Bakhtin first proposed to explain the social strata of the Renaissance and its appearance or representation in the literary text. The carnival is the loosing of the cry, abuse, praise, and laughter by the underclass within a *regulated* cultural context of the dominant—"the official, the authoritarian"—whose aspects are "violence, prohibitions, limitations" and the elements of "fear and intimidation" (Morris 209).

I equate the carnival with the house party, the juke joint, the southside Chicago blues club, and maybe even a few hotel ballrooms in a place called Hawaii, where the blues carries forth, Hell-burst and Hell-bent. The rhetoric of the blues is intent on carrying forth the cry and laughter of the bluesman and his audience. Indeed, as Bakhtin writes:

> It was the defeat of divine and human power, of authoritarian commandments and prohibitions, of death and punishment after death, hell and all that is more terrifying than the earth itself. Through this victory laughter clarified man's consciousness and gave him a new outlook on life. This truth was ephemeral; it was followed by the fears and oppressions of everyday life, but from these brief moments another unofficial truth emerged. (Morris 209)

This rhetoric of the performance to release laughter, to overcome one truth with another is only one act of the carnival's participants. Bakhtin looks at the usual elements of the communication triangle, its variations within the carnival's ephemeral life.

First, the audience. For Bakhtin, all classes of people frequented the carnival, but primarily the lower and middle classes, and other unorganized elements who belonged to no social group. He is making a point about a question that we discuss about the audience of the blues, whether its cultural importance is felt outside that culture, or felt in the same way, or whether the distance between the culture of the performer and the culture or color of the audience inevitably affects the rhetoric of the moment. We have heard bluesmen both affirm and deny the impact of the audience's color or colors, as well as the ambiance of the house. Albert Murray's binary of the concert blues and the dance blues is interesting in this regard; I think, however, Bakhtin's argument that the carnival, through language alone, upsets the dominant makes the point moot. The audience, in its very assembly, can overthrow (however briefly) the spirit of class culture by its mingling, its enjoyment of the somewhat "dangerous" text.

Between audience and performance—between the door and the dance floor, between the lobby and the first row—exists the space in which the bluesman or blueswoman performs. At Bakhtin's carnival there are several kinds of performers, and the blues knows each of them. Even though Bakhtin admits that the distinction between actors and spectators is nonexistent or minimal, "a free collectivity," he does identify the usual characters of the carnival's performance as clown and fool. One would never think to call, for example, Son House or Skip James a clown or fool. We might more readily see the words, in our usual understanding, to apply to other bluesmen who are consciously mining comic effects as part of their performance—I think of Howlin' Wolf, Guitar Slim, Eddie Clearwater, Guitar Shorty.

But Bakhtin is arguing that the clown or the fool is not the object of derision, but is the herald of an unofficial truth, the kind that is generated at the carnival through the artfulness of the actor. It is not comic, necessarily, except that the comic is diametrically opposed to the seriousness of the official culture, dominated, in fact, by church and state. According to Bakhtin, the clown derives his repertoire through what he calls "carnival familiarity" (Morris 203). I take this to be a kind of equivalent to Evans's study of local tradition, or what we call "discourse conventions," those ways of talking that we tend to expect from, and associate with, certain contexts—what Bakhtin would derive his "glossia" from. A working musician like Charlie Patton was voracious in his own listening, his own taking in and reinventing. It is the closeness of the carnival time—for Charlie Patton and Big Jack Johnson alike, the closeness of the audience—that leads to a close exchange of words, expressions, and the larger conventions of blues composition. This relationship of actor to audience in part explains, I believe, the breadth of performances of a Patton or a Jack Johnson: the wholeness of their view is due to the sense of communality which must be a precondition to the blues performance. This communality is, in fact, the precondition for the rhetorical act, in which expectations are generated in a space provided for the interchange of language.

I think Bakhtin's other important point about the clown—besides his deriving language from one's normal discourse with his audience—is the clown's self-mocking behavior. He is neither below nor above the rhetorical effect of the performance: he is "one of us" in the baldest of bad rhetorical phrases. He is literally in it, over his head, and we know when we hear it, in uttermost sympathy, that we are as well. What "it" is is the blues, and it isn't a mastery of the blues guitar, for example, nor is it a mastery of the harp or washboard. It is rather and supremely the feeling in the voice, the shock of recognition that Patton gives us when he sings "If I Were Bird Nest Bound":

> If I was a bird, mama, if I was a bird, mama
> I would find a nest in the heart of town
> (Lord you gonna build it in the heart)
> So when the times get lonesome
> I'd be birdnest bound

or when he delights us in "Hang It on the Wall," or when Big Jack Johnson sings "Daddy, When Is Momma Comin' Home?":

> "When is Mama comin home?"
> And she kept right on sayin, "Daddy, when is my Mama comin home?
> Oh daddy daddy, when is my Mama comin home?"

As Bakhtin argues, the power of the actor is in his verbal abilities, his linguistic heroism as Gates calls it, or, as Murray describes it, in the way he turns the rhetoric of the master into the weapon of the clown:

> Uncle Jerome and I was learning about verbs and adverbs and proverbs, and he preached his sermon on the dictionary that time, and he had is own special introduction to the principles of grammar: A noun is someone or something. a pronoun is anything or anybody; a verb is tells and does and is; an adverb is anyhow, anywhere, anytime; an adjective is number and nature; a preposition is relationship; and conjunction is membership; and interjection is the spirit of energy. (*Train* 71)

These linguistic abilities provide the tensile strength for the third angle of the communication triangle: the song itself.

It is difficult for us to extract the song from the performance when paying attention, as Bakhtin does, to culture. In addition to the transcriptions we have already noted, there are audio recordings, but they too cast a curtain over audience, and even filmed performances we have—while being helpful (I refer, for example, to Son House's lecture and songs as captured at the University of Washington, available as a video recording)—convince us that the ritual of the blues must revolve around the physical contact of performer and audience. Such contact becomes a blurred or fluid medium, in which sympathy and response turn the performance into a communal moment or moments. The song can be said to be performed as a collective rhetoric or discourse (i.e., as the sounds of the carnival channeled through the best orator in the crowd.

These sounds, according to Bakhtin, are ambivalent laughter, arising from songs and other verbal constructs which are of mainly three kinds: parody, abuse, and praise. The first is of least interest to us, unless we see the parody in less pejorative terms than does Bakhtin; for him, the parody is a clear and deliberate bending of official, often church, texts, for the purposes of eliciting laughter—the laughter of mischief.

But I find parody's absence in the blues significant, if we remember that Bakhtin's carnival audience is sliding down from the overclass, on holiday as it were, or slumming, for whom the references of the parody are clear. For the audience of the blues, a usual separation of audience from overclass was and is much more often in effect, so that what we can call parody in the blues is something very different (i.e., the endless recycling of songs within the tradition without the rhetorical purpose of parody—to specifically comment on that text's comic subtext—but with its surface qualities of repetition and variation). Parody is not for the blues then a comic or satirical term, but a condition of *imitation* and variation—in a sense, of honoring an ideal of free exchange. Imitation, one of the most time-honored canons of rhetoric, has to do with both tradition and excellence. Cicero writes that the student should "copy in such a way as to strive with all possible care to attain the most excellent qualities of his model. Next let practice be added, whereby in copying he may reproduce the pattern of his choice" so that he can "attain the most excellent qualities of the model he has approved" (2.2.22). In the blues it is, once again, the handing around and around and around the best of the blues, the songs that make people laugh and dance; it is the variations on theme, the "I lost my woman" lament that historians of the blues find with a dozen different names attached—like a Bible whose inscriptions upon the inner leaves has been passed from generation to generation.

Parody, however, is only used pejoratively in the blues, sometimes in reference to an overdone version, a "tasteless" one that comes from a Hollywood studio, for example. We see in Bakhtin's other terms—abuse and praise—a rich vein of discovery within the performance of the blues. African-American culture has among its verbal traditions a supreme form of abuse, the dozens; Paul Oliver has shown its relation to the blues where

> the purchaser is not challenged by a one-sided game because he feels a bond with the player-singer. Blues singer and listener are bound, through the medium of the record, whose mild terms they can interpret in a shared tradition of a more abusive nature, against a common opponent (*Screening* 245).

Oliver, without referring to rhetorical terms, has perfectly expressed the process of identification that ideally unites the speaker and listener.

There are, of course, far more subtle uses of abuse in the performance of the blues, from Charlie Patton's antics with his guitar to the misogynist lyrics of a song like Robert Johnson's "32–20 Blues":

> If she gets unruly thinks she don't wan' do
> Take my 32–20, now, and cut her half in two

or Jack Johnson's "I Slapped My Wife in the Face":

> I slapped my beautiful wife in the face this morning
> cause she only asked me where I've been.
> Oh, oh baby!

The latter shows how the song of abuse can be turned against the singer and become one of praise, albeit one with the usual sardonic twist of an oath against oneself. Songs like Johnnie Temple's "Lead Pencil Blues" are in this tradition of abuse and mocking self-pity, in which the laughter is freeing, in which a social consciousness of the audience turns the performance into a ritual of sympathy and joy, an unbaring of the singer's soul for all to pity.

Praise is a more subtle quality in the blues. In speaking of the carnival, Bakhtin refers mainly to the outlandish claims of the verbal artists for their own performances, again a kind of clowning that he said was based on "[f]reedom, frankness, and familiarity" (Morris 213). Playing the fool is a recognized part of the comic art, of course, but its appearance in the blues is, for me, more in the realm of *hyperbole*, a rhetorical figure of exaggeration that Aristotle calls a mark of the young, which displays "vehemence of character" (2.12). Such praise does not harm its effectiveness as commentary by its moving out of bounds. When I listen to Robert Johnson's "Terraplane Blues":

> Who's been driving my Terraplane now
> For you since I've been gone

and "Honeymoon Blues":

> Betty Mae, Betty Mae
> You shall be my wife someday
> I wants a sweet little girl
> That will do anything that I say

or Memphis Minnie's "Me and My Chauffeur Blues":

> Going to let my chauffeur going to let my chauffeur
> Drive me around the drive me around the world
> Then he can be my little boy
> Yes I'll treat him good

I hear this comic praise that has some sweetness in it, some sour, some self-pity and self-mockery, at its center an authentic cry of love that must be screened with art if it is to maintain what Bakhtin calls the "utopian ideal and the realistic merged" in the performances of the carnival (Morris 199). It is what Kenneth Burke calls the appeal of form:

> The rhythm of a page, in setting up a corresponding rhythm in the body, creates marked degrees of expectancy, or acquiescence. A rhythm is a promise which the poet makes to the reader—and in proportion as the reader comes to rely upon this promise, he falls

into a state of general surrender which makes him more likely to accept without resistance the rest of the poet's material. In becoming receptive to so much, he becomes receptive to still more. (*Counter-Statement* 140–41)

Burke's "state of general surrender" is the promise of the carnival, well-delivered into the hearts and minds of the audience, just as it is into the willing eyes and ears and bodies of the blues audience.

"Community, freedom, equality, and abundance"—these are Bakhtin's key terms for the value of carnival. I see these things in the blues. I think I have sensed them from the moment I heard my first blues—some Leadbelly my older brother had collected during the revival of the early 1960s. I heard it at my first blues concert (Muddy Waters, Portland, Oregon, 1968) to the last concert, Buddy Guy romping around a basketball arena in Honolulu, and between—to Otis Rush singing and playing for two hours on North Belmont. I have never before thought of it as *carnival* time—though my enjoyment of the Delta Blues Festival in Greenville, Mississippi might be explained that way—but there is a simplicity and generosity in Bakhtin's work that clarify the *importance* of the blues. It can elevate our understanding of the blues to that of other literary texts, other performances that have traditionally been given more space and energy in our learning and teaching: Bakhtin allows us to connect the blues to timeless rituals of community and freedom, to see in the clubs, parties, concerts, and on the porches a *social consciousness* at play, to see it blossom in the verbal lyricism of the bluesman, the laughter of the crowd, the darkness behind us and maybe ahead as well. The rhetoric of the carnival is a consequence of its own brief time in the air as dark laughter—before the man comes and closes the carnival down.

Bakhtin's formulation of *heteroglossia* and the carnivalesque suggests a dialogical rhetoric of the blues by which we as listeners can understand the music, the maker, the song, and ourselves. Bakhtin's helpfulness takes us up to but does not include the third part of our study of the rhetorical complex. This third range of the continuum I have gleaned from literary and rhetorical theories is the most current of the three, indeed is *predicated on the current* as a trope for the way power flows today (or is drawn) from colonized to colonizer, from possession to imperial, from oppressed to dominant. Postcolonial studies seeks to uncover the ways power *animates* us, how this habitation tends to wither those who have been taken, and how it swells those who are the takers, how language, act, and art mask and display this flow in both the context of imperialist text or the text of the colonized.

Jamaica Kincaid's *A Small Place* displays a particularly angry, politicized expression of this condition, within which, I will argue, the blues can be observed as postcolonial discourse:

> [W]hat I see is the millions of people, of whom I am just one, made orphans: no motherland, no fatherland, no gods, no mounds of earth for holy ground, no excess of love which might lead to the things that an excess of love sometimes brings, and worst and most painful of all, no tongue. For isn't it odd that the only language I have in which to speak of this crime is the language of the criminal who committed the crime? And what can that really mean? For the language of the criminal can explain and express the deed only from the criminal's point of view. It cannot contain the horror of the deed, the injustice of the deed, the agony, the humiliation inflicted on me. (31–32)

Postcolonial theories of culture are no more monolithic than critical perspectives in the blues. Kincaid can be critiqued as expressing an extreme and simplistic view of the condition that leads to the adversarial or conflictual model of discourse between colonized and colonizer. Jones's *Blues People,* if it had been made aware of a theory to come, would probably have availed itself of Kincaid's jeremiad, a rhetoric of anger and doom that pushes the listener into a position much like a cornered animal, whose only egress is straight through—or retreat from—the source of the fear or hatred. This leap forward is the only one left, Kincaid would say, but it is a leap backward through a history of horror.

A second position, less extreme than Kincaid's, is expressed by Homi Bhabha in such a way that we might see his as a post-structuralist version of Bakhtin's dialogic, in which there are counter-positions, but midpoints as well, which are reached by a conjoining of language, what Bhabha calls mimicry:

> *Almost the same but not white:* the visibility of mimicry is always produced at the site of interdiction. It is

> a form of colonial discourse that is uttered *inter dicta:* a discourse at the crossroads of what is known and permissible and that which though known must be kept concealed; a discourse uttered between the lines and as such both against the rules and within them. (237-38)

In addition to the interesting use of the ever-lingering metaphor of the crossroads, how reminiscent this description is of the ways three bluesmen describe their experiences in Alan Lomax's freeform sessions he called *Blues in the Mississippi Night*. Big Bill Broonzy, Sonny Boy Williamson I, and Memphis Slim are monumentally restrained in their comments about audience and freedom, yet we can hear at the very same time not a restraint but a *con*straint. Each man was simply prohibited by his time and cultural context from "speaking his mind." Instead, as with so many blues lyrics that we call, too easily, "double entendres," we have to look, as Bhabha says, between the lines for the real strength of the blues performance. By "strength" I mean its substantial double-edge, its power to go beyond the *literal* sense of Sleepy John Estes's

> Now
> Mr. Clark is a good lawyer
> He good as I ever seen
> He's the first man that proved that
> Water run up stream

to the metaphorical Mr. Clark who can keep Estes out of the pen, as a god or devil or good liar might, if Estes will just keep himself out of the grave.

Bhabha refers to this ability of the colonized individual or group or race to be not only "almost but not white" but also to have the quality of a *"metonymy of presence"* (239). He argues that what colonized discourse has to work with is the discourse of the colonizer, though access to it (say, the King's English) is simply forbidden, and is impossible, in fact, if coming from the wrong-colored face (thus, the reverse criticism aimed at English blues musicians, who sound decidedly odd singing blues lyrics as if they are reciting Cockney street rules). Only by devising a new language, or organizing the old to suit the requirements of English—only by doing this would one have a metaphor of the dominant English. Bhabha argues that by using Western forms the colonized are forging a metonym—a resemblance that has its own life, its own mobility and powers, rather like a created man who is a blasphemy to the one, a working presence to the other. What is being resembled (or mimicked) are the old forms—the forms of the master.

We can characterize this sense of resemblance, or mimicry, to a concept of the bluesman as a medial figure between two cultures unequal in power, a sublimely powerful one, which can assist us in understanding this famous line of Robert Johnson's from "Walking Blues":

> She's got Elgin movements
> From her head down to her toes,
> which is followed by one much less noted—
> Break in on a dollar most anywhere she goes.

The first, "Elgin movement," he borrowed from current white slang of the time, referring to clockworks on a literal level but, to the delight of the audience, having a reference to the movement of a woman's body. The drawing together of curves in clockwork and women is justly famous. (As an example of the power of metaphor to grow beyond a believable intention, we might turn to Eric Clapton's admission that he was first drawn to Johnson by this kind of language, which Clapton seems to have associated with the *Elgin Marbles,* an entirely different but understandably *British* measure of female beauty! (Guralnick 46)) But the third line has no clear "official" reference that I can discover, and displays both Bakhtin's *heteroglossia* in one stroke and Bhabha's metonymical presence: the first two lines resemble Standard English, the third line appears as a true "blues figure." The first two lines are clearly *indebted,* opening the door for the third, which I can only guess means that the woman will, one way or another, take your money if you let her, perhaps even if you don't know that you are letting her. It is symptomatic of so many blues lyrics that their meanings are partially hidden behind this "mimicry" that Bhabha explores. Rhetoric becomes a delicate construction of forms that plays with empowered figures while embedding them with—and within—the "unthought-of" that eludes the dominant discourse. Bhabha calls this resolution of contradictory positions or influences hybridity, a term which immediately calls to mind the very essence of American culture, but which for Bhabha means "a form of social and psychic recognition; it is an awareness of the graftings, transitions, and translations through which we define our present and articulate an ethics equal to the way we live now" (qtd. in Olson and Worsham 18). He argues that hybridity is about the "enunciatory subject" but *not* about the "politics of recognition"; I understand this to mean that the postcolonial subject is not himself "speaking" for or to the dominant; rather he is "a subject in performance and process, the notion of what is to be authorized, what is to be deauthorized, what difference will be signified, what similarity or similitude will be articulated—these things are continually happening in the very process of discourse-making or meaning-making" (qtd. in Worsham and Olson 19).

This "subject" is the whole discourse, forming itself through performance and response. Bhabha's work suggests for this study a way of understanding the blues as a rhetoric in continual search of these enunciations against all odds—those of its own presumed context of African-American culture (which overlooks the blues to a great degree) and the larger one of American culture (which tends to "possess" or recognize the blues as a fixed body of work). The "social process" of hybridization both ensures and endangers the existence of the blues—and authorizes this study to view the blues as a flow of rhetoric to and from "enunciating" subjects:

> For me, hybridization is really about how you negotiate between texts or cultures or practices in a situation of power imbalances in order to be able to see the way in which strategies of appropriation, revision, and iteration can produce possibilities for those who are less advantaged to be able to grasp in a moment of emergency, in the very process of the exchange or the negotiation, the advantage. (qtd. in Worsham and Olson 39)

A third position within postcolonial approaches to language and cultural positions denies that there's anything authentic or "masterly" about any discourse. Postcolonial theory becomes most postmodern in this third position in that "'I' is not unitary, culture has never been monolithic, and more or less is always more or less in relation to a judging subject. Differences do not only exist between outsider and insider—two entities—they are also at work within the outsider or the insider—a single entity" (Minh-Ha 218).

In reference to the blues, this means that African-American knowledge is not necessarily an *inheritance* of the African-American and is not necessarily forbidden to the non-African-American. Such a position floats aesthetic work like literature and music apart from any strict cultural tethers and instead makes it accessible to any individual who so chooses to take that path. Such a third position is attractive to many workers in cultural studies because any recognition of "authenticity" denies power to many who might therefore be considered "hybrid" or "outside." Gareth Griffiths writes:

> The mythologizing of the authentic [. . .] is [. . .] in many ways itself a construction which overpowers one of the most powerful weapons within the arsenal of the subaltern subject: that of displacement, disruption, ambivalence, or mimicry, discursive features founded not in the closed and limited construction of a pure authentic sign but in endless and excessive transformation of the subject positions possible within the hybridised. (241)

This is the rhetoric of the slippery slope, the hyperbolic course of the endlessly reproduced, warped, re-appropriated sign. This is not a comfortable position for a speaker of the blues (or any other represented reality)—but a continuum of possible positions, upon which the rhetorician can slide, but with no authentic or original center to which he or she can come *home*. But a hallmark of the beauty of the blues, especially as defined in work by Charters and Lomax in terms of the authentic *bluesman*, and in work by Keil, Spencer, and Evans in terms of the authentic *culture*, is this authentic *nature* of the blues. But when we face it with postcolonial understandings, the blues tends to slide and blur into a Frankenstein-like monster of hideously reduced intelligence, ugly repetition, primitive sounds and rhythms, what LeRoi Jones himself called "city" blues—"harder, crueler, and perhaps even more stoical and hopeless than the earlier forms" (105). How can the postcolonial "lens" be handled productively, so that we can understand the blues as authentic expression, as powerful as the most canonical drama or prose or poem?

Postcolonial rhetoric can deny that there is any such thing as assumed authenticity, if we take this third theoretical position; the blues is so much a hybrid itself that to speak of authenticity is to speak of a romantic notion that is denied not only by the nature of the music but by the nature of the bluesman himself, a figure raised under a culture not at all pure, but controlled, in fact, by white overlords, white industry, white commerce, white language, and so on. If there is authenticity, as Minh-Ha argues, it is a matter of the *subject judging*. We return, then, to the first part of our rhetorical-complex: the subjective critic, the audience whose powers include the response, the evaluation based on contextual—not only cultural—parameters. And, of course, we have the advocates of Delta blues as "authentic" and contemporary soul-blues as "non-authentic"—a fine example of the hybridized subject position.

But the conflict is not resolved for those of us who think that there is such a thing as the blues *itself*—springing whole-made from Baker's matrix, to be taken as new. Those who think there is such a thing as the blues itself do not need to say much about postcolonial thinking, or even response theory, or any Bakhtinian dialogics. Instead, these blues people think of the blues as "walking like a man" and always walking—a living blues entity with strength and beauty and power, existing somehow apart from the vagaries of critical perspectives, historical change, audience expectations. If the blues doesn't walk, it hangs in the air like a blue note sustained by a few hundred watts of electricity, a clean dark vibrato endlessly rising and falling and running from Yazoo, Mississippi to Chicago, Illinois, spreading east and west and just singing in the air, forever and always.

How is this cherished blues either subjective or dialogic or postcolonial? What crossroads can this study's rhetorical complex map for its meeting with the blues?

When Otis Rush played that night in September he was probably not thinking of any of these issues, certainly not the theories that formalize them. Perhaps in his off-hours, when questioned by critics, writers, and fans he would have to face them, but they surely become foreign objects when the amps are turned on. This is not an unusual situation, of course, in the world of criticism. The parasitic nature of much writing about art troubles some critics like George Steiner, who turns to the consolations of God for answers to difficult questions about the need for so much agonizing over meaning and presence in language, where "any coherent understanding of what language is and how language performs, [. . .] any coherent account of the capacity of human speech to communicate meaning and feeling is, in the final analysis, underwritten by the assumption of God's presence" (3).

Others see the critical enterprise as simply a part of the discourse of art and culture, an articulated response to the object or text or performance that "stands in for" or "complements" all the other responses to that object that are left invisible or merely felt or thought about in the minds of audiences or readers. Critics become articulate spokespeople, sometimes refining their own art beyond what general audiences consider reasonable response; hence, the division noted earlier—between pop and high culture—leads to critics writing to and for themselves and leaving mass audiences to their own inarticulate yet powerful responses, often measured only in terms of dollars spent, but more virtuously in the hours upon hours we call leisure time or pastime or entertainment time.

Mulling over these matters again, I find myself particularly affected by the fact that the blues is thought to be a pleasure of the underclass, a black underclass, often captured in history's sepia tones, but always a class removed from the *real* channels of power, the roads to freedom or riches. I think this rather romantic and melancholy image is also essentially true, and it is what draws so many people to the blues. It is disaffection from so many expectations in life, but a disaffection posed as damned and damnable fun. It is a *coup* against those who would make us sad—a middle finger raised at a woman or man or place or time that brings us down. When Otis Rush smiles his gentle smile, eyes closed, it is as if that "joy" of the blues has lodged itself very gently in his soul and it shines forth with a "You can't hurt me anymore" steadiness.

But Rush is just one bluesman. One watches Son House's furious performances and believes that this is a serious, necessary expulsion of sadness, regret, anger, disappointment. And Memphis Minnie luxuriates, in her hoots and relaxed picking, in a soft regret over loss, lust, and love. The blues are no more monolithic than the theories I hope to understand them by. All that these theories do is open new ways to understand, not ways to close other understandings or to imply that they are inadequate to the task. The blues is too rich to come under any single authoritative gaze.

What an adoption of rhetorical perspectives—the feeling audience of subjective response, the dialogical process of speech communication between performer and society, and the postcolonial context of language and identity under stress—allows the blues listener to do is this: to play with these perspectives and critical tools as each performance seems to offer ingress. The marvelous verb *seems* is deliberately chosen; there must be a certain threshold over which one must cross in order to analyze an aesthetic experience. These perspectives and tools await us beyond that threshold. Just as I earlier asserted in Chapter 1 that the rhetoric of blues criticism slides east and west upon a classical continuum of *ethos, pathos,* and *logos* (drawing unequally from these sources of rhetorical power)—so we can move now, I hope, to a series of assertions regarding the blues in terms of a rhetorical *event,* the performance of nine blues. We will couch the blues in relative terms of public or private contexts for the purposes of understanding the meaning of the blues, its power and beauty in its many appearances.

The *need* to understand is as mysterious as the *ways* we find to understand. It can arise out of love for the music, certainly, or love of the culture which one believes gave rise to the blues, or a curiosity about certain ethnic expressions, or an interest in generic explorations of music. One's initial position of interest is important in understanding one's need to go further into the blues, as Peter Rabinowitz notes in describing any act of "reading," "looking at readers' starting points can help us understand how interpretation comes about and what its implications are—not the implications of the particular texts at hand, but the implications of the very means we use as we go about making sense of them" (3). I would argue that the critical tools discussed here offer an instrument for any investigator, casual or scholarly, not only to understand but to enjoy (and, hence, *live*) the blues.

The next chapter, I hope, will demonstrate this range of understandings and enjoyments. The chapter does not purport to find the essence of the blues in nine performers nor to present a top nine of performers, nor to indicate the range of the blues. By my own critical apparatus and measurements, these nine performers are great rhetoricians of the blues, whose command of the blues text and the blues context makes them worthy of my study.

Many performers recoil from the complicated judgments made of them; others are flattered. Most, I would say, see the role of the critic in much the same way as he sees the role of the audience. She's out there listening and feeling. The critic is part of the audience whether you hear back from him or not. But there's special beauty in getting that critic off his seat and moving. It may be "just words," but you've reached into his soul nonetheless.

3

Cooking (with) the Blues

The emotive vibration between audience and performer can only be achieved through ritual sharing. As author and reader we may or may not reach a harmonic, communicative empathy. I hope that my study of enlarging the rhetorical view of the blues from an emphasis on a personal *ethos* of the bluesman and blueswoman to a communal *pathos* of audience and artist is demonstrated in a specific manner in this chapter, one that seeks to combine the thinking, feeling subject of the rhetorician (or bluesman) with the minds and hearts of the audience (repeating and reinventing the blues performance itself). This study has until now looked at general conditions and individual perspectives, but has remained for the most part outside of the performance itself; the performance has been understood as a rhetorical context for the interactions between speaker and listener, but has not been analyzed from within the performance except in first- and second-hand accounts of live performances.

This chapter hopes to draw the analysis into what traces of performances many of our culture have as their only access to the blues: recordings. I argue that they can serve as legitimate examples of original performance, and that they afford a recourse beyond the aforementioned appeals of face-to-face rhetoric with a third of *logos,* perhaps overlooked by many who are thinking of blues as "wordless rhetoric," as *affective* texts. Recordings, in fact, allow for the tempered, or reflective, experience of the blues, tempered or supported by printed lyrics, histories, transcriptions, scholarly readings, testimonials by audience members, and so on—many resembling the special topics of classical rhetoric, which are not available in the concert hall or club, but which can be accessed simultaneously with the recorded performance. In short, the recording can deepen the rhetorical dimension of the blues by offering *words* written in retrospect that suggest historical, social, and aesthetic reasons for the recording's existence—much like criticism but perhaps less argumentative, more transparent or expositional. I hope to provide, in several different forms in this chapter, a rational discourse acknowledged as present (if rarely emphasized) in the context of any blues performance.

Selecting the nine performances for this chapter's rhetorical readings was not an easy task. If I had depended simply on my own references, I could have filled ten chapters, but my sense of personal favorites has been only one factor. I have chosen performances that are canonical or relatively popular, and that are readily available to any listener determined enough to go to three or four shops, at most, to find these performances; many will also be available in academic library collections, All are readily available on compact disc. I have arranged these performances by date of recording; and while I can't argue that there is any straight-line logic to their plotting over the past seventy years, I will point to general modes of development in the blues from performance to performance. The predominant work in these readings, however, will be within the parameters each artist has set for these recordings and within the parameters with which the blues has enabled us to see, especially, the rhetorical effects I have described in the preceding chapters. Some of these readings have considerable supplementary material included—biographical details, for example—while others stand nearly alone, or within purely musical contexts.

Geographical coverage is quite narrow; I have made no attempt to distribute my readings across the Piedmont to Texas, or to Los Angeles or Africa or London. In fact, my choices appear to lie, with two radical exceptions, up and down the main North-South axis of the blues. Similarly, gender notice was not given to these readings, though in hindsight the ratio of eight men to one woman would seem about correct in reflecting current numbers of blues performers, if not blues audiences, which, especially in clubs, are more evenly gendered. Race as well was not a key factor in my choices, although I do believe that the postcolonial dimension of the rhetorical power of the blues mediates against white bluesmen—or marginalizes them in an already marginalized discourse. Since I have described this dimension in the preceding chapter, it is not surprising that only one of these performances is by a white musician.

These nine choices do, of course, reveal my interest in displaying the rhetorical power of the blues. As I argue, three modern rhetorical views of language—subjective criticism, dialogics, and postcolonial language-use—when combined with elements of classical rhetoric, allow us to analyze the blues performance's meaning and power. I do not argue in any of the cases to follow that the bluesmen and blueswomen whose work displays this power were necessarily aware of their skills as *rhetoricians*—as *artists*, yes, who are aware of their effect on audience, but not necessarily in the terms of rhetoric that we can employ. "Purposiveness" is perhaps the better word to describe one mindset of the effective, or rhetorically strong, speaker; we can also lodge this "purposiveness" in the audience, in the whole community of blues people who—in various ways—acknowledge the power of the blues in the way the blues moves it to thought, feeling, and dance. "Preaching the Blues" is a well-known Son House blues—it is also a famous Bessie Smith blues. Perhaps it is a title that best suits the rhetorical grounding of this music, in the "sermonic" power of language.

Finally, where possible or appropriate, I discuss other performances by the artist that I think illuminate the chosen text; these other performances may include other recordings, video or filmed performances, other versions by other artists, and my own personal recollections or those of other blues listeners.

Nine Performances of the Blues

Charlie Patton, "When Your Way Gets Dark" (1930)
Source: Charlie Patton, Founder of the Delta Blues (Yazoo 2010)

Patton is still a cult figure, underlined recently by a certain amount of hype surrounding the reissuing of his music on compact disc and notice of these releases by national music publications. This cult status carries with it a certain pleasant cachet of elitism among his hardiest fans, a "told-you-so" among the oldest, a torrid worshipfulness among the younger. The holier-than-thou spirit that infects so much cultural criticism these days finds Patton to be much more hip than Robert Johnson, for example, who is too much the spiritual leader of *white* players and casual listeners of the blues, or Blind Lemon Jefferson, whose own wave of adulation was tuned to the earlier folk blues revival of the early 1960s.

Patton is the authentic bluesman to end all discussions of authenticity, the flashpoint of discussions about the power and depth of the blues. Patton achieves a double intensity of significance to his cult members because he is unknown outside of the blues discourse he is credited with founding; unlike Robert Johnson, one cannot expect Patton on the *Billboard* charts anytime soon. He is inclusive of the blues' deep center, yet exclusive of its inauthentic fringe.

The cultishness of Patton's current following can be attributed as well to the less-than-pretty condition of his recordings, his less-than-pretty voice, his less-than-pretty guitar playing, and his unfocused repertoire. Only the first factor was beyond his control; it is too bad he recorded for Paramount, which used inferior equipment. The other factors I note were clearly of choice (although the ragged voice may have been because of a throat-slashing: more grist for the mill), and the Patton cult today valorizes these choices, of course, into arguments of artistry and commitment and scope—while feeling itself lucky that Patton would have none of, for example, Robert Johnson's elegant refinement when playing his blues. Johnson's blues were dark, but they were still sweet.

Patton's voice, guitar, and repertoire all suggest an extensive rather than intensive spirit, a performer who, in Son House's opinion, would do any crazy thing he could in order to get the attention of his audience. I would add that this "craziness" is in fact an intensely focused rhetoric of such pliancy and such contextual sensitivity that we can see in Patton the first great recorded rhetorician of the blues, one who could read his audience wide open, speak back to it in a dozen different ways, and could mimic the voices of his time with such ease that, as one listens to him, it is easy to imagine three or four Patton *brothers* gathered around the microphone:

> a double articulation; a complex strategy of reform, regulation, and discipline, which 'appropriates' the Other as it visualizes power. Mimicry is also the sign of the inappropriate, however, a difference or recalcitrance which coheres the dominant strategic function of colonial power, intensifies surveillance, and poses an immanent threat to both 'normalized' knowledges and disciplinary powers. (Bhabha 235)

It is not too much to argue that this dangerous strategy that Bhabha defines is what still attracts the potential cultist to Patton while keeping most others at bay. What I called "sweet" in Johnson is the sense that this "wild spirit" of Patton's is somehow uncivilized by comparison—not uncaring or oblivious, but tuned to an audience that has, for most of us, disappeared into history. His unpalatability in our time is palpable; if I seem ready to "orientalize" Patton into the exotic figure that the early blues-finders were always seeking, then I am also ready to rhetoricize the effort, and assert that such a figure of renown *within* a discourse, who remains unknown beyond it, must speak with an eloquence of some refinement, of a repertoire that suggests a formalism forbidding to a general audience; yet Patton knew all kinds of music and, according to Calt, was successful at dance, gospel, and minstrel forms.

Gospel, ragtime, preaching, and a folk sensibility can all be found easily in Patton's limited number of recordings. The hybridity of the postcolonial figure, either cast as a "mimic man" or as one who must speak to an "Other" in accepted (though radically altered) tongues can be found in Patton, beginning, as I noted above, with the voice.

I can hear three voices in Patton, and a fourth if you add the speaking voice of the brief sermon he issues in "You Gonna Need Somebody" and "Prayer of Death." I know of no other bluesman with this capacity, certainly no pop singer comes to mind even if we count the falsetto and the spoken passages of Motown singers and soul artists. Howlin' Wolf derived that gruff growl from Patton, and could do the upper register croon now and then for contrast, but in Patton there's a middle range that establishes Patton's abilities not only to deviate but to center as well.

The main tool is the rough baritone, which is throaty, rugged, at times "wet" sounding as if the singer has too much phlegm in this throat, at other times woody and muffled, though the latter may be a result of the poor condition of the recordings we have. To my ears the voice is not particularly expressive in itself; at times, there is even a monotone that creeps into the singing as if Patton is going over the lines in his mind as an exercise in memorization. What emerges during these flat passages is, instead, a rhythmic genius that finds obvious outlets in songs like "Hang It on the Wall" and "Mississippi Boll Weevil Blues," in which the words are more spoken than sung, but spoken with such obvious rhythmic attention (as they are in rap) that their lyricism is revealed the way a musical instrument will reveal the rhythm of a song accompaniment.

What Patton can do is blur the lines between words and rhythm. In jazz the *tour de force* version of this blurring is scat singing, but Patton would never entirely lose track of the lyric-based blues. Instead, he seems to deliberately frustrate our expectations (frustrated by many blues performers, of course, but Patton may be the fount) of linguistic competence in our singers.

When we consider that Patton was also the writer of most of the songs he recorded, with the clear exception of the gospel numbers, his methods become even more clearly tilted toward the deeper text of the song: its rhythms, which can be amplified with guitar and the body in performance. Patton had a sense of rhetoric as a totalizing effect of performance, not lyric, not guitar, not even voice; he is the equivalent of the elocutionist who has learned not only the niceties of language and argument, but also the minutiae of body language to create a full presence, a "thickness" of effect.

An example of this melding of effects, this time from the instrumental context blending into voice, can be found on "Spoonful" and "Prayer of Death," in which the powers of Patton's mimicry are given to guitar, the former in replacing the title word "spoonful" with a bottleneck figure that mimics the inflection of the word, and in the latter, the guitar showing us the sounds of bells rather than naming or mimicking with the voice. In rhetorical terms, this bringing into play of elocutionary effects—in short, gestures other than those of the voice—suggests that Patton was aware of the repertoire available to the performer beyond the given of words and music. Patton not only seems to have blurred the lines between the word and the sound, he did as well the line between his body and song:

> Patton's uncanny liveliness as a performer gave his music an intangible and inimitable dimension that elevated it above house "frolic" entertainment and probably made him the singular attraction he was. "Oh man, he puts *all* his-self into it," Booker Miller said of his performing style. " [. . .] Sometimes it 'looks just like he's gonna fall outta his chair." (Calt and Wardlow 20)

What Calt and Wardlow call the "intangible" quality of Patton's excellence they later attribute to Patton's "buoyant" power of expression, an intensity that is not "taut" like his unnamed rivals, although they have particularly harsh words for Son House (who, it could be argued, *was* certainly taut in his delivery). The pejorative take on this "buoyancy" is the clowning that others, as Calt and Wardlow document, accused Patton of using in order to hide what was a barely-present musicality.

This argument of clowning, as the game of a fool who has no other game to play, in no way suggests the carnivalesque "clown" I discussed in the preceding chapter. His critics are speaking pejoratively; "clowning" is a cover-up. For Bakhtin and this study's use of his view of the carnival, we may say that Patton was the *perfect* clown of the blues because, in Calt and Wardlow's words, "No other Mississippi bluesman took his approach of manipulating his level of intensity during a song" (20) and in Bakhtin's words, clowns "stood on the borderline between life and art, in a peculiar midzone as it were; they were neither eccentrics nor dolts, neither were they comic actors" (Morris 198).

What better description could there be of the rhetorician's ability to "manipulate" his position so that it stands not apart but "between" life and art? It was this very "betweenness" that so irritated Son House and others into thinking that Patton was an impostor who didn't care enough about the seriousness of his art to make it, indeed, serious in performance. The echoes exist today, where the showmanship of figures like Jimi Hendrix or a Prince (or a Leonard Bernstein, for that matter) often lead to a blanket condemnation of his work, as if it couldn't exist legitimately under or within those conditions of performance; Howlin' Wolf's dressing down of Hendrix is a famous and particularly ironic example, given Wolf's own clowning skills (Charles Shaar Murray 134). The rhetorical exaggeration of style, for example, can mislead readers into a sort of atomistic appreciation for the "turn" of language, without a larger understanding of the whole movement of the argument. Style, or "stylishness," such as Tom Wolfe can produce—or a Cormac McCarthy—can lead readers astray, or into a sort of subjective reverie on the beauties of expression, or form, with little perspective on larger outlines. Patton, however, is sufficient in the voice and guitar, in the songwriting—divorced from clowning in the flesh, he does not need defending.

As blues' first and perhaps greatest appearance of what Bhabha would call sixty years later the "mimic man" of postcolonial conditions, Patton was still deep in the pocket of the blues. He is today reduced to his recorded performances and the biographical and critical work of others, as "founder" or "father" or "king" of a tradition that cannot fairly be said to have a single progenitor. On one performance we cannot possibly hang this genealogical burden, of course, but in "When Your Way Gets Dark" we can hear not only the high *seriousness* of the blues as we want to call it, but also the buoyant comedy of it, and Patton's rhetorical command of its authentic core of blues communication.

On first hearing, "When Your Way Gets Dark" is high bottleneck, choked vocal, and wistful leave-taking. While this can describe, in these general terms, a goodly portion of acoustic blues recordings, the listener moves from this general recognition of an expectation met—the repeated guitar figure, the gruff, half-spoken vocal, a sense of loss—to the particulars of this performance. The move is from a kind of extensive acknowledgment that "Yes, this is the blues and only the blues, from a 'mournful' bottleneck on down" to a careful response to specific moments in the performance. Reception theory refers to this as "consistency-building." Iser argues that in our reading a text we first recognize its parts and then find ways to enwrap these parts in a consistent vision of the whole. The operation is akin to doing a jigsaw puzzle, which we assume has a consistent whole encoded within it. Listening to the blues, I would argue, demands a similar kind of consistency-building, although the reading is not so linear. Listening to a blues, even a solo blues, there is perhaps more than one "line" of text we read as we go. I hear Patton's voice, his guitar, and his lyric's images at the same time, or as nearly simultaneous as I can make them. I am building a "whole" or a *gestalt* out of the performance beyond pointing out the musicological elements—the beautiful bottleneck, for example, and the way it fills in Patton's dropped-out vocals at the end of several stanzas. This consistency-building proceeds impressionistically, beyond our conscious awareness, often as a lightning-fast process, so that we have to slow down in order to "see" or feel it (Iser 72*ff*.). I hear the descending guitar figure at the beginning suggesting the blues itself, remembering that classical and popular music almost never begins with a descending figure (and I burrow further into my memories and find that Brahms copied Beethoven in doing his first symphony's opening bars to that rare effect—a tragic "fall" rather than initial rise).

The effects of Patton's first stanza—

> When your way gets dark, baby, turn your lights up high
> What's the matter with 'em?
> Where I can see my man, Lord, if he come easin' by

—are sufficiently frustrating to any conventional, or traditional poetic, sense of consistency. It is easy to slide the vocal back behind the overall effect of the performance and remain in an impressionistic mode of "That's the feeling of the blues; do the words really matter?" Transcribing this stanza is like deboning a fish, yet a part of the bluesman's repertoire is the words he speaks or sings, even if only for a phrase to catch, or a question to halt the listener in his tracks. For me, the spoken second line, "What's the matter with 'em?" is utterly comic, the flat speech of the singer sounding almost like another man thinking out loud on a literal level that has nothing to do with the theme of the lyrics to come. I take this aside to be comic because it is an example of Patton's serious clowning around his own position of performer; he finds another voice, comments inventively on the song's first, rather sentimental line. The effect is one of confusion, then self-mockery, as if Patton is not going to go wholeheartedly (i.e., without irony, into this conventional lyric of leave-taking). Bakhtin's verbally astute clown obtains at this moment of disruption in the lyric, and at one stroke shows me that Patton has a double voice, a heteroglossia that would not be silent for long.

As if to double this sense of vocal acrobatics, Patton follows the high bottleneck figure with a repeated, heavy bass line. There seems to be very little music in the middle except some occasional strumming behind Patton's voice. What I hear is the keening guitar voice at the front, and the bass stumble at the bottom. Inside this wide opening is Patton's voice, which is never consistent in either pitch or timbre, but wavers, chokes off high notes, drops into the speaking voice, and gives way to the guitar at the end of stanzas.

Without anything more to guide a listener, forgetting for a moment all that we know about Patton, we are left with a blues that we can't dance to (Calt and Wardlow call "When Your Way Gets Dark" one of his few non-dance tunes). His rhetoric of doubled voice (irony in the making), descending lines, high and low guitar is capped by the obvious doubt of the lyric itself:

> I'm goin' away, baby,
> Don't you wanna go?
> I'm goin' away, baby, don't you wanna go?

I wonder if the singer will go away if he has to go away alone. He may stay, and the magnanimous tone of the earlier line, "What made me love her, you will come an' love her, too," may eventually be withdrawn as mere braggadocio. His boast, too, that his old lover will call after him, "You'll call at me, baby, and—an' I'll be gone," is delivered by Patton with little enthusiasm, so that its transparency as boast is clear to the listener. Patton, while not immune from the macho image of so much acoustic male blues, here seems to once again undercut the expectation of a general blues feeling with a commentary of irony or disbelief. Caught between art and the real, Patton's ability to deliver the blues and his own criticism of them creates a rhetoric of ironic, yearning distance, a playfulness or "buoyancy" that manages to catch the blues and, like Patton's own stunts, kick them around a little in a dance of the wise fool.

Skip James, "22–20 Blues" (1931)
Source: Skip James, *Complete Early Recordings* (Yazoo 2009)

As early as Sam Charters's 1967 *The Bluesmen,* Skip James has appeared in the blues world as a kind of dark angel of blackest blue. Charters describes his heavy use of mordents and minors, of irregular rhythms, suspensions, and echoes of field hollers contributing to an overall sense of "introspective brooding," of "lonely introspection" (*Bluesmen* 71; 79). Recently, another chronicler of the blues called James's recordings "downright *supernatural*," his voice "curiously detached" signifying "something . . . chilling"; he calls James's songs "[d]ark stuff, musically adventurous and morally unforgiving" (Davis 111). Earlier, David Evans called James's music "some of the strangest [. . .] in this genre" and refers to his guitar playing as "eerie" and" hollow" and songs with "bleak, morbid themes" (51). In another recent text, Robert Santelli calls James's voice "haunting" and his guitar "melancholy" (207; 208). And most recently, Stephen Calt's biography of James, *I'd Rather Be the Devil,* creates a disturbing portrait of the man as, indeed, a fallen figure, "within the context of his own society, a profoundly worthless person" who had evidently spent most of his life in a state of barely repressed rage.

Calt's demythologizing of the dark and melancholic figure we have had of James, of the Keatsian figure who lives "in embalmed darkness" and who provides for the contemporary blues audience a kind of bad dream of the blues-context within which Calt argues that James festered for fifty erratic years—this figure of James responds to an imperialist guilt as does Keats to the nightingale:

> Darkling I listen; and for many a time
> I have been half in love with easeful Death,
> Call'd him soft names in many a mused rhyme,
> To take into the air my quiet breath;
> Now more than ever seems it rich to die,
> To cease upon the midnight with no pain,
> While thou art pouring forth thy soul abroad
> In such an ecstasy! (51-58)

Calt goes after an "Orientalism" that has infected much discussion of the blues since Charters, an Orientalism that describes a love of the exotic for the sake of repositioning one's guilt and one's desire outside of one's culture, to seek in other places a love object that will not threaten but will have already bent its knee to that origin: "Orientalism depends for its strategy on this flexible positional superiority, which puts the Westerner in a whole series of possible relationships with the Orient without ever losing him the relative upper hand" (Said 90). Edward Said goes on to describe the complex implications of such positional superiority in the way the blue listener can romanticize an especially unique individual like Skip James:

> a whole series of 'interests' which, by such means as scholarly discovery, philological reconstructions, psychoanalysis, landscape and sociological description, it not only creates but also maintains; it *is*, rather than expresses, a certain *will* or *intention* to understand, in some cases to control, manipulate, even to incorporate, what is a manifestly different (or alternative and novel) world. (90)

These "interests" Calt skillfully describes in his biography as those created by young white blues scholars, entrepreneurs, and cultural historians when confronted by aging yet in a sense "virginal" bluesmen like Furry Lewis, Bukka White, John Hurt, and Skip James. The blues revival of the early 1960s could not have occurred around textual or recorded evidence alone. Flesh and blood survivors like James were living proof that an Orientalist romance of "worship" within control zones was still possible, despite a creeping awareness of a passage of America's own innocence within the oppressive 1950s. White men tracking down black men, as a schematic, has the look of a new slave trade, and it is Calt's intention, I believe, to suggest this doubling of an Orientalist control for purely self-serving reasons.

James responded to his rediscovery, Calt says, with good "technical ability," or what other commentators have referred to as James's virtuoso musicianship, but was also "simply unfocused and apathetic." Calt reasons that feeling is at the heart of the blues expression

> because blues music is not intricate enough to remain interesting without a performing aura of passion or energy, his detachment amounted to a more severe debilitation than the alcoholic tremor of Son House. The perceived greatness of Mississippi blues had rested solely on their palpable intensity and forcefulness. (332)

Calt then reveals that James never really thought of himself as a blues singer, but only played at it:

> What was striking about James's disclosure was not so much his calculated attempt to be cunning and thereby obtain the spoils of both worlds, but the failure of blues commentators to so much as sense that James had been striving to impersonate a blues singer, rather than become one. What was to James a swindle on his part had come across as an expression of heartfelt sincerity. (333)

There is in this passage much revealed about the nature of postcolonial rhetoric—to say nothing of a Sophistic one of self-aggrandizement or deception—one which we must be aware of when commenting on the blues, to say nothing of understanding the cultures from which the sense of the colonized and colonizer arise.

Calt, without saying so, is very close to a position that Said would like us to be able to see, given our ideological shortcomings as Occidental readers. Calt spends much of his book belittling all who would overlook the essence of the blues life—working for a living, making dance music—for its delusionary world of romance, adventure, lyricism, and liberatory rhetoric. But in this passage Calt refers to the "disclosure" as made to Calt by the bluesman shortly before James's death, as if once again to place the object of James within a controlled frame, this time not a large frame of capitalist or Occidental proportions, but a small and privileged one, again, of white confidant. This is an unfortunate replication of that attitude that Calt rightly criticizes in those who apparently exploited James in the 1960s; furthermore, it problematizes all that Calt says in James's behalf, and creates a taint of condescension that seems always to creep into those texts which go too far to project an aura of benevolence toward their subject.

But Calt is anything but a benevolent voice, and he erases all sentiment from this world of the bluesman and can be forgiven a few cases of "now-the world-may-be-told" hyperbole for the genuinely fresh wind of reality he brings to our understanding the world of the working bluesman. The passage continues with the observation that James had "calculated" his blues performances without spirit or feeling, and that critics, in their rush to embrace this "virginal" bluesman, had failed to note his diminished powers.

Calt turns the tables on the blues critic here, suggesting that the work of James since his rediscovery was "bad rhetoric" in its adherence to a relative truth of "faking the blues" while assigning the professional critics a second "bad rhetoric" of an Orientalist desire that blinds the critic-as-truthteller. We are left in a bad place, no doubt, where the lies of the performer are taken as truths generated by a deluded audience. Truth is destabilized, or lost, put aside in this implicated performance of sheer delusion.

My brief discussion of rhetoricality in this study's Introduction may be recalled when dealing with the reverberations of Calt's assertion, since that nihilistic outcome—the hole of or (w)hole of rhetoricality swallowing up standards or foundations of truth upon which we can base judgments—leaves us wondering what can be grasped here and held to with some certainty or comfort. It would seem that Calt's understanding of good rhetoric is contained in the *pathos* of the bluesman's desperately difficult life, one that is somehow transmuted into the "passion and energy" of real feeling in the music, "qualities [. . .] fueled by emotion" (332) that would make James's association with greatness a highly specific one, "a momentary greatness" (142) that would transcend blues as merely a "dreary social or racial document" and instead remain as "art or entertainment" (216). Calt returns to the reliable early recordings for this expression of greatness and, while not sentimentalizing those days in which James was creating great music, does find in an earlier time a truth of expression that would always, according to Calt, elude James thereafter.

The move is a typical one for many blues critics, who turn their backs on recent recordings as nostalgic re-creations that lack the force and originality of early recordings. The charge is a common wisdom, rooted in an ideology of the subject who, confronted with a numbing array of forces counter to it in modern society, responds with as much sheer passion—unleashed, unharnessed, uncontrolled—at least in part as a subjective "cry" of withdrawal. This near-reflexive cry is not understood by blues critics to be a recognizable part of the bluesman's repertoire; rather, it springs from the body's spirit itself, becomes in fact the spirit of the blues. It is a good rhetoric of the soul, torn out and shaped by the conventions of the genre but reflecting, nonetheless, "the concentrated, underground singularity of experience that results in a blues desire's expressive fullness" (Baker, *Blues* 152).

James's almost entirely unnoticed recordings of 1931 perfectly illustrate Houston Baker, Jr.'s description of the blues art. In "22–20 Blues," the first sound we hear is a light-hearted piano figure which soon gives way to James's vocal, an opening stanza as instantaneously fulfilling one's sense of the blues' dark romance as any:

> If I send for my baby and she won't come
> If I send for my baby and she won't come
> All the doctors in Wisconsin, sure won't help her none.
> And if she gets unruly, and gets so she won't do
> And if she gets unruly, and gets so she won't do
> I'll take my 22–20, I'll cut her half in two.

The rest of the lyrics are for the most part a comparison of pistol calibers, one too light and one about right. On paper, which is not a very notable locale of the blues, the words seem to indicate that there is a great violence waiting the girlfriend who, for whatever reasons, is uncooperative with the singer whom, we like to assume, is James himself.

This assumption is unfair, to begin with, because we should be ready to grant the bluesman as much ability to deny his identity to others as any poet can; indeed, the rhetorician who cannot understand the psychology of his audience, and so work his own character into a fellow of it, will not succeed as long as that audience flows freely to and from his view. The so-called primitive nature of blues lyrics—their vernacular cast, their simple rhyme scheme—do not and should not restrict our understanding them as imaginative constructions.

Beyond just this one objection to nailing James down with his own lyric are, as I noted, other contextual clues in the performance as to the meaning of "22–20 Blues'" entire "weight" or force. But for a moment we can take the lyrics alone and still make trouble for the "dark" reading we are familiar with. We can interpret the lyrics, for example, as the mere braggadocio of a man whose girl is beyond his control. Thus, the leisurely comparing of calibers becomes a fantasy of revenge, an obvious substitute for the real thing, which would be more along the lines of a narrative in the past tense, of what "I had to do." As the lyrics stand, the threat has the feel of an empty boast as much as a clear plan of action.

Other rhetorical devices for the understanding of the piece all point away from the "haunted" label so much of James's work receives, and points instead to something more subtle, to what Calt calls James's ability to "stun" his listeners, a rhetoric of disturbance or alienation moving away from, not a reaching toward, his audience, as if the blues were hellfire sermons of early American Puritan preachers:

> [T]he verbal content of his songs was second to their ability to assault the senses. He conceived of blues as having the mesmeric effect of spirituals. Instead of uplifting listeners, it would stun them. "Why did I like the blues?" he once asked. "Well, I'll tell you . . . The blues will take more effect than any other kind of music." Unlike other blues singers, he was able to project forlornness even when performing spirited, uptempo music. (32)

This is precisely the effect of "22–20 Blues" on this listener. I think the song is both spirited and uptempo, but it is not the lyrics that convey this sense; furthermore, a sense of being "stunned" by the number is the cumulative effect of cross-effects (i.e., a confusion of effects that produce a sense of distance, intentional off-putting—a rhetoric of dissonance or fragmentation that, far from Patton's "thickness" of unity, is a broken scatter of effects).

The first such effect follows the piano-playing, which is indeed "zany and unpredictable" and frustrates any sense of "brooding" or melancholy or romantic, dark haunts and instead suggests a drunken spree, what Calt calls "pell-mell pyrotechnics" (145) and Charters calls "a hard-rubbed gem of country blues playing" (*Bluesmen* 73). The piano is so intrusive as to be comical, another tongue so divorced from the apparent threat of the lyric that I am reminded of Bakhtin's heteroglossia here, and suggest that the voice of the piano is the true soul of the singer's intention: to lurch ahead with blustering punctuations and rappings like a drunk throwing his arms around while he plods down a back alley. Calt believes these pyrotechnics create a sense of "apprehension" or "stress" and I would agree to the point that they *disinvite* a participation in the music by frustrating expectations and creating a welter of sounds that deliberately do not create a harmonious whole.

But this may be the way we understand James's greatness. The voice, for example, in its famous falsetto does not sound threatening at all, but lonesome, somewhat passive or impotent. Compare it to the great growl of a Howlin' Wolf, the rasp of a Charlie Patton, even the high-flying scream of a B.B. King, and you feel that James is in his own corner somewhere, singing alone, and perhaps only to himself. "22–20 Blues" does not sound especially falsetto to me, perhaps only in parts, revealing the middle register of James's voice to be unremarkable, mild, not quite as abstracted as the falsetto and not with the soulful lonesomeness of another bluesman, Robert Johnson, who seemed also to court a lonesome sound.

We are left with a patchwork sound, perhaps "haunting" to some but to this listener a rhetoric of alienation borne out of a repressed rage, as Calt says, against the world he thought had abused him. He is, almost impossibly, a perfect mold for Ralph Ellison's invisible man:

> When one is invisible he finds such problems as good and evil, honesty and dishonesty, of such shifting shapes that he confuses one with the other, depending upon who happens to be looking through him at the time. [. . .] Too often, in order to justify *them*, I had to take myself by the throat and choke myself until my eyes bulged and my tongue hung out and

> wagged like the door of an empty house in a high wind. Oh, yes, it made them happy and it made me sick. So I became ill of affirmation, of saying "yes" against the nay-saying of my stomach—not to mention my brain. (*Invisible Man* 572–73)

This is the "bad rhetoric" of the false truth given to those who are deluded by it, and the voice of Skip James is the invisible man's caught in a whirlwind of deception, dishonesty, and alienation. Houston Baker, Jr. calls this process a recapitulation of slavery's "scarcity and brutalization" and blues' "movingly expressive" response (*Blues* 63); listening to Skip James I hear an eternal regression from a still point in front of me where the blues always is. James seems to retreat from that point, although his sound and feeling echo there.

Memphis Minnie, "My Strange Man" (1936)
Source: Memphis Minnie, *Hoodoo Lady (1933–1937)* (Columbia CK46775)

This medium tempo blues is, according to Paul and Beth Garon, about the blues "personified," "waiting at the back door" or already on the road heading for the next stop on an erratic but predictable course from heart to heart (167). The "strange man" of the tune has come into the singer's life, turned it up a notch because he's "got something that I really need" and then disappeared one night. Then, early in the morning of the day or night on which the singer sings her song, the stranger has returned to stand over her. The singer feels "happy" once again, and threatens to lock the door and leave if he should ever do the same.

> Next time you leave me,
> I'm gonna walk out and lock my door.

How is this strange man the blues personified? The blues here is a sense of happiness paired with its dark opposite, lonesomeness. The blues is a pull between the two, the sense of the inevitable bounce from one to the other, the elevation of the blues and its sudden deflation at the moment when any more happiness would simply burst the boundaries of believability.

The personified blues is always walking in and out of the singer's life, as it did for House, Johnson, and many others before and after

Memphis Minnie. This man or woman inherits most of the narrative thrust we associate with the balladic plot of many blues lyrics, and instead of a development of plot that may go years in length, or through several episodes, comings and goings, risk and rescue, we have the timepiece of "My Strange Man," in which the blues walks and stands, leaves—and, most importantly, simply *is* in his or her silence.

Silence, in terms of the audience, is rapt attention or disapproval, an extreme state probably very rare in the dancehalls, and more European in its figuration of approval in concert hall performances. In terms of the bluesman, silence is indicative of fear, flight, and rootlessness, as Baker explains in his metaphor of the blues matrix's crossroads. But if the blues itself is silent, personified into a human figure who then stands wordless, the performance can then be seen as a ritualized bringing forth of speech, an unleashing of the words by the bluesman himself, an invoking of what is repressed by fear or loneliness or rootlessness, a bringing back *into the room* the words of the blues that, for audience and bluesman alike, are often inarticulate thought and feelings. When these thoughts and feelings are made articulate, lyrics spring forth with the kind of elegant power that Robert Johnson's have, or, on the other hand, the vernacular songs of the earth that Memphis Minnie performed.

Giving voice to the voiceless blues is a cultural effect of slavery—a liberatory rhetoric of, for example, Kenneth Burke, where

> The *Rhetoric* must lead us through the Scramble, the Wrangle of the Market Place, the flurries and flare-ups of the Human Barnyard, the Give and Take, the wavering line of pressure and counterpressure, the Logomachy, the onus of ownership, the Wars of Nerves, the War. (*Rhetoric* 23)

One can argue not only with the civic release of a soapbox speaker, or a political broadside or even a Sunday sermon, but also with the subversive, backwoods "Whoo!' with which Memphis Minnie underscores so many of her performances. Hers is a dialogical rhetoric that sidesteps a Bakhtinian carnivalesque (in which dominant discourse would be ironicized and mocked) and steadfastly remains in an expressive-poetic mode of the subject (and subjected) woman applying all the rhetorical effects at her command to confront and in many cases overcome what had become a man's world of the blues, blues that "[present] an individual female experience of pain within a relationship and [transform] it into a collective naming of the social quality of black women's domestic experiences" (Davis 136).

Classic blues—dominated by the female figures of Smith, Rainey, and Ida Cox—was effectively brought to an end with the folding of show tents and the American economy in 1929. Not coincidentally, the rise of the lone bluesman as record-maker and performer appears at about the same time. There would be more great sessions for Bessie Smith to come, of course, but the die was cast for the blues in the thirties to be the lonesome blues of the single male, in or out of the Delta, with dance bands like Cannon's Jog Stompers being a significant but still wholly male phenomenon in the cities. The working bluesman of the time brought guitar and harmonica with him, found a piano in the joint, and sometimes a second guitar as Minnie did (and married more than once), and made do with that. The blues aesthetic had taken the poetic (read *lone male*) turn that Charters and others would try to revive thirty years later when these young bluesmen, if still alive, were fifty years or older. This phenomenon of the 1930s was not so much a conscious turn as an economically-driven one. But it led to a curious doubling of the European ideology of the lone artist, the romantic sensitive in search of meaning that would, as I note, lead to the blues having greater value to whites in the 1960s than it might have if the "loner" bluesman had never become ascendant. Jazz, by contrast, is almost never viewed as a solo art, with the significant exception of solo piano—for which two hands perhaps serve as two "voices." Blues went solo.

Minnie was never a blues queen or empress, honorifics for the blueswomen who preceded her. She in fact much more fills the mold of the blues*man;* despite her love of jewelry and occasional flashy gowns, her performances were strictly business, as this account by Langston Hughes attests:

> Memphis Minnie sits on top of the icebox at the 230 Club in Chicago and beats out blues on an electric guitar. [...] She grabs the microphone and yells, "Hey now!" Then she hits a few deep chords at random, leans forward ever so slightly over her guitar, bows her head and begins to beat out a good old steady downhome rhythm." (qtd. in Garon 54)

There is nothing particularly feminine found in these descriptions of Minnie's performing, even if one associates only the feminine with a less forceful, less aggressive *elocutio* than male counterparts. Her singing conveys only a narrow range, for which "My Strange Man" serves as an excellent example. Her voice, while not quite harsh, is flat, with a burr on the edge that keeps any conventional descriptions of refinement away. Any sense of pleading or submission, which we might associate with the written lyric, "Won't you please come back to me?" is erased with the actual falling pitch of the recording, so that the mood is one of sadness but not weakness or passivity. The last line of the song, "I'm gonna walk out and lock my door" also contributes to the sense of clear direction or forcefulness in Minnie's performances. This forcefulness can be attributed not only to the frank admissions of sadness but to the more obvious use of the double entendre, which could locate the feeling of the lyric not only in an abstracted quality of sadness or happiness but in the gut or loins, a literal physical craving—like many of the food images that Minnie uses—that belies any prettiness in her work.

The guitar playing, still acoustic in 1936, is similarly "manly" in the relatively unornamented style that "My Strange Man" employs, and in the strong bends that adorn the riff that Minnie fills with between lines. The bass is unobtrusively placed behind her, strictly on the beat. The performance ends abruptly and simply when the line ends; there is something about this simplicity that, ironically, becomes extremely *forceful* in the mode of a Muddy Waters years later, when he pumped electricity and sidemen into this straight-ahead earthy blues and said that Minnie was "out there, doing the job" and that he was "doing the job she's doing" (qtd in Garon 68). There's never any mournfulness in Minnie; one might say, in recent vernacular, that she's too *bad* for that.

But this last description suggests a difficulty for the contemporary blues critic who, when considering the bluesman as a category which subsumes the blueswoman not for the sake of easy stipulations but ideological blindness, must confront a new repression of what Ann Ducille calls the "primitivism and exoticism of the thoroughly modern moment" which nevertheless overlooks female sexuality:

> red-hot mamas punned, parodied, and played with black female desire. They in effect plumbed, and inverted their positions as long-exploited, fetishized

> commodities. But identifying women blues artists as the site of a struggle of black female subjectivity necessarily raises complex questions about agency and interpellation, self and subject, person and persona. (428)

What Ducille questions is the complex relationship that exists between the blues and the culture from which it sings, and now, the different culture which hears it.

It is hard to say whether the gender of the blues performer matters. *Matters how?* is a first question. It seems to matter to the blues audience as a whole today. Besides the blues shouters like Koko Taylor and Shemekia Copeland (who suggest traces of the classic blues), acoustic-based singer-players like Susan Tedeschi, and female guitar-slingers like Debbie Davies and Sue Foley, there are very few women in the blues; contemporary tastes suggest traditional ones that divide along lines of vocal or instrumental focus. In both areas, however, the force of the performance is suggestive of a masculine profile, either in the singer's frankness about sexuality and love or in the musician's interpretations of *male* guitarists. And why are there no women harp players? I would suggest it has to do with the harp's disallowed obscuring of the woman's face, her soulful sign of difference, a sexually-charged one, within the masculine rules of the blues.

What matters about gender in the blues is difficult to pinpoint at this time in our history while listening to the blues of fifty or sixty years ago. We can forget that the woman performer was more at risk than the man, that the very occupation of musician for a woman was synonymous with good times and crime. Minnie herself was probably a prostitute, and it is this kind of life experience—worse or simply gender-specific, if we remember the law-breaking lives of Robert Williams, Skip James, Bukka White, and Leadbelly—that suggests an alchemy of passion in the blues that is not in itself unique to the female performer but particularly precious. For many reasons, the blueswoman either did not initiate nor did she survive the rigors of the working blues musician's life. Ducille's suggestion of how females traded in on their sexuality for the favors of audiences is exactly true; Minnie's life attests to that, and what is not evident in a single performance like "My Strange Man" must be noted over a range of experiences of listening to the blues. Extractions of the blues from their cultural contexts are forever creating only traces of the lives that gave rise to the blues, and this study adheres to the rule of contextualizing when possible:

"At the heart of the matter is *desire,* always the first victim at these class rites, for it is perceived clearly as dripping with subjectivity, a drenched and humid poetics that recognizes passion in order to embrace it, not to tame it. It is this passion that is at the heart of the blues" (Garon 128).

Even in the recordings, however, one can hear Minnie's passion. It comes unexpectedly, but it is not particularly "feminine"; rather, to adopt the Garons's position, it speaks of a passion or desire withheld from the bluesman, or perhaps transmuted into other rhetorical gestures or instrumental figures. (Little Richard, a hybrid himself of musical and gender signifiers, may have found in his falsetto shriek a 1950s equivalent for that cry of passion that others found in over-amped guitars, but which could be heard in the blues as well.)

For Minnie, this passion would all of a sudden be expressed in a verbalized, almost orgasmic "Whoo!" or "Hoo!!" or "Wheeeooo!" This expression invariably makes me smile because it goes beyond the English of the lyric, and goes into the body of the singer herself for an expression that nonetheless has universal connotations. In grammatical terms this word "Whoo!" is an interjection, its definition revealing for its transcendence (or avoidance) of English syntax or, in fact, any other system, as "emotive words which do not enter into *syntactic relations.* [. . .] Ah, Boo, Oh, Ouch, Sh, Wow" (Huddleston 246, emphasis added). The blues, indeed much of American popular music, is full of interjections, though with less emotive impact than Minnie's "Whoo!" For example, "ah" and "oh" and "oooh" are common pop and soul devices, though some of these uses seem more keyed to filling rhythmic holes than always expressing the emotions of the singer. Performers such as James Brown, Sam and Dave, and Al Green, however, use a dynamic range of interjections to comment upon the emotional content of the lyrics or the impact of the song's meaning upon the singer himself.

The blues has had full use of the interjection, Murray's "energy of the spirit," for its whole history. While Minnie's is perhaps its most joyous use, bubbling with carnal delight and simple joy in living through and with the blues, many examples come to mind to indicate the *wordless*—and so more directly expressive, or pathetic—rhetoric of the interjection. Blind Willie Johnson's gospel-like hum and moan on "Dark Was the Night (Cold Was the Ground)" is not a momentary commentary on the syntax or meaning of the lyric, but wholly enters the blues as its only verbalization, the emotion of that sound becoming meaning not as a marginal comment to comprehensible lyrics but as its core content in dual force with Johnson's guitar. Howlin' Wolf's "Moanin' at Midnight" takes the sense of interjection as outcry to a level of ironic menace, a sad protesting sound from deep down in the diaphragm. Otis Rush's yapping and barking on a live performance of "Every Day I Have the Blues" sound like the breaking of a compact with sense, propriety or any other stricture placed on the bluesman by the laws of English. Rush uses the interjection to react in the manner of one of Bakhtin's carnival clowns who suddenly gives up on the rules of good behavior and goes nuts not only for a few laughs but also to thumb his nose at the expectations of the usual ideology governing such performances. Not even satire will do.

Add to these examples Memphis Minnie's "If You See My Rooster (Please Run Him Home)" in which Minnie does a full-throated rooster call that starts way back in her throat, unlike other interjections in "Has Anyone Seen My Man?," "Caught Me Wrong Again," and "Good Biscuits." "If You See My Rooster" also contains a more conventional interjection "Eeeeooo!" full of comic sexual relief and a guitar riff that skillfully mimics the clucking of barnyard hens. As a songwriter, singer, and guitar player, Minnie displayed the bragging sexuality and swagger of the classic blues queens while adding to that primarily "sung" format the guitar playing that sounds today as clean and economical as a Scrapper Blackwell or Robert Junior Lockwood.

Albert Murray's discussion of the dynamic that exists between self-expression and public, traditional ritual is instructive in understanding Memphis Minnie's importance in the meaning of the blues. Murray does not cite the dialogical rhetoric of Bakhtin, but Bakhtin could serve as a subtext to Murray when he writes:

> when the speaker's speech plan with all its individuality and subjectivity is applied and adapted to a chosen genre, it is shaped and developed within a certain generic form. Such genres exist above all in the great and multipharious [sic] sphere of everyday oral communication, including the most familiar and the most intimate. (Morris 83)

"After all," Bakhtin continues later, "our thought itself—philosophical, scientific, and artistic—is born and shaped in the process of interaction and struggle with others' thought, and this cannot but be reflected in the forms that verbally express our thought as well" (Morris 86).

Bakhtin's dialogic can illuminate Murray's comments on the role tradition plays in the formation of the "expressive" or "original" artist:

> The self-portrait (and/or the personal signature) [. . .] is not primarily a matter of such egotistical self-documentation but rather of the distinction with which they fulfilled inherited roles in the traditional ritual blues confrontation and purgation, and of life affirmation and continuity through improvisation. Incidentally, the revolutionary nature of their innovations and syntheses were not nearly so much a matter of a quest for newness for the sake of change as of the modifications necessary in order to maintain the definitive essentials of the idiom. (*Stomping* 252)

"Definitive essentials of the idiom" are the repertoire, the shared knowledge of artist and audience, what Davis calls the "collective property of the black community" (136). They are the canons of a rhetoric of the blues, which this study seeks to enumerate and explore.

Memphis Minnie pioneered the Chicago electric blues, and lived a career remarkably parallel to Muddy Waters's in a stylistic breadth aided by her traveling north from the Delta at a critical stage in her life. But while Waters's career was essentially a straight arrow upward, Memphis Minnie's failed and fell to earth. In her music, however, we hear a great synthesis such as Murray speaks of, absolutely the blues in idiom and element, but innovative and precious in the words and wordless rhetoric of this blueswoman.

Little Walter, "Blues with a Feeling" (1953)
Source: Little Walter, *The Best of Little Walter* (Chess 9192)

A band of bluesmen is not a single sound but a collaborative sound, a collective of voices that, ironically, more approximates what I take to be the African roots of the music than the more "primitive" sounds of the acoustic South, what is an aestheticized response to the social order:

> This controlled freedom took place within a moral order in which daily interdependence was the normal state of affairs. It was, in Davidson's words, a "robustly collective" society. Based on collective responsibility, it was a society in which exceptional individual achievement was expected to serve the community. This was its moral imperative. (Floyd 34)

Floyd is discussing the performance qualities of the African ring dance, its collaborative qualities of call and response—and echoes even Weaver's intertwining of the rhetorical and the ethical, the "moral imperative." It is not difficult to see that if this is a cultural trace, pushed north by those African-Americans like Memphis Minnie and Muddy Waters who wanted to move north and make a better dollar with their music—it is not difficult to see or at least to imagine that the African nations to a degree reconstituted themselves in the guise of the blues band, whose versions of call and response were spurred on by great individual talent like Little Walter and great leaders—or chiefs—like Muddy Waters. Even the sense of the dancing audience, a critical part of many performances, can be felt in listening to great Chicago blues like Little Walter's: it swings not so much in the rhythm of the heart but in the rhythm of the feet, the stroll and the shuffle and the skip, hop, and jump.

The blues band is the African culture in its clearest return within the context of the blues and blues performance. Electricity is a new magic, and the deep tradition of the African reed instrument—lost, until Little Walter and other electric masters like Junior Wells, in the amplified waves of guitar, bass, and drums—was resurrected by a Western technology which, when driven through Walter's harp, provided the blues with the full and present power sound only heard, until then, in the acoustic spaces of a back porch jam.

In this dovetailing of African and western motifs we can see what Franz Fanon called the "cultural nationalism" that must try to surmount the racial or ethnic divisions that entail a delimiting of resources and rhetorical power; voices turn to conversation, and there is not the lone man speaking outward, but the many speaking inward, a collectivity that subsumes the individual voice. This nationalism follows an assimilationist phase, in which marginalized cultures are threatened with a subtle erasure by their having borrowed so heavily from the dominant culture that their own productions are largely identified by their resemblance to the colonizer's art or literature. This phenomenon in African-American culture is suggested, I believe, in its history of jazz, in which sophisticated Western forms, some drawn from classical music, were utilized by great figures such as Duke Ellington, Gil Evans, and George Russell—and currently, some say, to too-formal effect by Wynton Marsalis. Blues, always a recessive form, did indeed move to the concert hall with figures like Leadbelly's and John Hammond's concerts in New York, but its assimilation would seem to me to have been more consciously carried out by the white rockers of the 1950s. In other words, the blues was taken by rock rather than the other way around. The blues was transformed for urban audiences by an urban or Western phenomenon of the electric amplifier. Blues performers, by adopting this technology, fought against a cultural bias that had reduced the blues for mass audiences to the sophisticated sounds of a Louis Jordan or Billie Holiday—in other words, to an assimilation that had led the blues to a sort of grandfatherly position *vis a vis* jazz and pop music.

In the Chicago blues of Little Walter I hear a nationalism that has a hint of violence about it, of playing along the brilliant edge of the band toward the goals that Fanon sees for the new "enclosed" nationalist, which is not African as much as it is a new hybrid: "The historical necessity to which the men of African culture find themselves to racialize their claims and to speak more of African culture than of national culture will tend to lead them up a blind alley" (qtd. in Amuta 159). These are, literally, the blind alleys of west and south Chicago that would be the scene of demise, even death. Fanon is attempting to push the men of a new national culture away from looking back at African roots and toward the present and future, which is inevitably intertwined with that of the colonizer. The colonizer gave the blues the violence of electricity, the city centers that so many great bluesmen moved to; and there they forged a new blues of amplification and lives of violent endings that were caught between cultures, even as they blended the powers of each.

Walter Jacobs was already recording as a teenager for Parkway Records in 1950. Moving quickly up the Mississippi River Valley from Louisiana, he had played with Rice Miller and Muddy Waters, Baby Face Leroy, and other figures of the country and city blues, moving on to his own R&B hits like "My Babe" in the mid-1950s. Was there any hint of the cultural nationalist in Little Walter as he moved north into the mean streets, where he plugged in and blew the competition away on harp? According to Chidi Amuta, Fanon saw the great pitfall—or the "blind alley" of a cultural nationalism—a "romanticization of bygone days corrected by philosophical traditions and aesthetic conventions borrowed from the world of the colonizer" (159). In other words, one would be caught in trying to revive an older culture using new tools borrowed from the bad guys.

Blues is very much a hybrid, of course; I have discussed hybridity earlier in this study, primarily from a linguistic perspective using Bakhtin's dialogical rhetoric. But that view is largely an apolitical one, existing in an innocent world of aesthetic production dominated by the subjective response of a listening audience. Performers' opinions are notoriously flippant or deliberately provocative, but it is worthwhile to look at one of Little Walter Jacobs's remarks as reported by Studs Terkel and repeated by Buddy Guy: "Little Walter said once, 'If George Washington Carver could make all his medicine out of a peanut, I can get something out of this harmonica'" (Obrecht 87). The remark betrays a sense of the self as heroic figure, the profoundly impressive achievements of a Carver, which became part of a rhetoric of hope for African-Americans, as exactly that man who Fanon suggests will see himself as part of a cultural phenomenon, not just an aesthetic one. If Little Walter saw the playing of the harp as analogous to Carver working on the peanut, then Walter would also have seen himself as a new African-American whose works, like Carver's, would have global influence but forever be "housed" by, or attributed to, a particular culture's contextual pressures to create, invent, push forward and rhetoricize (as Jacobs does with this remark) its achievements.

Jacobs had a sense of his own achievements: he was soon to leave the great Waters band and tour with his own, returning to Waters only to record. He knew he was good, and he may have seen that the nation of the African-American was such that a Carver and a Jacobs were on equal footing in a culture that looked for speakers, leaders, eloquent sons and daughters. The great blues band, like Muddy Waters's, manifested itself in Chicago in mid-century for perhaps this purpose of establishing a sense of nation, of a new enclave, a growth of national and cultural spirit that, when infused as Fanon says with the tools of the oppressor, became a sound that actually predates the hard electric rhythms of rock 'n' roll and, more tellingly, anticipates some of the critical political moments for the African-American in the mid-1950s.

Walters compliments white instrumentalists (he enjoyed Lawrence Welk, for example) but reserves "soul" not for blues or jazz, but for the African-American, of whom he says:

> you've got to live it to know it. You can pretend but that ain't the soul of it. All of your music has to have soul, without it it's just pluck, pluck, pluck. It's the same in what they call jazz. when Louis Jordan was making records and Nat King cole has his trio and Erskine Hawkins and Lionel Hampton had swinging bands, there was some soul. (qtd. in Glover *et al.* 231)

It isn't only the culture; it is the collective, *banded* voice of that culture that has "soul."

The first thing I notice about just about any Little Walter performance is the band. This is a *band* I'm hearing. There were bands before the Chicago bands, of course, so it isn't as if I am hearing an entirely new phenomenon; it has to do, rather, with the sense of the band being not only a band, but *a band of. Of:* a preposition that, in grammatical terms, introduces a phrase that will modify the headword; the grammatical intricacies of my subjective response to Little Walter or Muddy Waters or Howlin' Wolf is of some importance to me. It means that I am having both worlds—a band sound and the sound of the *parts of* the band—for my enjoyment of the Little Walter "sound." This is a great blues band, made up of blues virtuosos like Jacobs, Jimmy Rogers, and Otis Spann, and we return to Floyd's description of the root value of collective expression enhanced and deepened by the individual talents of the community members. They were all riding a groove laid down by the great drummer Fred Below, and Little Walter would step up in turn and *wail*—a term rightfully associated with the reed instrument, especially the saxophone, which Robert Palmer argues was a kind of template for Jacobs's sound, especially the jump sound of Louis Jordan's band (*Deep Blues* 201–2). When Walter split to do his own recording (and surpassed his boss Muddy Waters's popularity on the R&B charts in the mid-1950s) he turned to fronting his own band, and writing and singing. The almost perfect balance of the Waters band is often missing, but on a performance like "Blues with a Feeling" from 1953 the elements of the great blues band are there, as well as the individual heroics of the great harp player.

When I first hear the harp on this tune—indeed, Walter's harp on almost any tune—I hear something very different from the other paradigmatic blues harp sound, that of Rice Miller's (or Sonny Boy Williamson II, as he is more commonly known on recordings). Miller's stayed in the country, round and pure, water-like or transparent, smooth and bubbling; the metaphors of fluid—of air and water—are indeed what the reed instrument is associated with, but Miller's *blues* sound, I believe, is more in the phrasing and idiosyncratic rhythms of the playing. In Little Walter's there is the electricity that gives the harp an extended range of sounds, and it is in this extended range that I hear a rhetorical—or underlined, emphatic, gestural—groan, hum, and growl that is so characteristic of the blues voice. In *Blues People,* LeRoi Jones argues that the blues is a sort of parent of jazz, primitive and simple, from which grew the unruly son jazz, but we have also heard that Jacobs looked *to* jazz for his sound. These genres are clearly interdependent and, while putting aside Jones's argument about parentage, we can look at another point he makes about the pure "sound" of African-American brass that might illuminate Walter's:

> The purity of tone that the European trumpet player desired was put aside by the Negro trumpeter for the more *humanly expressive* sound of the voice. The brass sound came to the blues, but it was a brass sound hardly related to its European models. The rough, raw sound the black man forced out of these European instruments was a sound he had cultivated in this country for two hundred years. It was an American sound, something indigenous to a certain kind of cultural existence in this country. (79, emphasis added)

That "cultural existence," of course, was a hybrid one when pushed into the urban centers of the north, framed in a white enterprise like the music business, pumped up with electricity to reach the back of a club. Jones, understandably, does not wish the term "primitive" to be applied to African-American arts of the 1950s, but he recognizes their roots in a time and place of a black culture.

Little Walter, borrowing from jazz as it had borrowed from blues, brought the reed together with electricity and created that sound that was raw and guttural, high and silvery—chromatic tumbling and perfect sustains that sound even today as "free" as any instrumental flights in jazz. If the metaphor of "freedom" is more often applied to jazz and its political and aesthetic conceits, perhaps Walter Jacobs is due some of that metaphor as well, along with a handful of blues musicians who manage to rhetoricize the blues in flights of hot virtuosic passages while tumbling back into the groove of the band. The rhetoric of the hero, Gates would say, is the signifying, a reflexive commentary on the art itself:

> the principle of self-consciousness in the black vernacular, the meta-figure itself. Given the play of doubles at work in the black appropriation of the English-language term that denotes relations of meaning, the Signifying Monkey and his language of Signifyin(g) are extraordinary conventions, with Signification standing as the term for black rhetoric, the obscuring of apparent meaning. (53)

For one understanding of a blues figure like Little Walter Jacobs, Gates's theory of a black rhetoric indicates once again the "doubleness" born of two or more cultures. Little Walter's very words and instrument are of the West, yet the apparent meaning of such a figure is "doubled" or deformed or subverted, made larger than life, and made a signifier of another life; Walter's genius, his ability to push the sound past its accepted limits and then back again, showed what he could do but didn't have to do, to "show off" and get away with it. His rhetoric is one of exaggeration or deformation—and then a return to the collective norm of the band.

"Blues with a Feeling" is a quartet performance, with the Myers brothers, Louis and David, on guitars, Fred Below on drums, and Little Walter on harp and vocal. Walter's voice, even at the young age of 23twenty-three, is raspy and mature, and threatens to cut out (as with older reed players), if the vocal is not made muscular, hard-edged. His voice is not in the supple groove of the band, nor is the full voice of the harp, but in another groove, closer in fact to Memphis Minnie's in the way it seems to come through clenched teeth, at other times dropping back into the throat at the end of the line "That's what I have today," a slight drop in pitch sounding a blue note of the subtlest kind.

His playing is restrained, relative to the virtuoso pieces like "Juke," "Evans Shuffle," and "Lights Out" in which the absence of a vocal seem to shift the role of the voice straight *into* the harp. But Walter does take an instrumental break, and for its relative modesty it is still hard for this listener to believe it is played on an instrument we can carry around in our pockets. Indeed, the harp is the most democratic of instruments of the blues, after the voice, and it can be argued that, for its size, position, and the fact that it is a wind instrument, most closely joins it to the human voice. Its rare mastery, however, suggests that the harp is indeed an instrument *too* close to the voice, the latter having a logical primacy in blues expression. The guitar and piano, on the other hand, are clearly "Other" in their size, complexity, and variation, and thus are more alternative to the voice and not eclipsed by it.

Typical of the Chicago blues of the period, there is nothing remarkable about the tune's three chords and twelve bars; the lack of a bass player is noted, but the Myers brothers double up on high and low rhythm, with one providing fills to Walter's vocal lines. Fred Below eases along beneath everything on drums and provides, with the Myers brothers, the kind of "pocket" Little Walter can escape from when he wants and to which he returns easily after the break. In the manner of Gates's signifying monkey, he repeats the form, then tropes away (with a sense of improvisational freedom) to comment using the beauty of his sound and structure—his rhetoric of hyperbole—then coming home again with the line "I'm gonna find my baby, if it takes me all night and day."

It is easy to romanticize a figure like Little Walter in urban terms, as Charters did the country figures in rural or pastoral terms. A fighter dead at thirty-eight from the complications arising from a street beating—a steel pipe over the head—Walter Jacobs in his heroic guise as the George Washington Carver of the blues harp becomes a figure of tremendous charm, magic, and significance. But romance? Probably not, unless there are still traces in the blues criticism of our time that finds a special cachet in violence and death and self-destruction (as the boom over Robert Johnson might indeed indicate). Listening to Walter's last recordings with the so-called "super blues band" of Bo Diddley, Muddy Waters, and himself, recorded in 1967 should remind us that Little Walter had almost nothing more to give. His gesture was complete, and in 1967 it might have already occurred to him that the great blues bands he had been a part of were themselves bridges and tropes for a new consciousness, of a power of urban black that he would not himself be a part of.

Jimi Hendrix, "Red House" (1966)
(Source: Jimi Hendrix, *Blues* (MCA 11060))

"Red House" is one of only a handful of blues compositions of the American guitarist's short but legendary career in the spotlight of America's counter-cultural flowering of the mid- to late-1960s. The number was a standard of Hendrix's stage show, a kicking back, typically, into a roots position that the audience seems—on hearing tapes of those live shows—to appreciate as *little* as anything Hendrix performed.

Applause is desultory, for example. on the concert disc *Live at the Winterland* recorded two years after the number's first studio recording in 1966 (which is analyzed here). After a long guitar introduction, employing the Delta-like seventh of Robert Johnson's repertoire, Hendrix—on stage—presents the blues in a slow, loping fashion, not especially well aided by either his bass player's behind-the-beat elementary bottom, or his drummer's odd snare accompaniment. Hendrix's band members, Noel Redding and Mitch Mitchell, were, respectively, primarily rock and jazz players, and neither seem especially comfortable with the route Hendrix had chosen on this number, which was slow, exploratory, and inscrutably structured (or, better, unstructured) around Hendrix's enormous technical prowess. This prowess would get Hendrix into performance hot-water many times, leading him into areas that had no back doors, or closed front doors which would lead to flabby middle sections of unending jams and unneeded riffing while the band got together again. Somewhat like Charlie Parker and John Coltrane, Hendrix seemed to immerse his sensibility in pure sound, a timbral universe that left his audience, even his consciousness, behind at times.

The Winterland performance is not all bad, but its rhetoric is a hybrid of a kind different from that which I have been exploring in the bluesmen who formed a part of Hendrix's musical heritage. The hybrid is a familiar one to any rock music listener of the 1960s and since. Indeed, the case has been made that almost all of rock is blues-based in its simple chording, its pentatonic scale usage, its lyrical content of love and lost love. Seminal figures such as Little Richard (with whom Hendrix played as a mere band member), Presley, Berry, and Diddley have toes if not whole feet in the blues, and these figures directly influenced later giants in rock, such as the Beatles, Rolling Stones, and Bruce Springsteen.

This hybrid is called blues-rock by some, bluesy rock by others, rock 'n' roll by others (the "roll" being that loose and easy swing of a blues beat). Its performers were mainly white, as was rock itself in the 1960s. Coming from a black performer like Hendrix, blues-rock was what inflected his live performances with both simplicity and "authenticity" and—unfortunately—the kind of excess that marred much of his performing material. The *studio* recording of "Red House," made two years earlier, will be discussed below; the rhetorical hybrid of the bombastic blues is what concerns me now: the hybrid that drew so many fans toward the blues but away from its unembellished essence.

I am struck by the irony of Hendrix's still debatable position among blues listeners and critics, who acknowledge his ability to play the blues but perhaps not his ability to feel them. A similar charge sticks to white blues players, but in the latter cases the discussion inevitably adheres to racial lines and cultural wellsprings. Hendrix is a unique figure, whose musical stride seems to have been large enough to scuff away any lines one thought he saw between the music of the "arena" and the music of the jukejoint.

But hybrids are ungainly creatures at times, and Hendrix's live performances of "Red House" see him striving mightily to give his young, mostly white audiences chorus after chorus of blistering guitar, bracketed by cool vocals, always providing a contrast between, as he notes in the song's lyrics, his voice and guitar (his baby's left him alone, but he still has his guitar). This contrastive (or better, *bi-polar*) rhetoric is what gives much of blues-rock its distinctive power, since it is based on a blues scale, and instrumental breaks—but a "white," sanitized lyric, sometimes psychedelic, often banal love tales that don't resemble the blues lyric except in simplicity. Among those whose contributed to this blues-rock hybrid most importantly were Johnny Winter, early Fleetwood Mac (Peter Green), Mike Bloomfield, Eric Clapton, and, somewhat later, Stevie Ray Vaughan.

Hendrix never campaigned for the blues in the way his white counterparts did, perhaps because he didn't think he needed to—he needed no self-justification for his choice of music. But he was very much in touch with audience response—I think as a result of his long tour of duty with traveling bands like Little Richard's and Curtis Knight's—so that his blues numbers were relatively few and far between. Instead, the blues-rock hybrid was given out, and in performances like "Red

House" at the Winterland, become lumbering guitar exercises and clumsily improvised lyrics.

The guitar, in addition to the unimaginative, stiff accompaniment of Redding and Mitchell, sounds thin and trebly, initially like Albert King's Fillmore performances in the deep bends and turnarounds, but then Hendrix leaves the blues for extended chorus after chorus of upper register playing that—even though devoid of the manic vibrato work that marks his greatest live performances of rock guitar—leaves the audience sitting on its hands when Hendrix finally returns to the lyrics. The soloing has neither the propulsive force of his best playing nor the interior logic of his true blues playing on the song's *first* recording.

The lyrics, too, are presented less economically on the live recording, with interjections like "Well" and modals like "might" intended, I believe, to be more cool or less pointed than the rhetoric needs to be, especially in reaching a large live audience, and topped off by the embellishment of the last line, the punchline—"I know her sister will"—with "sister" being modified with "big fat"; Hendrix chuckles after rushing the words and says what sounds like "I messed up the words" in a typical Hendrix mumble.

The performance dissolves into a sense of miscalculated proportions—too low an energy in the voice, too much in the guitar, stiff backing, and a not surprisingly cool audience. In short, the power of the blues, although Hendrix has certainly attempted to evoke it here in an unfriendly context, has failed him, and he has failed it. His hybrid sound—born of a rock sensibility but an obligation to the blues sound that nurtured him—is mismatched halves, so that the pocket Little Walter enjoyed with his band is entirely missing, replaced by a compensatory elocution (and enunciation) that turns almost parodic, too "hip" for the blues.

What is the blues "voice" exactly? Is there only one? Are there great voices—and then, by comparison, "thin" voices like Hendrix's? Or can any voice touch upon the blues?

The notion of a "thin" voice has nothing to do with the tone of the voice itself; rather it has to do with the relatively context-bound dialect with which that voice sings the blues. The "thickness" of the blues voice is the one we normally associate with the Delta, the hum, growl, and shout, the elisions, the falsetto, the slurs and groans of the deep blues. Working away from this ground zero of the blues voice is not necessarily a moving away from authenticity or "real blues" performance. Black English, we know, is not a geographical phenomenon at all, but a racial and cultural one; it is not surprising that Junior Kimbrough, from the hill country of northern Mississippi, considered Taj Mahal the most exciting bluesman he had heard. Taj Mahal was born in New York City. John Lee Hooker considers Jimi Hendrix "the greatest blues singer" he has ever heard, though Hendrix was born in Seattle and spent very little time in the South, despite rumors to the contrary. Charlie Patton's ethnic heritage is a matter of some debate, but his immersion in the African-American life and speech of the Deep South is not.

We can see that the *idea* of the blues voice is not racial or racist, but rather a cultural, aesthetic identification. We can separate, however, the effective blues voice from a less effective one: the difference can depend, often, on being born into, or close to, the dialect of Black English. The thinness of Stevie Ray Vaughan's voice is only relative to those he would copy, like Albert King's, whose ease and comfort within with the blues lyric, despite a limited vocal range, is as thick as they come; they make Vaughan's vocals "thin" and forced by comparison. A brief comparison of Vaughan's "The Sky Is Crying" with King's will illustrate the point that King *speaks* the lyrics, while Vaughan *enunciates* the words with characteristic fervor but little ease; (a third version, Clapton's, takes an interesting turn in that Clapton tries to talk the lyrics toward the brink of crying them, a rhetorical strategy of understatement that, characteristic of Clapton, concedes King's privileged position as "authentic" blues singer).

The blues voice displays dialectal inflections we know to be Black English, a dialect with its own hierarchies and politics but one we associate with the cultural materials it produces and inhabits. According to Ronald Davis, "The delta vocal style tended to be hard and unrelenting, producing rough, growling tones, although the falsetto was frequently employed for contrast. Blues singers elsewhere moaned, hollered, murmured, or declaimed" (qtd. in Floyd 77–78). Idiom, I would argue, is directly available only to those whose lives, not ears, are immersed in it.

This assertion raises the specter of authenticity, a concept found illusory by much postcolonial thought, which is in part guiding my reading of the blues. When Margery Fee, speaking of Maori experience and voice rendered by the non-Maori, asserts that "the ideal of 'authenticity' has been proven to be, like so many others, relative and context-bound," she is eating and having the cake that every culture wishes to keep on its own table (i.e. a holy identity, a sacred place where the Other is excluded). But Fee does not throw out authenticity—she slices it up like the cake on the table and hands it around to yet another conceptual minefield, which is *difference* (242 *ff.*).

We may be exchanging one difficulty for another, but the position I would like to take on the question of authenticity and the blues is a more literal understanding of my thin and thick metaphor. There *is* authenticity in the blues, but it exists in relative amounts that depend, in part, upon the immersion in African-American culture that any performer can demonstrate. Demonstration is by performance, which can lead, therefore, to an Englishman being more authentic in his blues than a black Southerner. This can come about, as I argue, by one's immersion in the culture. The critical component of the immersion, almost invariably, is the voice, the language, for which there is no substitute. The musical "dialect" of the blues can be studied, loved, copied, internalized, as Eric Clapton and a few others have done to the point of there being a real blues there in the air. This is simply the result of education, which we hold out as one society's greatest promises of peace, harmony, and intersubjectivity: a way to take difference and exchange it for knowledge, to know each other as they, almost, know themselves. It is what Kenneth Burke would call one "accessory" in understanding the modern rhetorical situation, *identification,* which "is affirmed with earnestness precisely because there is division. Identification is compensatory to division. If men were not apart from one another, there would be no need for the rhetorician to proclaim their unity" (*Rhetoric* 22). Hendrix, as rhetorician, proclaims that blues and rock cohere; yet they do not so *easily.*

Hendrix looms as an especially interesting case in determining the authenticity of his blues. Fee's lateral move to the notion of difference now becomes useful. Authenticity, she argues, "denies Fourth World writers a living, changing culture" (243). I have tried, above, not to deny authenticity to young white kids from, say, North Dakota, who copy their old Muddy Waters records, but I have clearly given the big slices to Southern blacks and their progeny up North. I imply an authenticity while I deny its simple inheritance. Fee shows a way out through difference, and Hendrix plays us a way out *beyond* difference by providing us with an imperfect example of the desire, the need—but not the execution—of a rhetorical consubstantiality, a pure "meeting" of rock and blues that join them while retaining traces of their division.

Hendrix playing "Red House" in 1966 in England for his first album (subsequently left off the American version *because it was blues*) was not producing the hybrid of blues-rock, as he did later in live performance, but was instead producing an indigenous blues displaying those differences directly attributable to Hendrix's cultural life, which was neither Southern nor Northern, but black working-class. Hendrix displays on the original "Red House" a full blues repertoire, a vocabulary of the blues from the Delta turnaround to the occasional overamped blur of a Buddy Guy, the multi-vocality of a Muddy Waters, a tight 12-bar framework within which his same sidemen stay back, simple and thereby understated—as is everything about the performance.

This *under*statement (like the rhetorical figure of the *litotes,* in which the speaker might say of Hendrix, "He is not a poor guitar player," thus reining in the intended effect of an exclamatory display of admiration) I would argue, is the rhetoric of Hendrix's best blues, and works against the usual fury he and others often used to get "inside" the blues from an obvious outside position. Ellison, in fact, calls these "rhetorical understatements" African American *signifying* ("Blues People" 249)—in a sense much different from the more current understanding of a Gates or Baker. Hendrix was, in effect, eventually seduced by his larger audience's needs, away from a course of playing that could have given us more blues; instead, if the *zeitgeist* of the times is any indication, Hendrix drove himself toward bigger and bigger audiences like Woodstock and the Isle of Wight, and left the locale of the blues far behind.

As a rhetorician, then, Hendrix may have seen the blues as understatement—perhaps even as protest, counter to the times, which demanded a politics and ethics of the hard edge or radical freedoms. He wedded the blues to rock and forged massive attacks like "Hear My Train A-Comin'" much to the dismay of those who knew he could play quiet, exquisite guitar in the manner he does on "Red House" (or the acoustic version of "Hear My Train"). Hendrix's rhetoric was above all else polymorphous—engaging many discourses of music from folk to jazz to pop—and led to the kinds of hybridity I have already discussed. The absence of hybridity is what separates a studio recording like "Red House" from the live performances. Blues with a feeling—from a black musician: authentic, indigenous, but different in its eventual trajectory into the arena rock of enormous white audiences looking for noise and flash.

One important difference even in this understated performance is that Hendrix is all alone as singer and guitarist. The blues band implies response, conversation, a careless but careful dialog of voices, calls and responses—and there is no "talk" in this performance. This is clearly a star turn. One would be hard pressed to assign a truly responsive band of equals to a player of Hendrix's power, but one hearing of the Muddy Waters band in the mid-1950s demonstrates what a *heteroglossia* of tone and timbre can do for the meaning of the blues conversation.

Another difference is the formality of the arrangement, related to the relationship of players noted above, but having, I believe, more to do with the ideology of the rock world toward which this recording was being directed. The rhetorician's sensitivity to audience led Hendrix to the politeness of the structure. Some of this rigidity might be blamed on the backing, but I am persuaded to hear in Hendrix's cautious vocal delivery a desire to lay down a basic blues as a way to persuade his audience that the blues is an appropriate subject for Hendrix. I think, though, that he would fail with his audience in this and, as I note, lead him to infuse a blues spirit with the performance excesses of rock music. Typical urban blues of this period was informed by a sense of a party, dancing, horns, shouts, and raucous backing punctuated by a dominant bass track (for example, Albert King's Stax recordings or Guy's early Chess sessions as leader), features missing in this performance.

Hendrix creates a curious inversion of conventional values by his being black, playing rock, and retreating politely to the blues. This inversion I have referred to as difference because he is obviously playing the blues as a bluesman—but as one *who would prefer not to*. Compare Hendrix to Clapton, for example, who is white and playing the blues—and *retreating politely to rock,* but *who would prefer not to*. For their audiences in the 1960s, these great hybrid figures were rivals for our affection and respect, and yet, in retrospect, Hendrix seems much the more poignant figure in his relationship to the blues. He was always far more willing to please his audience than was Clapton, and thus was led away from certain musical forms like the blues and toward forms more "popular" in demand (and witness Hendrix's "showmanship"). Clapton, by contrast, wore his love for the blues like a badge, and always directed his musical rhetoric toward its eventual recuperation in the musician's performances.

Hendrix's solo on "Red House" is concise and packed solid with vocalisms, the bending and glissandos, jumps, drops and whoops of his guitar kept within a traditional structure of a break (although the instrumental break is one of those "hot" features not often found in vocal country blues); like Coltrane and Parker he was not one to play with silence. He sounds at ease in the lyric, singing lines like "Back over yonder across the hill, that's where I came from" with ease and naturalness. The images and comments themselves—the red house, not seeing his woman in a long time, the key that doesn't work, bad feelings, and the sly but happy ending of a convenient sister—are down-the-middle blues lyrics, unremarkable in themselves but notable for the way Hendrix has assimilated them, as hundreds have before him, in creating a "new" song.

Hendrix's last words are caught in the song's fade out. I presume his question, "How's that?" is to the engineer or producer, as if to say, "I *told* you I could play the blues, but now I want you to tell it *to* me." But the question is clearly rhetorical, requiring no response because the answer is already evident to those present: you can hear the satisfaction, the pleasure, in Hendrix's voice.

J.B. Lenoir, "Down in Mississippi" (1966)
Source: J.B. Lenoir, *Vietnam Blues* (Evidence 26068–2)

Something happened to J.B. Lenoir's blues that makes his music, of all the modern bluesmen's art, stand apart as an example of the inquiring nature of the blues, its rhetorical search for answers through words and music, its affirmations of simple truths and old joys in a time of upheaval and pain.

When Lenoir recorded "Down in Mississippi" and eleven other tunes on September 2, 1966 in Chicago they would be his last; he would die less than a year later from injuries suffered in an automobile accident. His last recordings would be released in Europe through a German label, but would remain unreleased in America for almost thirty years. Lenoir's reputation among American blues audiences would stand on his easygoing Jimmy Reed-like shuffles of the early- and mid-1950s like "Let's Roll" and "Slow Down Woman" and his handful of "protest" blues from the same period, "Eisenhower Blues" and "Livin' in the White House," which were as close to a cause celebre as blues music is likely to produce. Lenoir, even then, was a sort of Janus figure among bluesmen. His two faces were turned, as it were, toward the two audiences he discerned in the blues—or more precisely toward their two venues. Albert Murray concisely calls these the dance hall and the concert hall, and with minor changes accepted for the simmering counter-cultural scene of the mid-1960s, we can see that at the time of Lenoir's final recordings he was as aware of these two scenes as he was when he began recording in 1951.

In ancient Rome, these two faces of Janus represented doorways, beginnings, and the rising and setting sun. For the Romans, obviously, Janus was a figure of great power, of the promise of openings, the future, the power of opposites that are dependent on each other for their identity as powers—like dark and light, hot and cold. I want to develop this metaphor of Janus in the work of J. B. Lenoir because he seems to me to represent better than any bluesman the blues' modern strength *and* challenge: to invest the rhetorical power of the blues—its community, tradition, and locale—with the elements of the new and the topical.

One hears, listening to "Down in Mississippi," one of the strangest duets in blues history (as one hears on the whole collection, twenty-four songs from two sessions, all on *Vietnam Blues*): drums and acoustic guitar. It is only strange, though, for our not hearing it on record very often, if at all. Charlie Patton, for example, used rapping for a drum equivalent, and John Lee Hooker cracks out a beat on his plywood resonator; indeed, many acoustic guitarists would use the body of the guitar as a drum or "second" rhythm instrument. It is not at all strange to anyone who has sat around somebody's living room or front porch or street corner and literally drummed away on a pants leg, lamp post, briefcase, or lunch box in private accompaniment to a lone guitarist and singer. If there is anything similar among all the performance videos of blues in clubs, where one has a good view of the audience, it is the keeping of the beat. This interplay of audience and performer is unremarkable for its commonality. Yet, on record this sublime conversation between the bluesman and his beat-keeping, rhythm-popping audience is almost non-existent. Why?

I think it is because we categorize the blues in such a way as to disallow this crossing of forms, but Lenoir in his Janus-mode found the solo acoustic sound of his last work and married it to the urban band sound of the great Fred Below, a timekeeper for Muddy Waters and many of the Chess stars of the 1950s. Lenoir's ability to sum up the "ontogeny" of the blues is striking and, while other bluesmen were performing acoustically at the time, reminds us that in the middle of the electric and folk sounds of the 1960s Lenoir was displaying roots and innovation at the same moment—in short, working once again across what David Evans calls the tradition.

There is something strange about the drum sound of Fred Below, creating on first hearing not only a sense of something "different" about it but exotic as well, since the rhythms themselves are regular but syncopated between the bass drum and the tom-tom (played with hands, I believe) and the trebly sound of finger cymbals, which conjure up associations with Eastern or Middle Eastern clubs and marketplaces. Below was trained as a jazz drummer, but there is none of the light swing feel that he brought to many of the great recordings of Little Walter and Muddy Waters or even Chuck Berry on these recordings. Instead, Below has adopted a "less is more" aesthetic, and is more interested in timbral invention than rhythmic invention. What one hears is a small percussive band, cleanly separated by pitch and timbre. Below's sound, in short, is ironically avant-garde for its regression to a polyglot primitivism.

It is Lenoir, however, who works at the center of the performance, with his guitar and voice in almost constant play. His playing is mostly single-string, with occasional chording, although the chords sound fragmentary. On other songs, Lenoir uses the guitar as a drum; on "Round and Round" he raps and thumps out a beautiful duet with Below. On "Down in Mississippi," however, he uses the guitar to repeat a few simple single-string figures that ornament or comment upon the vocal and its words.

It is Lenoir's voice that always arrests me when I listen to a Lenoir performance. For the good guitar playing, the rolling rhythms, even the words of both love and anger—for all of these strengths in Lenoir's blues it is the voice that I can hear afterwards. High-pitched and clear as a bell on the early recordings, it had by 1965 and 1966 caught a little rasp between its smooth sides so that in the louder passages, or when Lenoir is hitting a particularly high note, his voice breaks into a curious kind of kittenish growl, creating a double sense again of sweetness and dark, of a Janus looking for the bell-tone of a Robert Johnson falsetto or the gruff bottom sound of a Howlin' Wolf. He ends up somewhere between, not caught but, like Janus, comfortably looking into both doorways of the blues. Comparable voices are those of Little Johnny Taylor and Jimmy Johnson, with Taylor's soul blues a delight for their humor and self-deprecation, and Johnson's a similar, though Chicago, sound with a throatier quality than Taylor's or Lenoir's and a guitar that is purely electric. Lenoir's voice is always front and center.

"Down in Mississippi" is typical of about half of Lenoir's last recordings in its subject matter and its rhetoric. The subject is the South and the lives of African-Americans in the south. Unlike the earlier protest songs like "Eisenhower Blues" that were working class in tone—or suggestive of a class distinction driving the blues, of poverty and privilege but not explicitly racial in content—the latter songs of protest like "Alabama," "Alabama March," and "Shot on James Meredith" are clearly racial in perspective. This perspective may have followed years of racial injustice in the South and Lenoir's home state of Mississippi, but was not made so evident in any other bluesman's performance of the period that I am aware of. Of course, the "evidence" of Lenoir's performances was largely available only to European audiences who were listening to Lenoir as a part of the folk blues revival of the early and mid-1960s.

The irony of Willie Dixon's supervising these recordings is exquisite, since it was Dixon who, with a great talent for the bombastic, comical blues of the preceding fifteen years, dominated the tone of the blues coming from the studios of Chicago. Dixon sings low harmony on "Down in Mississippi" and creates a subtle, almost shadowy echo to Lenoir's sweet voice singing a lyric about the agonies of black life in the South.

Does this mean that Lenoir's approach to the blues was not only unpopular but "dangerous," subversive? Probably so in the sense of a likelihood of a shift in public perception. This shift in any performer's life is dangerous in that expectations are not met, new ones are offered, and the gap between the two can be seen as a reader's confusion between what was and now what is. In reception theory this confusion is overcome by "correction," in which one is constantly adding to a picture or understanding and thus inevitably changing or revising it. If the addition is smooth, like a brick to a growing wall, the reader will assume that she is building a good structure. When the brick doesn't fit the next space, a problem of indeterminacy can result, in which the reader looks at the new brick and says, "Where does this go?" For any performer, especially one dependent on such a small audience, as all but the most popular bluesmen were, to give up the electric sound, and the good-time sound, was "dangerous"; if it was a "good" move or a safe move it was to the tune of Lenoir's German angel, Horst Lippmann, who knew that the black bluesman performing in Europe (such as Bill Broonzy, who promoted himself as the last bluesman heroically waging a war against time and enemies as if he were a throwback from another age) was a powerful symbol of disaffection, a romantic cipher of American experience that was as strange and evocative to European audiences as Edith Piaf was to America.

One wonders where Lenoir could sing a lyric about being "a lucky man to get away with my life" in escaping Mississippi except to the interior exile of Americans who had moved north in the years between the First World War and 1930:

> White Southerners were reluctant to acknowledge the message of self-determination and protest they dimly perceived in the mass migration of half a million African Americans between 1915 and 1920 and a million more during the 1920s. The migration demonstrated that African-Americans could participate in the historical process, act in protest against their lot in the South, and change their destiny. From this perspective, white Southern resistance to and attempts to impose restrictions on black migration were informed not only by economic demands but also by Southern racial ideology. White Southerners did not wish to acknowledge the protest against Southern racialism and the evidence of black agency that were implicit in migration. (Lester 129)

This protest took many subtle forms, none subtler than the protest blues of J.B. Lenoir, but none more direct in their charge that the Mississippians of his youth had made "a hunting season for a rabbit" but that the "season was always open on me." Yet few in this country heard this tune and Lenoir's other protest blues, and I wonder if anyone save for the white, liberal lover of the folk blues could have sat still for these protest blues. If given a choice, and if the market for Chicago dance blues was a good indication, then Lenoir's protest blues were fated for failure, or in response theory terms, "lack of uptake" by an audience who, as white as it was in 1965, took to the folk blues for deep thoughts and distant history, and to electric blues for dance.

Yet if a theory of the blues is understood in terms of the genre's rhetoric, it would seem that these protest blues would be among the genre's most popular products. In other words, here is rhetoric in visible form, civic rhetoric in which the bluesman comes forth from any kind of aesthetic shell and takes on the very commonalities of existence: where I come from and where I was lucky to have escaped from, alive. Isn't this the rhetoric of the blues—and if so, doesn't the relative failure of protest blues suggest that the blues is, by contrast, so passive as to resist a rhetorical dimension?

Paul Oliver concludes his study of the blues with a similar suggestion, though he would relate the blues to a protest of the soul against human reality in a way that far exceeds what I call the blues protest song, or one rooted in violence of white against black:

> By the 1960s there were signs that the blues as a truly creative folk song were already on the wane, for the tragic themes of suffering and misery that had arisen from poverty and destitution, from disease and disaster, violence and brutality, from bad living conditions and aimless migration, were less frequently heard than in former years. (*Meaning* 289)

Oliver is correct in noting that the blues seemed, even in the 1960s, to have lost an audience, but he is wrong to assume that the general context of the blues had begun to disappear and thus its aestheticized representation. Far from it, the 1960s were full of misery for African Americans, if only in the terms Oliver uses. The social upheaval of the 1960s certainly did not exclude the African-American and surely the rise of socially conscious music like that of Marvin Gaye's and Curtis Mayfield's, and of course later the meteoric rise of rap music—these song forms suggested that the message was the same, but the vehicle had changed. Oliver's argument that things were getting better and thus the blues wasn't needed anymore sounds naive in retrospect, especially if one looks at contemporary black music lyrics. There, the passion of the blues has been turned into anger.

Lenoir's passion in songs like "Alabama" covers anger in a sadness that contemporary audiences may have found as a sign of weakness or resignation, at best a Stoicism (Lucas Beauchamp-like, as in Faulkner's *Intruder in the Dust*). Audience response was perfectly predictable for the time because there was in the polarized rhetoric of the 1960s (of quite emphatic political camps of liberal against conservative) an ethic of action that was built on a premise of confrontation or adversity. The sweet and sad protest blues of Lenoir confront, *but do not dissipate,* a disastrous reality in the South which, as Lester says, resulted in a migration north, but do not confront the bringers and masters of that reality to such a degree as to *sound* confrontational, let alone combative. A song like Dylan's "Masters of War" is homicidal by comparison, yet does not draw on the kinds of racial power that the bluesman *could have* drawn on. The focus remains on the character of the singer, not the men to whom the song reacts.

Ethos, as I have discussed earlier, is the character of the speaker, the sense of the essential "way" of someone's interaction (linguistic or not) with the world; it is how we learn, or choose, to interact with an environment that contains a multitude of potential audiences. Larry Neal writes that the blues had indeed been miscast as "resigned" toward life. This resignation was admirable on one level, because it was a Christian message of acceptance in a way similar to the message of the gospel song, whose lineage runs so parallel to that of the blues. But Neal disagrees with a critic who sees this attitude as

> the essential function of the blues, because the blues are basically defiant in their attitude toward life. They are about survival on the meanest, most gut level of human existence. They are, therefore, lyric responses to the facts of life. The essential motive behind the best blues song is the acquisition of insight, wisdom. (55–56)

Neal, in language reminiscent of Ellison's, sees the blues singer as a "ritual poet" who "reflects the horrible and beautiful realities of life" (57). The lyrical content of the blues anchors its message as literary, yet the realities of the lived experience, largely specific to a culture whose history is a marginalized and colonized one, reveals an *ethos* of the rhetorician whose very existence is incumbent upon a close community of audience and listeners and performers, their power derived from the consensus—and, most importantly, reveals an *ethos* that is as emotionally powerful as Cicero and Quintilian argued, evoking not rage or anger or hate, but "calm and gentle[ness]," and which "requires a good and even-tempered person" (Quintilian 6.2.18). This sense of calm is not of course directed at the situation described in these blues, but at the singer himself, who feels the *ethos of the audience*, moved, rebounding upon him. The wisdom of the audience is thus given freely, as it has been given to the audience by the singer.

J. B. Lenoir is such a rhetorician as Neal describes because he is not only a "calm and gentle" speaker but a ritual poet who reflects "the ideology of a new 'proletariat' searching for a means of judging the world" (59). Neal unites the personal and the collective, as this study has attempted to do, in cultural terms of performance rooted in African-American traditions that utilize Western linguistic conventions. He says, as if speaking about Lenoir's most personal statements of political reality, that "even though the blues are cast in highly personal terms, they stand for the collective sensibility of a people at particular stages of cultural, social, and political development" (59).

Poet and rhetorician. The lyric and the speech. The personal and the collective. The dialogical life of the individual word, in Bakhtin's view always *anticipating* a response, and so in part defined by the future, seem to have found a certain resting place in J. B. Lenoir's blues. Working in a kitchen at the University of Illinois at the end of his life, the working-class Lenoir could not have anticipated the future life of his words and music, the flat thrust of "Down in Mississippi" and the clear truth it tells, the sheer beauty of the voice and drums and guitar, fixing for a moment a boundary of the blues: Janus in the archway of the world of words, poetry on one side, rhetoric on the other, a sign of beginnings and endings, the sun always setting and rising on the blues.

B.B. King, "Gambler's Blues" (1967)
Source: B.B. King, *Blues Is King* (MCA 31368)

This study does not hesitate to be ethnocentric when necessary. Despite the clear sense of the blues being a culturally specific phenomenon, and its practitioners by a wide majority members of that culture, I have argued that in the audience of the blues lies indications of different ways to understand the blues. This study has used classical and contemporary rhetorical theory, verbal or discursive difference and dialog as first formulated by Mikhail Bakhtin, the subjective or phenomenological encounter with the aesthetic first described by Rosenblatt, and the politicized or colonial rhetoric of oppressed cultures. These have been tools for understanding the meaning and power and beauty of the blues. These broadly-defined ways into the blues have been largely determined by the white or Western culture that gave rise to a print-based "critique" of art forms. Even the last and most recent, postcolonial discourse, is written largely by Western-educated scholars who then turn or invert western critical thought upon itself in order to serve Others, whose new form of rhetoric, if they have any, are historically oppressed or, at best, crippled.

The audience is a critical factor in any study of performance, and for reasons stated in many excellent studies of the blues (Barlow; Palmer; Keil), the whiteness of the blues audience is not new; indeed, early figures like Patton and Sam Chatmon played as much for white parties as for black. Following the blues revival of the early 1960s, the blues became framed within a white attention, while black audiences turned to rhythm and blues, soul, and Motown.

Our understanding of the blues is a white understanding if by "our" I mean the bulk of the blues audience today. But to validate a black reading of the blues does not seem to invalidate one which uses exclusively white or Western means. As I argued earlier when speaking of Bakhtin's theory of discourse, the blues is so embedded in a Western culture as to be obviously Western in such features as electric instruments, auditoriums, and, above all, the English language as the linguistic currency of even the most "country" of blues. The blues is a beautiful hybrid, as the postcolonial critic would argue, which eludes a simple binary of dissection:

> the functioning of language in a colonial universe is preternaturally dependent on the instability of its own facts. For colonial facts are vertiginous: they lack a recognizable cultural plot; they frequently fail to cohere around the master-myth that proclaims static lines of demarcation between imperial power and disempowered culture, between colonizer and colonized. (Suleri 112–13)

This "vertiginous" quality of the blues is what gives it a power of universal attraction, I believe, for its elements are impure in every sense of the word, and for that we feel its alchemical power to transcend a single place, voice, sound, or listener.

This listener has always thought that the "good man" of the blues was B.B. King. In my role of audience I was soon of the conviction that King was an embodiment of a general virtue we call "generosity," and whose abilities to "move" me toward him was answered by me with a reciprocal gesture of "giving"; one might even say "giving in"; but I had no African-American frame by which to articulate this sense of King as the good man. I felt it, *only* felt it, when I attended a performance of his in the late 1960s in Portland, Oregon. Twenty years later, with a history of Western rhetoric as a part of my graduate education, I began to connect him to a rhetoric characterized as "oratory" that resides within, and emanates from, the soul of a particular individual. a masked *ethos* of the blues Larry Neal earlier quoted in this study, and described two millennia ago by Cicero:

> "Nor does any thing seem to me," he added, "more noble than to be able to fix the attention of assemblies of men by speaking, to fascinate their minds, to direct their passions to whatever object the orator pleases, and to dissuade them from whatsoever he desires. This particular art has constantly flourished above all others in every free state, and especially in those which have enjoyed peace and tranquility, and has ever exercised great power. For what is so admirable as that, out of an infinite multitude of men, there should arise a single individual who can alone, or with only a few others, exert effectually that power which nature has granted to all?" (1.8)

Cicero earlier in *Of Oratory* makes a key observation of the skills of an orator, and would seem to be looking straight into the heart of the blues:

> [T]he whole art of speaking lies before us, and is concerned with the common usage and the custom and language of all men; so that while in other things that is most excellent which is most remote from the knowledge and understanding of the illiterate, it is in speaking even the greatest of faults to vary from the ordrinary kind of language, and the practice sanctioned by universal reason. (1.3)

But Cicero was still in my future when I was "moved" by B.B. King to see him, in the moment, and in the big picture, as an orator. An approximation of that moment is captured on King's album *Blues Is King* in 1967 at the International Club in Chicago. This live album is overshadowed by the far better-known *Live at the Regal* recorded three years earlier, but the former, in my opinion, is a blues document that shows a more intimate club audience and performer interacting with each other. The Regal date sounds like an Otis Redding warm-up, with shrieking adolescents and unison response that is a sign of a time when electric performers were a good excuse for audience shenanigans or—in their best light—audience *performances* that were *presumably* attuned to that of the performer. But the Regal crowd goes too far for this listener and approximates, unfortunately for the blues, a pop audience more in touch with adulation than music.

I had the ambiguous fortune of hearing King in a concert hall. What was good about that night was the acoustics. King's guitar and voice were sharp and thick at the same time, and his band—close to that playing at the International—were tight and clean-sounding. What I didn't like were the seats, the proscenium, the curtain, the distance. But King's oratory won out.

Oratory is rhetoric that is both science and art, and that exists in the performance of the lone speaker in communion with his or her audience. Cicero says that such practitioners are rare because they combine a commonality of the everyday with the learning of the scientist and artist. King is the great orator of the blues for me because, as Cicero implies, King speaks *for* his audience and yet moves them beyond the position of "now" to a place that only the blues can get you to. That night in Portland I knew the rambling introductions were old formulas, the gestures were all twenty-years old, the licks were old figures, the inflections, tone, and pitch of the voice were nothing new—and yet I knew that by taking these "everyday" tools of King's he was showing this particular audience that he could make it happen for us in great sweeps of *movere*. The *commonality* of the blues experience seems to have been King's great love, even finding itself proverbialized in his most familiar song, "Every Day I Have the Blues." At Portland I watched him put his hands on his hips and smirk, I watched him put his hands behind his ears and look wide-eyed at the audience—and I knew all of these moves and was delighted to be moved by them nonetheless for their familiarity. King never pushes too hard, yet that is all he does—works hard—as any viewing of his numerous video appearances will attest. His repertoire is small—many of his "tools" already noted above—in that the vocabulary of his performances has remained relatively stable all these years. I take this as a sign of an authentic or "natural" speech in King that has few rivals in popular music—a limitation of expression that presents King with the orator's challenge to be *of* the community and *above* the community at once, like the lovers of Plato's *Phaedrus,* who Socrates argues "find in themselves traces by which they can detect the nature of the god to whom they belong [. . .] so that they take from him their character and their life" (60).

I remember the guitar and voice as equals that night. The guitar was fat and stinging, round and thin, with the stuttering chord fragment (or double-stop), set off by the short glissando, the vibrato, of course, like a small cry inside either pain or desire. The voice was big and roaring, small, pinched, and suddenly talking, comically falsetto one moment and the next shaking out a last word like a dying gasp. King just stood there, and, like the great orator, spoke through the blues about the commonest of subjects in common voices that moved me.

King is well-known for his spoken introductions to songs, and "Gambler's Blues" on *Blues Is King* is a good example of a more obvious kind of oration than the song itself. King often uses "we" as the subject of these short talks, and seems to stand both for the band as a unit and for the regal "we" of the performer himself. When I hear "We—-" I am, like Cicero's intended audience, immediately aware that the speaker has begun his address, a *direct* address, and that this is not only music this time, but a performance—a speech—about people: people in groups, people alone, performers, and audiences. King seems to place himself in a regal posture with "We" but at the same time he grounds his reason for performing: "We're going to do our best to move you." The admission is both modest and dangerous, modest in its unassertive "do our best" and dangerous in its flat declaration of an approaching affective, rhetorically-grounded display of *movere* that creates a momentary and apposite objectivity. (Imagine, by comparison, folk, pop, classical, or jazz musicians saying, as they tune up, "We hope this moves you"; more likely, "we hope you like this," which is something very different: an aesthetic conclusion rather than the process of response itself.)

Then the qualified invitation comes: "If you like the blues I think we can." For there to be a community, there needs to be an outside as well; the blues community is welcomed in; others are forewarned. Prior and shared knowledge of the blues is important. The audience is invoked by its ritual object: the blues. King's "I" is a momentary subjective spotlighting of the center—the authorial core—of the performance to come, the "we" widens again to the band, and the music begins with what Charles Sawyer calls "a tour-de-force guitar introduction," several bars of slashing guitar as hard-edged as any King plays on record, I believe, with a mid-solo change up the neck that is hair-raising. That stuttering double-stop jab is there, as well as the long sweet bends; the rhythmic control is impeccable and comes down into the vocal that marries gambling and love into a metaphor of luck and loss.

Sawyer argues that King's oratorical skills came from the church; there is obviously no better place to learn the art of spellbinding for good: "The craft he borrowed from Reverend Archie is based on two principles: maintaining the entire performance, singing, playing and talking between songs in a conversational mode, and repeating a dramatic cycle of mounting tension, climax and release, in ever-increasing swings" (177). Indeed, Sawyer's whole chapter on "The Music Alone" in Sawyer's biography of King is essentially, and superbly, a rhetorical analysis of the effectiveness of King's performance art. While delving deeply into such things as guitar tone-control, Sawyer is returning time and time again to "the musical conjuring act" that does not allow the audience to be passive but "active collaborators" (178–179). Sawyer calls this the "conversational mode" and is more accurately in the terms of this study a rhetoric of *controversia* by which is, in Bakhtin's words, "[s]ome kind of specific outer expression that is directly included into an unverbalized behavioral context and in that context is amplified by actions, behavior, or verbal responses of other participants of the utterance" (Morris 60). It is this mode that makes King not only an effective orator of the blues (i.e., establishing a clear sense of community and speech, of the making of meaning within the community—but also the ambassador of the blues that time and country asked him to be.

Quintilian, much under the influence of Cicero, did not think that such a perfect orator existed:

> So let our orator be the sort of man who can truly be called "wise," not only perfect in morals (for in my view that is not enough, though some people think otherwise) but also in knowledge and in his general capacity for speaking. Such a person has perhaps never yet existed. [. . .] (1.*Prooemium*.19)

This, indeed, does not seem to describe many living individuals even now, but Quintilian allows him to practice some moral choices we might call "relative"—the orator "has no need to swear allegiance to anyone's laws" (12.2.27)—so that we can understand a public speaker's need to change his tune at times (as King does when trying to record with pop stars). These real-life pressures are turned to the orator's advantage—and to society's advantage—as the orator's reputation grows, so that when he is old,

> young men will frequent his house, as in the old days and learn the road to true oratory from him as from an oracle. The father of eloquence will educate them, and, like a veteran pilot, teach them the coasts and the harbors and the signs of the weather, what reason prescribes when the wind is fair and what when it is contrary. (12.11.5)

The parallels to King's current position as the elder king of the blues is obvious, given the endless stream of testimonials directed at King by younger musicians, and even those of nearly his age.

"To do honor to the world": this is as lofty a mission in life as one could imagine, yet B.B. King in his practice of the art and science of the blues oration has created our acceptance of that honorable role for him. His blues is the rhetoric of a generous authority that does not patronize but inspires as Reverend Archie inspired, with passion, giving, those ears turned out to listen for the response, such as these few pages that capture in calmness one vibrant night in Portland. "Gambler's Blues" represents in miniature that night and the good man and orator's long career.

Muddy Waters, "Can't Get No Grindin' (What's The Matter With The Meal)" (1972)
Source: Muddy Waters, *Can't Get No Grindin'* (Chess 50023, CHD3-80002)

One of Muddy Waters's last recordings for Chess Records before moving on to Johnny Winters's productions for Columbia, "Can't Get No Grindin,'" cannot be said to exactly recapitulate his career—but instead is instructive for its rhetorical intelligence in the face of what Muddy knew to be a case of diminishing returns at Chess Records. The song doesn't recapitulate as much as it refracts Waters's own history of the blues—as great a history as has ever been created in the genre. I have chosen this performance over his others even as I call it a kind of creative capstone to his career for a few reasons: one, his reputation will always rest primarily with his Chess recordings; two, the early 1970s was a period of relative popularity for Waters as a stage act, even while his recordings began to wane in their availability—his less noted recordings of the period, therefore, can profit from increased scrutiny; three, the Winters-produced recordings that followed are generally very good but to this listener veer too often toward the excess Waters was never party to during his earlier career; four, the sound is rich and light, as Waters always was as a master of the blues, unlike the later recordings produced by Winters who, I believe, understood Waters's powers and sympathetically went about overstating Waters on records.

"Can't Get No Grindin'" is not Chess-produced, but produced by Ralph Bass, responsible for the horrendous brass sessions that were one of Waters's few failures as a recording artist. When Bass produced Waters again for the "Can't Get No Grindin'" album several years later, he displayed Waters in a more conventional setting, though when one hears Pinetop Perkins's electric harpsichord, one immediately wonders what destruction the music business is about to visit upon Muddy Waters.

But the song "works" not only in itself (i.e., as a comic blues about all the things that can go wrong in a day, from making a living to being cheated by preachers, and even nonsense about bushels and pecks, and a man "with a cornfield around his neck") but in the way I suggest above, as a lens on the past that, in the case of Muddy Waters, was a long and rich past, and one that he carried with him after his resurgence in the 1960s as a father figure to musicians and the genre as a whole. The sense of retrospection in any art is an inevitable consequence of success and endurance and stamina, and Waters had all of these qualities as an artist, and turned this burden into an almost endless performing tour in which (as I witnessed in 1968) the blues became the object of his burden to be danced away and blown away on a current of pulsing rhythm, telepathic communication among the band members, and a rhetorical stance toward his audience of utter dignity and warmth, a unity of body and voice that shook the back of the hall so that we, the audience, seemed to be feeling exactly what he was feeling.

What more can be said about this rhetoric? It is certainly an ethical one, grounded in that value of the blues as single among collective, a dynamic that is played out in performance that allows the tremendously rich voice of Waters—the greatest in the genre—to ride over the top of the first verse of a frankly silly song like "Can't Get No Grindin'" with a conviction of the "I" that does not necessarily obtain in other performances of the clowning blues singer. The attitude is the typical self-pity the blues has seen since Charlie Patton, leavened by an obvious case of hyperbole, so that the fool knows the fool to be himself and so is rather too wise to be *only* the fool. This leavening is present even in Waters's gorgeous version of "Black Night" (the horns removed), as chilling a message of doom as any bluesman ever recorded. Waters smiled through his blues for the most part, and "Can't Get No Grindin'" is an excellent example of the bluesman's rhetorical coup: if I'm singing about it, then it's not going to get me—I got *it*.

Waters's rhetoric is experienced-based, I think, out of which grew the experiential truths that were entirely persuasive as *testimonies* of life:

> Testimony [. . .] is the foundation of history, which is occupied about individuals. Hence, we derive our acquaintance with past ages, as from experience we derive all that we can discover of the future. [. . .] Testimony us capable of giving us absolute certainty [. . .] even of the most miraculous fact, or of what is contrary to uniform experience. (Campbell 55)

George Campbell's eloquent 18th Century rhetoric establishes a clear path for the aestheticized testimony of the "contrary" experience of our great artists, including the bluesmen and women of this century.

Waters's use of language as consolation can take many forms in the blues, not just the comical or self-pitying. The classic blues of a Bessie Smith seemed often to point to the future, when her man would come home or—in short—her luck would turn. As a song of faith, the blues is a kind of secular gospel in this way. Implied consolation is in the blues' ability to "top" or "out-do" (a form of boasting, or the dozens common to African-American linguistic play or signifying) in songs of misery like Eddie Boyd's "Five Long Years" or Buddy Guy's "One Room Country Shack." One listens to these extreme delineations of misery with the full knowledge that each wishes to be more dramatically *effective* than the last, to employ a rhetorical *amplificatio* upon the audience's nods of recognition. The tradition of consolation implies a renewal of past injustice with a contemporary stroke of still deeper blue. Muddy Waters's consolatory rhetoric was sometimes comic, sometimes dark, and always delivered with a sense of the offer—the generous "me too" of the boast—as being made from the *ever-present past* of the performer himself.

This quality of the ever-present past in Waters is perhaps what sets him off from other bluesmen who worked out of country or solo settings into urban band settings. His only rival for this sense of depth and breadth is perhaps B. B. King, but King's blues are not only urban now but sophisticated as well. By "sophisticated" I mean welcoming elements of jazz, brass, and pop music to such a degree that King accommodates them. Waters, by contrast, was defeated by brass (and white English musicians, although *Fathers and Sons,* done with white Americans, is fair listening) in such a way (clearly desultory vocals, most obviously) as to imply to his audience, "I don't want to do this." King's achievement is partly in his ability to adjust—a sure power. But Waters's relative inflexibility says, "What I have here is enough"—or, in broader terms as he often sang them, "I love the life I live and I live the life I love." What that life was, the audience knows and feels every time—harpsichord or not. Waters's deep-bottomed voice sings out:

> [H]is mastery of the fine points of intonation is the true glory of his singing. Those infinitesimally flattened thirds, majestic falling fifths, and glancing slides between tones all mean something, just as the slightest shift in the pitch level of a person's speech means something when someone who hears as acutely as Muddy does is listening. Exactly how flat he

sings a note will depend on where in the melody line that note falls (a purely musical value) and on the emotional weight of the feelings the line is meant to convey. As in the singing of the Akan of Ghana, the flatter the pitch, the more intense the feeling. One recognizes in the artful pitch play an unmistakable reflection of the African preoccupation with music as language and, more specifically, of the pitch-tone languages so many Africans spoke when they first arrived in the Americas. (Palmer, *Deep Blues* 102–3)

This study asserts that observations like Palmer's are really about rhetoric, what Palmer says is the "meaning" of the blue note, that flattened third. When Waters brings to bear all of his tonal weapons—face, lips, tongue, throat—in a famous song like "Mannish Boy" the performance slows down to a *tour de force* crawl while Waters amplifies the meaning of the "man" in the "boy." By contrast, "Can't Get No Grindin'" swings like much of the mid-1950s recordings with his classic group of Little Walter, Jimmy Rogers, Fred Below, and Otis Spann. It swings along, and the "meaning" of the song is not as deep, not as serious, and so the rhetoric of that great vocal instrument is muted and more subtle, with only the hint of that big bad shout Waters could give to the last syllable of a line. The voice is undeniably raspy and rich, but in this performance he is not varying that natural quality, or deviating from a kind of middle ground. His rhetoric, to echo Palmer, is tied to the meaning and the feel of the *total* performance: the comic blues, requiring less, not more, of the speaker's power.

What is not a part of this recorded performance is audience, and it is safe to say that its presence for Waters provoked an intensity of vocal performance that Palmer relates in *Deep Blues* and which several live audio and video recordings can attest; as an example of the latter, even the utterly formal surroundings of The Band's *The Last Waltz* extravaganza gave Waters, very near the end of his life, a chance to squeeze the English language into and out of a lyric so that his body twists and shakes in accompaniment. His 1981 appearance at the Maintenance Shop, an Iowa TV production available as a videorecording, also shows an aging Waters having to put up with a restless but adoring white audience and finding—this time seated—that his eyes are fixed somewhere "back there" as he urges an uneven band back through some classic numbers. The rhetoric of these performances is consistently attuned to purpose (i.e. invested with the life experience of the performer) but meted out in such a way that the rhetorician's sensitivity to surroundings and audience response is both appropriate and correct. Waters's *ethos* is centered in the meaning of the music as it could be *conveyed*—not created—with greatest effectiveness, out of the past and into the present of this time and place, carried by this aging figure, "so that people still know that I am Muddy Waters, you know" (Rooney 121).

He called the blues "tone—deep tone with a heavy beat" (Rooney 122). Waters found that tone in a musical setting of the great bands he put together, not only in the voice alone. He could get that "deep tone" in his voice, but he could double or triple it too with the sound of the band. His own slide playing is missing on "Can't Get No Grindin'" but it is clearly a second voice on most of the classic recordings. The slide in the hands of early players like Tampa Red and Blind Willie Johnson allowed for a duet feel to the solo performance; the slide could whine, hum, moan, or grumble just like a voice could, and when Muddy Waters played his, it responded to his vocals as a wordless language, a new tonal range within which Waters and the other slide players could almost "hear" a human voice but remain outside of its signs, and instead concentrate on the instrument's strengths, its thrilling swoops and sudden chordal voicings: its imitations of the voice going beyond what the natural voice could actually achieve.

Waters seems to have played much less slide in his later years, giving it over to one or two lead guitar players. (On the Maintenance Shop video, Waters *does* play some excellent slide.) On "Can't Get No Grindin'" Waters sings but does not play. The guitar, in fact, is handled by Pee Wee Madison and Sammy Lawhorn, neither of whom do anything beyond playing a modest rhythm background that sounds a lot like Little Richard's "Tutti Frutti," especially when matched with Pinetop Perkins's strutting harpsichord solo. The performance does, however, have a second voice, if not Waters's slide or anyone else's. James Cotton's harp plays a second solo and, like Little Walter before him, infuses the Waters sound with a suggestion of jazz, reed, and the wild "outside" that is missing from the rest of the performance.

Just three years earlier, in 1968, Alan Lomax had seen the Waters band perform outdoors near the Lincoln Memorial. He called it "America's newest orchestra [. . .] an orchestra built around singing, highly rhythmic yet subtly supporting and amplifying the vocal part, going back through Son House to the one-stringed diddley bow, to the very roots of African-American music in Mississippi" (421–22). Lomax notes the echo of the Delta and Son House, who Waters called his "copy" as far as a bluesman could "model" for Waters. Robert Johnson was important, too, but House was the man who had given Waters the deeper groove into the tone of the blues. If Robert Johnson was silver, Waters was gold. House was closer by, and Waters watched him as a good student will, and Lomax reports that Waters practiced one-and-a-half to two hours a day, and built a repertoire for white audiences as well as black, country western as well as pop. Waters's favorite radio performer was Fats Waller, he started on the harmonica, could play the piano, thought black music better than white "because it has more harmony" (Lomax 413). Lomax paints a portrait of Waters that overthrows the misconception often created about the bluesman's primitive beginnings. Difficult, yes; primitive, no. Waters denied having the blues all that much, although his first blues, "Country Blues." came to him after losing a woman. He was clearly a student: working at being a musician, and making it work, and making money at it, and hardly ever looking back as soon as the chance to leave the Delta came.

This sense of purpose, of shaping one's skills to meet a need, does not withhold an honoring of the man as a genius of music, but suggests instead what the genre of the blues should be recognized for: a musical and word-filled rhetoric that is as highly evolved in its way as any other musical form, whose users are first students, then practitioners—and from those practitioners a few masters rise like Cicero's desire. Only the faintest hint of Waters's artistry can be gleaned from the abstracted lines of even his best lyrics:

> Well, now, some folks say
> The old worried blues ain't bad
> That's the miserablest feeling,
> Child, I most ever had.

The "deep tone" he gave to the blues is there—as you recite these lines you can hear your voice slipping into a drawn-out last word, an inner logic that the blues lyric seems to create in any reader's mind. The ground, or foundation for these lyrics—the soil, if you will—is the "new orchestra" that Waters gave signs of creating even at his first recordings with Lomax in 1941 and 1942. Waters recorded alone and with the Son Simms Four, with and without a second guitar, with two other vocalists, and with violin and mandolin. Compared to Robert Johnson, whose repertoire seems to have been as wide-ranging if not more so, Waters never held to the romantic loner role that the blues has, unfortunately, been saddled with in discussing some of its greatest artists.

The rhetorical artist is alone and is not alone at the same moment—in that his performance is *his* performance, but only in a dynamic context of culture, language, audience, and received and posed meanings. Neal's *ethos* of the lightning rod figure is just right for Waters, in that Waters knows the blues, but does not sentimentalize it; he can rise above or beyond the milieu of his own audience. The African *ethos* of the collective voice channeled through one is perfectly right for Waters as Neal understands it in *American* terms; Waters's use of the band, his easy acknowledgment of other masters, his belief that the blues is a *tonal* phenomenon beyond simple technical reach, his joy of expression—all of these elements of Waters's blues are in themselves identifiably personal but derived too from a kind of idealized discourse of the blues from which one feels that all the great ones drink. Near the end of his recording career, Waters could sing a lightweight song like "Can't Get No Grindin'" and be perfectly sanguine about the effortless sound—the practiced lightness of the rhythm over which his voice is really the hard beat he wanted. He parceled out the meaning of the blues into his band, no matter which group he was working with, as a symbol of the blues feeling itself, a universal sadness washed free with the rhythmic rise and fall of water in a deep bucket. He amplified that rise and fall with a rhetorical genius for watching himself, his audience, and his band, pulling all of these elements together into a call-and-response of unmatched power and beauty.

This call-and-response, its greatest amplitude reached in the 1920s market for the classical blues singers, was what Waters recovered in miniature for the parties and jukes of the war years in Mississippi, later gone north and electrified for audiences in clubs, festivals, and tours. And even on recordings, this dialog of man and group, singer and listeners, speakers and talkers, guitar and harp, guitar and drums—even on late recordings can this collectivity of the blues be heard. Waters achieved a signifying of the deep blues in its saving context of the recording, saving for any future audience the code of his culture captured in the technology of an Other. Waters, as he says to one interviewer, seems to have been intent on "patching up" whatever the human heart had found broken apart in our time.

Eric Clapton, "Groaning the Blues" (1994)
Source: Eric Clapton, *From the Cradle* (Reprise 9 45735–2)

Charles Shaar Murray, writing a biography of Jimi Hendrix, considers Hendrix's rivals in the 1960s, and delivers to Eric Clapton the kind of backhanded compliment that any "white bluesplayer" should consider himself lucky to receive, given the difficulty—some would say the *synoeciosis*—of the label. Murray believes that Clapton is to the blues as Vladimir Nabokov is to the English-language novel (144). Murray draws the analogy in order to show that Clapton's skill, whatever the degree we are to grant him, is an acquired one, done through diligent study in a sort of hothouse methodology. He points to Nabokov's English, like Joseph Conrad's, as almost too perfect, not in its textbook-like correctness, but in its almost overly systematic *inventiveness*. The formality of this invention suggests a sort of textbook education, as if Quintilian's students had actually gone on to form a sort of academy of rhetoric, fully charged, and those outside (where all bluesmen reside most of their lives) would sound unschooled, yet not necessarily laconic, by comparison. This objective distance of artist and medium, Murray suggests, has given Nabokov and Clapton a certain dryness at the center, a bloodlessness that can only be attributed to the accidental conjunction of natural voice and chosen medium.

The argument is an interesting one, not only for what Murray says but for what he does not say and perhaps could have if he had carried out implications of his remarks. What I find most valuable in Murray's argument is the admission of blues to a global audience and, secondly, his drawing a literary figure into the discussion. Murray, a fierce defender of Hendrix's blues (and, indeed, almost everything of Hendrix's) nevertheless argues quite plainly for a heart of the genre to be the American South, in particular the Delta, against which any other blues must be measured for power and authenticity. As I discussed earlier, authenticity can be a matter of degree or proportion when dealing with a complex musical performance; in other words, it can have *some blues* in it. Murray, I believe, would agree with this approach; thus he can give and take away from a figure like Clapton a mantle of blues. Clapton's blues, though, will be "dry" or, in essence, *merely* acquired.

But it is the blues and, as B. B. King, Robert Junior Lockwood, Ike Turner, Otis Rush and others have testified, what Clapton plays is the blues. The double remove for Clapton—his global distancing—is not comprised only of race but of geography as well. I have argued that the blues is a hybrid of a peculiar kind, vividly local in its heart but stretching through a linguistic medium around the world. Of course it was Clapton who participated in the blues revival in Europe in the late 1950s and early 1960s and whose early band The Yardbirds accepted the difficult task of backing Sonny Boy Williamson II (Rice Miller). To look at a figure like Clapton, even in the first stages of his blues with John Mayall's Bluesbreakers in 1965, is to remind oneself that the blues is no more restrained by culture than is classical or folk music. Its quality, however—its power and beauty as it rebounds upon local and far-flung audiences—perhaps is reserved for those few who learn the *need* to communicate.

Murray's mention of Nabokov is redolent with a condescension with which any national literature naturally endows itself. Nationalist literature is based on political differences, cultural hierarchies that, even today, may deny there is any such thing as American literature, since its medium is English. To speak of Nabokov as an emigré or an exile is theoretically sound—he exploited the labels himself, I believe. But for a discussion of the blues, Nabokov's position (and Clapton's as well) suggests the bluesman's own dilemma of dealing with African roots and Western surface. Clapton and Nabokov are dealing with the words of a New World. Murray is wary of formal technique in place of intuitive or idiomatic expression; most critics of the blues would have no quarrel with this wariness. But the question is not, for Murray, whether or not the exile can inherit the Word. For Murray, he cannot; he can only pretend to, and it is a degree of brilliant *invention* (not *conveyance*, as I argued for Waters) by Nabokov and Clapton that the audience recognizes and applauds.

And it is here that the distances grow again between Murray's assertion of cultural disjunction and my earlier argument that the bluesman, too, is working with a foreign medium of English. The distinction is obvious: the bluesman, the most rural or the most urban-bred, is still immersed in this linguistic medium of English from his or her earliest days; the artist like Nabokov has truly to acquire English, while an artist like Muddy Waters has only to use it.

And it is all Waters has to use, and there lies a second important difference between the exiled figure and the colonized figure. Waters and the bluesmen had to forge a difference using the Western tools at their disposal; it is this task that Bhabha describes so well by his use of "mimicry." To copy and then to bend: that is the colonized artist's way, found within the colony, not—as in the case of Nabokov or Clapton—from without.

We can move beyond Murray's discussion to what it implies: the problematical relationship of not only race to the blues, but also *text* to the blues. I have discussed both of these issues throughout this study, but Clapton's blues seems to bring both matters into high relief, and are worth summarizing briefly before returning to him.

Assuming that the blues is rooted firmly in African ritual and performance arts, we may see its American emergence as a musical genre as rooted in those African-American figures who gave birth to it and which, through specific cultural conditions, nurtured and evolved the blues down through the twentieth century as an art form that reflected and reflects the experiences of the African-American. Our second assumption is that the study of the blues has been mainly textual through the availability of recordings, transcriptions, oral and written histories and interpretive works, and at the same time understood by audiences within and outside of blues communities as a marginally literary form of the lyric, which is extracted from the form and studied as a text *about* the blues experience and not, in fact, the blues itself.

Clapton stands at the very crossroads of these two problematical pathways of the blues. I call them pathways because it is obvious to me that the blues is moving, and has moved for quite some time, away from a determinate cultural bias and toward its capture by a literary or "high cultural" posse for its interment within the covers of yet another interpretive agenda. Do these two directions have something to do with each other? Does the move from a clear racial root to an extracted study of the lyric in English graduate programs exist, in fact, on the same continuum? This question will be answered in the next chapter on teaching the blues. For now, we look at a single figure that illustrates these issues.

Listening to Clapton's performance of "Groaning the Blues" immediately fractures one's sense of the present time and place, and thus illustrates our first problematic. The song is by Willie Dixon, and was first performed in 1957 by Otis Rush. The retrospection in the performance is not unique; we know, if we know the blues, that Clapton is turning backward. This is the retrospective rhetoric of the epideictic, in that we are being asked to look at something that is past but that must be brought into the present view for praise, worship, meditation (Vickers 57). Of course Clapton worships his blues heroes, but so do many who cannot also play them. Clapton can play them, but in that transcendence of a renewed beauty in such a performance as "Groaning the Blues" there is a double-vision that Clapton does not deny and which for the audience suggests something of Murray's *caveat*. The audience knows this is not Clapton all the way—but neither was it *Otis Rush* all the way (but B.B. King before him, whose style Rush was listening to and imitating).

Some blues purists repeatedly call white blues performers "interpreters," a gentle code word for the color of their skin but suggesting the "remove" from the music, as if the true bluesman is singing in a booth somewhere in the United Nations and the white performer is "interpreting" it for another audience. All performances are interpretations; some are more interpreted than others—or so the purist terminology suggests. But those who would not equate Rush's interpretation with Clapton's would point to the sense of voice that eludes the white performer whose life experiences are outside of black culture. When Waters said that "[t]hey got all these white kids now. Some of them can play good blues. They play so much [. . .] but they cannot vocal like the black man" (qtd. in Palmer, *Deep Blues,* 260). Waters was pinpointing the idiomatic use of the English language that is ineluctably tied to regional, social, and racial variation. The guitar, in other words—and like writing—is a *technology;* the voice is grown out of the soil.

History has burdened Clapton, and performers like him who are not black and perform the blues, with a history of performance that issues like a dark river from a certain source. There is no denying that Clapton must go to the river to drink, yet the passion of voice displayed on "Groaning the Blues" suggests that Clapton's social or class experience—raised by grandparents, his father unknown, working class—can do much to erase those regional or racial roots that are missing. I am reminded again of Junior Kimbrough's surprising remark that he found Taj Mahal the most exciting blues performer he ever saw. If there was ever a dismissal of cultural "purity" in the blues, Kimbrough's is it. His is only one opinion, but a cursory look at the men who recorded, promoted, or lived by and off the blues is so racially mixed as to make the question moot to most of us except those who still believe that any culture must stake a claim to its art as one way of living in a political world fraught with those forces who would appropriate any such art if it threatens or, especially, if it offers profit. It is a crowning irony that Clapton's album, from which "Groaning the Blues" is taken for this discussion, is the genre's biggest seller.

Clapton has called himself a historian of the blues; I think his rhetoric is at times too self-deprecating; in the past he has cast himself as a supplicant at the shrine of his heroes so that among his earlier blues were almost note-for-note tributes to Otis Rush, Freddie King, and Albert King. I think the force of this study can suggest we look at the white blues performer as *responding* to the blues, not only interpreting it. In the act of response, elements of classical rhetoric, dialogical rhetoric, and a reception aesthetic assist in the *recuperation,* not appropriation, of the blues by a performer from "outside." Thus, the call-and-response trope of an African superstructure is troped to the outside to create a multiracial, multicultural discourse of the blues. It has always been so with the white audience, among which were the white blues performers themselves.

Does Clapton respond to the blues as well as play and sing the blues? I think he does, in such a way as to suggest the unequal discourse of the carnival, in which, according to Bakhtin, members of the court or church join the audience of the street for a period of forgetfulness and merriment. To accomplish this response, Clapton brings a somewhat different aesthetic to the conversation. First, he compensates for his English roots with an emphasis on the guitar. This is Muddy Waters's argument, and taken in its most generous sense, Clapton reveals that the voice of the guitar speaks across any cultural gap. His version of "Groaning the Blues" is more than twice as long as Rush's, yet the vocal is very much the same in tone. What has been expanded is the guitar intro, solo, and coda. This comes as no surprise to any blues listener who also listens to white blues players. Compensating for a weakness with an acknowledged strength is part of the game; Count Basie couldn't write jazz but he could punctuate its lines with such emphatic rhythmic lyricism that an obvious weakness was put aside in our respect for him.

Clapton, nonetheless, sings with a fervor that is not imitative of Rush but, I would argue, in the tradition of the Chicago bluesman like Rush and Buddy Guy who put their vocals "over the top" in part to match the amperage of the electric performance and in part to talk out of the blues tradition of felt expression. When slavishly imitative, or *falsely* emotional—one might call this sentimental—the vocals in white blues are laughably crude and do not sound responsive but *possessive*. Trying to sound "black" is not the point, of course. What *is* the point is Clapton singing the lines "My heart gets so heavy/I shakes down in my bones" in such a way—a five-part melisma on "heart" and "shakes," a characteristic upturn on the last word, here "bones," an adherence to the colloquial "shakes" even though for Clapton it is a convention—in such a way that we can sense conviction and utter commitment to Clapton's *listening* to those lines in order that the response be valid. Palmer suggests that Clapton is unusual in this respect because he "seems to hear so much more of the music's recondite intricacies than other white blues musicians, who often sound to these ears as if they think blues is a diatonic, equal-tempered music, instead of a modal, microtonal one" ("Baby Blues" 121). Palmer finds Clapton's playing to be idiomatically authentic, aggressive, raw. In reviving older blues and recasting them in his own sound, Clapton—by remaining faithful to the words themselves, down to colloquialisms that are obviously foreign to him—manages to create the sense of "I feel that way too, so much so that I can do that blues to show it" or as he remarks to a questioner, that "it's a question of listening with empathy to everything and anything, and then applying that" ("Eric's First Online Chat"). From out of the audience comes this response to the call of the blues.

There is a pleasingly innocent tone to Clapton's love of the blues that denies any mastery, any appropriation when, in fact, his reverence for the music is what some critics dislike. It isn't, they say, *work* for Clapton, it's love—and that will forever separate him from his working heroes. Clapton, a millionaire, must nullify his place in the blues by virtue of his success: the argument is elitist, yet present even in shadow form when black bluesmen like B. B. King reach a level of success that seems to deny the contextual correctness of the blues, which is lower or middle class.

The song's theme of loss—the singer cannot bear to think of his woman in another man's arms—is a common one in the blues, and is particularly common to Clapton's blues which, for many, reached its apotheosis a quarter-century earlier with the songs clustered around the story of "Layla" who, in Clapton's life, was a lover he could not love without suffering. Clapton's several recordings of Freddie King's "Have You Ever Loved a Woman?" form in themselves a portrait of a blues obsession that for Clapton sustains him as an artist who does not seem so interested in originality as in origins, which he clearly paints in blue.

As the most respected white bluesplayer of his generation, Clapton forms a kind of linchpin for a blues lifeline to a white audience that does not want the blues to die. Interviews commonly reveal the black bluesman's belief that white audiences are keeping the blues alive, and figures like Clapton show white audiences the way back as well as the way forward into the music. If the blues is still just a part of the carnival for most of us—to go to in order to have fun, to feel bad and good, to wonder at the *pathos* of the performance, the clowning of the bluesman, the great preaching of a harp or shout—it is because we hope to feel that we are more alive than a single place or position or art or even language can afford us. We go into the full world of the vernacular, as Bakhtin says, to shake off "this seriousness" (Morris 208).

It is ironic that the blues is a way for many of us to give full vent to our seriousness about this seriousness, and thus to find "song, gesticulation, laughter" (Morris 208) on the far side. Blues is not for Clapton or any white audience an excuse to stay blue, but to accept, as a gospel, its *curative powers,* its Platonic ladder up which each of us as subjects can move when immersed in the rhetoric of truth and beauty. In accepting the blues, bluesmen like Clapton, white or black, are not taking it away or appropriating it. I used the term response earlier, and I return to it: to talk in the vernacular of the blues *to* the blues is to wrap oneself in its substance. I can hear in Clapton's opening notes of "Groaning the Blues"—a discordant scraping of the guitar strings down by the bridge, three times and a downward gliss—a call to the blues, to Otis Rush and Willie Dixon, beyond and all the way back to other heroes, who listen then to the listener and seem to say, "*That* is the blues."

4

Teaching (by) the Blues

It is impossible to teach anything with total disinterestedness; conversely, it is dangerous to teach anything with total conviction. The blues in any pedagogical situation is beset by the same problems that any classroom text is: it is being used for some reason or reasons that do not necessarily match those intended, implied, or imagined by the producer of that text.

My attention to audience-oriented rhetoric and criticism, their subjectivities, has allowed me to see that the reception of a text or song or speech—its transformation through the encounter of a reading or hearing—can be understood as a response, and does not have an obligation to retain or imagine itself as "faithful" to the text that was produced; in fact, through the persuasive powers of this text or song or speech, the response may take the form of new texts, new songs, new speeches. The empowerment of the audience motivates a responsive rhetoric: in miniature, the shouted repetition of a line of blues, in grander style, the evolution of a tradition through imitation and variation by new artists and new, engaged audiences. This cycle of engaged rhetoric and responsive interpretation allows for a resummoning of creative energies on the part of audiences, to make art from art, to hear in the blues or poetry or novel a new music, a new meaning and power.

The plasticity of reception—if we allow for it in the ways we teach, the ways we set up encounters with culture—places tremendous, not less, responsibility upon the teacher (who is herself the leader of her "course," an appropriate term for the choreographed *movement* of speaker and audience). For this plasticity might allow for a hundred receptions for every hundred listeners, and so take the work away from author or collective or race or culture and hand it piecemeal, broken, under-determined (under-rhetoricized), to a future history.

Interpretation will exist in any context, but in the pedagogical one it assumes a greater presence through the relative inequality of teacher and student—and the mysterious weight of the aesthetic object itself. One assumes as a teacher a certain social responsibility to enact certain conventions of learning. Their ultimate aim, almost without exception, is to further social values, and develop those personal ones that have a congruence with social rights and privileges. Therefore, interpreting a text like the blues in a classroom will always have hanging over it a certain expectation of *usefulness* to person and community. This expectation is really very much like the expectation we have when we go to hear the blues—we expect great sounds, a good time, responsive joy.

But the abstracted quality of much of our teaching is predicated by institutional requirements, such as walls, desks, pencils, and paper. This dryness extends to our working with many texts, not only the blues. Even the most writerly and readerly of texts—say, an epic poem like *Paradise Lost*—has lately been interpreted anew using "New Historicism," a critical methodology that hopes to account for the force of a text by understanding written and unwritten texts that existed at the time of its writing and reception, to see this text as inextricably caught in a web of contemporaneous words and forces. But this work is still an abstracted task in the classroom, miles and centuries away from the moments of creation, the hard work of constructing, revisioning, producing texts—and the similar components of their reception. Some teaching the New Historicism believe that by a thorough grounding in context, so shall we know the text better. The argument is persuasive, except that the text becomes a massive complex that, if anything, continues to mushroom beyond any clear boundaries, any sense of closure or certainty.

With the blues, teachers—those I mean who treat them as texts, fixed constructions of linguistic substance, including the language of music—find the stakes even higher because the written text of the blues (as I argued earlier) is itself an abstraction of a performance that has absolutely no written text involved in it. Take away the walls, desks, pencil, and paper—and you still should have the blues. But to study only the vernacular language-as-lyric—of which the blues is a kind—as a classroom text is to invite failure, or worse a travesty of simplification or misinterpretation, a disservice to the rhetorical and aesthetic power of the blues that many teachers wish to make a *literary* object on par with other literary elements of the American tradition that have been made a part of the literary canon—narratives of slavery and captivity, literacy narratives, the rhetoric of Douglass and DuBois and Sojourner Truth, the rediscovered fiction of Nella Larsen and Zora Neale Hurston, the vernacular poetry of Sterling Brown, the jazz sounds of Langston Hughes.

Can the blues fit? I believe that they can, despite all of the danger signs I have raised here. The risk of abstraction, of overdetermined or underdetermined meaning, of preciousness, of exploitation—these risks, as I argue, are always the risks of teaching literature in the new classroom, but can be turned back as the blues itself has turned back these forces in other contexts. To paraphrase Houston Baker, Jr., the teaching of the blues is a mediation between creativity and commerce, a walking of the ways between saying too much and too little, too much situation or too little situation, too many meanings or too few, no beauty or too much, too much love of the blues or not enough.

This chapter will explore ways that the blues can be taught in a university setting—with or without a grounding in rhetorical theory, a subject of some marginality, surprisingly, in many English classrooms. I take this setting to be then, most likely, the literature or expository writing classroom, but much of the rationale and methodology presented here should be relevant to teachers in other disciplines such as African-American studies, American studies, ethnic studies, and music—a disparate collection of disciplines but one showing, in all its members, an interest in the relationship between peoples and their cultural products. The rationale and methodology will necessarily draw upon those same theories that I have employed in understanding the way we as individuals hear the blues; the move to the classroom, however, asks that these rhetorics and critical methods be supplemented by our seeing how *instruction* can be made to be a part of the blues—not so that it become a Marxian tool of institutional critique, for example, but so that the blues can instruct as a complex of rhetorical and aesthetic roadways to, into, and through the American cultural tradition.

My first try at teaching by the blues was a clear failure. I taught a senior seminar (meant to be a kind of capstone for English majors at my university) in the "documentary literature" of the American 1930s.

We read proletarian novels and poetry, looked at the great Depression Era photographs of Lange, Evans, and Rothstein, and listened to the blues. I used a then-recent collection in the Columbia series Roots 'n Blues called *Telling It Like It Is: News and the Blues,* a blues compilation by Lawrence Cohn from the 1920s forward on topical matters like floods and unemployment and the atomic bomb. We sat in the classroom as the tape played on my portable cassette player; students had also purchased the tape at our bookstore and were expected to study it at home.

The discussions were flat and lifeless. Great performers like Bessie Smith and Patton were just voices and hard-to-hear lyrics, tinny guitars issuing from portable players or the family stereo. We sat in class and did our best to connect these performances to those we had already read or seen. In my efforts to round out the sense of "document" to include photos and music, I had committed the error of meliorating differences, to say that there was something special about these blues, but nothing more or less special than this novel by James T. Farrell, or this photograph of Walker Evans. Unlike the written text and printed photo, the voices of Patton were totally effaced by the hard bright walls of our classroom and sounded as foreign—or abstracted—as a Mongolian folk song, or the cry of a strange animal.

I had no plan for this *strangeness.* Yet this strangeness is what I should have been able to teach *by.* Instead I toiled mightily to show that even the vernacular arts like the blues were interested in becoming rhetorically powerful and that the users of these arts were politically conscious, intelligent, and committed to showing how the blues could comment on the world's *specific* miseries, and not just its eternal verities; in effect, I was taking Neal's *ethos* of the blues and particularizing it. But my students had little or no grounding in the historical realities that gave initial rise to the blues.

I take my intentions to be honorable ones; I was motivated out of a new understanding of the blues (at the time) in the way it reflected a 1930s aesthetic of oral history that could supplement a crippled commercial—or dominant, accepted—history. I thought I was arguing that even such "primitive" art forms as the blues could turn their attention to the world's topical ills. And the blues did, but in making this argument I ignored the *sound* of the blues and focused entirely on their *meaning;* I was looking for their rhetorical force in the *ideas* they might contain—but entirely overlooking the rhetorical *elements* that make up the blues: the arrangement, the style, the ways of getting at effects of sound, word, and melody, the identity of audience, and so forth. I was stubborn enough to believe that I could never be wrong just to talk about *meaning* (it was a final goal of our reading, wasn't it?) until much later when I discovered that the meaning of the blues could not be seen as solely inhabiting its lyrics or musical "impression," but was, in fact, much more easily understood as a rhetorical act, with purpose, intelligence, feeling, and effect.

A hard lesson, but a lesson won nonetheless. A sense of trivialization—or at least reduction—has accompanied me ever since when dealing with any but the most formal art in the classroom. I can teach quite freely a novel by F. Scott Fitzgerald, for example, because it was produced so confidently as a part of that culture that expected, revered, and centered the novel-as-art—the same culture that I inherited from my parents and their standing as middle class European-Americans. This is what I mean by "formal art"—attractively packaged in book form and long held to be a traditional object of the American culture.

But what is this blues object, and how can we fix it for study and teaching? I was defeated initially, but I spent several classes experimenting with *recuperating* the blues in my own teaching of literature, deciding finally that these conflicts of conscience and method could become the basis for my pedagogy of the blues. I understood my role as "audience" of the blues (stretching back to my brother's Leadbelly recordings, through the Waters performance at my college, through Otis Rush in Chicago and a blues festival at Greenville, Mississippi, and of course the enormous crazy quilt of my collection of recordings) and felt too what I have described in this study as its double rhetoric: a classical rhetoric of emphasized subjectivity, overlaid with one of call-and-response, the Bakhtinian dialogue of the one and the many, the dynamic energy of its common speech augmented by the power of its musical vehicle—and the second of the encircled culture, the colonial voice itself responding to the deafening call of the European mainstream.

These ways of speaking about language power—as we respond as audience and as we enact our thoughts and desires through dialog and as cultural representatives—I have called rhetorics in this study, and I want to continue to use this term with an important supplement at this point in my thinking about teaching the blues. That supplement is the rhetoric of representation, by which I mean the ways we understand that which is unknown or not present.

These ways are the methods by which many teachers overcome or transcend the obvious barrier that exists between classrooms and society. The text itself is a representation—for many—of that which is not here, or which is unknown but knowable now through this language of "re-presentation." The importance of this rhetoric to the teaching of and by the blues is that it admits to a *lack* of authenticity in its presentation of the blues, but asserts that the blues can be known, if not ideally or truly known, in the confines of the classroom. Most importantly, this rhetoric allows teachers to point to those same roadways that the blues points to: the tracks of the blues can lead *to* the blues, back through time or just downtown.

Teaching *by* the blues is what teachers can do in reading and writing classrooms. The difference—between teaching the blues and teaching *by* the blues—is important and can, in fact, become one if we assert, as Baker does, that the roadway *is* the blues. But I will return to that pedagogical turn after investigating first the powers of performance in the classroom.

If we consider the blues to be oral poetry at its heart, as David Evans argues, then at the very least this poetry of the blues must be made oral again—not only in the recorded sense but in the fresh event of the words and their performance in the classroom. All that is being accomplished by this performance is the making of the words in the moment of their utterance by a performer or artist or interpreter. But that making, or re-making, represents the essential improvisation of their origins. The words that were made up at the moment by artists like Lightnin' Hopkins or Bukka White, or those more carefully composed like those of Willie Dixon, have power only in their eventual *expression* as words in close proximity to audience, re-made for that audience, and re-made again for the next listener. Their instability, their variation or difference, constitute the important improvisational quality of the blues or, as many like Gates argue, of all African-American linguistic expression.

So it is certainly not sufficient to *listen* to recordings in classrooms—though many teachers can do no more than this. Videos are used as well, performance tapes that seek to break that membrane that seems to surround the classroom with a sense of distance or ill-suited academic objectivity to the arts. Oral poetry (with ritual as Ellison's formula of the blues secret) is a device by which tradition is both created and preserved, a sort of discourse that risks momentary disruptions in the way a lyric can be bent, unbent, reshaped, exploded and pieced back together again in a four-minute performance by a master, apprentice, fool, or clown. It is this discourse that the blues employs to keep itself alive, a discourse of invention-within-collective-memory, set afire by Albert Murray's blues hero, the survival "of whom depended largely on an ability to operate on dynamic equivalent to those of the vamp, the riff, and most certainly the break, which jazz musicians regard as the Moment of Truth, or that disjuncture that should bring out your personal best" (*Blue Devils* 16).

To have a bluesman come to a classroom and sing the blues is not, of course, a perfect situation either; it isn't perfect because "blues in the schools" is somewhat of an oxymoron. The blues-complex is freedom, roads, trains, love, loss, and joy—metaphors themselves for a vernacular context of which school is an interruption, a blocking figure, a state apparatus whose ideology is in some ways still opposed—as the church is—to the meaning and force of the blues.

Yet the school is a place for instruction, a place to find young people somewhat at bay, perhaps trapped, if skeptical at least attentive to those who would change their way of thinking and feeling. Education is a cultural universal, and those cultures who are at bay themselves must find ways to talk back, to talk louder about themselves *for* themselves. No one has to hear but an audience of a culture's choosing. This is one value of the blues today: to show young people where much of their beautiful music came from. Just show it, and let them—the students—do the rest. "Showing them" is at the heart of performance—a "show" that combines art with event, sound with language, turns the linoleum floor into a stage and the teacher into an artist—a creative disruption in the rational plodding of so much of our learning.

Teaching the blues is what Billy Branch, a blues harp player, has done for the Urban Gateways program in Chicago:

> The initial, the primary purpose, is music appreciation. I incorporate a lot of history. I make sure the kids are knowledgeable of the blues greats. Because you have a limited amount of time, you can't get, real, real thick into history but I quiz 'em and I introduce 'em especially to the name people. [. . .] But the focus has to be a lot on the actual instruction,

> because the culmination will be performing with our band on our big show, you know. (Underwood 69)

Branch sees appreciation preceding performance, or finding a process by which observers can become participants. This process is similar to any active reading scheme, in which a passive role is made active by forcing, or encouraging, the creative juices to flow, and to flow back at—to create a dialog with—the first voice, in this case Little Walter or Koko Taylor or whomever Branch wishes his audience to "appreciate" through response, not just contemplation or private feeling. In short, Branch doesn't want his students to only see the blues, or say the blues—he wants them to *show* the blues as a "show," a true performance that speaks the same language:

As for cultural roots, Branch admits to a grand theory:

> What I want them to understand [is] that all the music that they hear on the radio came from this rich, neglected treasure that we call the blues. And I want them to be able to appreciate the men and women who created this music. [. . .] For black youngsters especially, I want them to understand that they have something to be immensely proud of as a part of their heritage, and somethin' to maybe give you a little bit more confidence and hold your head up a little bit, that all the music that you hear, that was made in America, your forefathers and your ancestors created it. And with that in mind, it's somethin' to be proud of. (Underwood 70)

I find Branch's distinction between *appreciation* and *understanding* deliberate and important. He is applying *appreciation* to the critical posture of listening to music and backgrounds, the lives of the greats, distinguishing historical meanings from aesthetic ones. He is applying *understanding* more to a creative or intuitive knowing born out of performing the blues. He implies that this understanding is a deeper knowing, *into feeling,* that can only be reached through the active participation of the student in the blues; Branch has rhetoricized the blues to the extent of claiming its primacy among all American music: its effects are historical and contemporaneous.

Branch also suggests a motive of black pride in his advocacy of the blues, a political rhetoric that he as an instructor must direct at his black audience, to show that the blues is not only a *formal* object, redolent of great achievement, but is also a *cultural and racial* object, an aesthetic representation of a reality specific to African-American culture. Indeed, this representation of the blues is still only an object, released finally into performance by Branch, his band, and his students.

But the blues can co-exist with white appreciation, white performance (or, more precisely, by those who are not African-American). Branch does not wish to exclude any audience or performer from a sense of the blues, although his sense of authenticity seems grounded in those elder bluesmen whose commercial successes have been the slightest, the taint of commercialism being his measure of *inauthenticity*. Branch does not wish to exclude white blues because he sees this form in much of the rock music young audiences have venerated over the past forty years. He is once again connecting current modes of appreciating music with historical processes, although I doubt if he would characterize this process as appropriation, as postcolonial theory would suggest he should:

> It's just as important, if not more important, for white children, actually white America in general, to understand black history as it is for black people to understand it. 'Cause, see, it's been the part of history that's been erased. Just take it from a musical standpoint. I mean, if you're not into the blues you have no idea that the Rolling Stones took their name from a song by Muddy Waters. You have no idea that all the Led Zeppelin, most of their hits were blues covers. And the Stones and the Doors and the Who and Cream, and even the Beatles. They cite the bluesmen as their influences. And you know [. . .] what makes a people proud and respected is the accomplishment of their culture. (Underwood 71)

Branch's use of *understanding* is intimately tied to performance, to making and re-making the blues not in the passive posture of the good listener or critic but in the posture of artist, of getting up there and actually blowing that harp. Much like the educational revolution begun by Donald Graves, Jane Hansen, and Lucy Calkins—which argued forcefully for "publication" of work so that reading, writing, speaking, and listening would lead to a closure, but a public closure of "author's chair," literary journal, and bulletin board displays—so Branch is showing us that the performance must form a process of learning that is an understanding of and from the inside of the blues. In only a few hours, Branch reports, the blues are being written, practiced, and performed by youngsters who would otherwise not find linguistic and musical expressions as ones of choice.

This need to perform presents a severe roadblock for those teachers working at the university level who are caught in their own universe of academicized or specialized discourse to such a degree that the performing arts are inevitably segregated from others that are text-based. English, for example, which used to include, routinely, the study of rhetoric, speech, and drama and theater, has been reduced in this century to text-based inquiry into literature and composition; rhetoric has survived—though in reduced form as, often, a single undergraduate class—and speech, drama, and theater have become departments or disciplines in themselves. English studies includes drama, but always as based on a foundation of the authentic text. Recently, as a part of post-structuralism's and New Historicism's influence, English has shown an interest in the oral tradition, and in other cultural artifacts like diaries and oral histories, and in the study of sign systems such as film and still photography. It is through these recent trends—supplemented in part by interest in postcolonial literacies—that we may be able to find a region of reconciliation between the text and performance. The blues, I believe, can be found there.

Houston Baker, Jr.'s work on the blues matrix—a powerful symbol that facilitates the "tropological energies" of his or any other creator's wish to invoke, "constitute and explain phenomena inaccessible to the senses"—is a very important addition to our understanding of the way African-American culture is made and represented, and for this current study points a way to integrate performance into the study of the vernacular. We can make this study essentially performative—as music and rhetoric—to draw on our creative resources as teachers and students, to act as subjects of the blues and makers of the blues:

> As driving force, the blues matrix thus avoids simple dualities. It perpetually achieves its effects as a fluid and multivalent network. It is only when "understanding"—the analytical work of a translator who translates the infinite changes of the blues—converg-

es with such blues "force," however, that adequate explanatory perception (and half-creation) occurs. The matrix effectively functions toward cultural understanding, that is, only when an investigator brings an *inventive attention* to bear. (*Blues* 9, emphasis added)

First, the "blues matrix" isn't only about blues music; it is a master trope like Gates's signifying monkey, an attempt to find a sort of core "ethic" for the way African-American culture has created itself. Baker believes that the blues music we hear is one phenomenon of the matrix—a very important phenomenon, of course, but not the first or best or most central. The matrix as a metaphor is, as Baker asserts, fluid and weblike. Blues music is there, but so is the novel, so is riding the rails, so is the poetry of the Harlem Renaissance and the essays of DuBois, and so is the slave narrative.

What Baker means by the "driving force" of the matrix is that it can erase "dualities" of understanding and creativity. Here, Baker's use of "understanding" is different from Branch's, and refers instead to the analytical work of the critic, the scholar, the commentator or interpreter who stands somewhat outside a culture in order to critique its effects. Baker asserts that such a position disables us from knowing the energies of African-American culture, which are highly "jumpy" or "tropological." It is only through working with the trope of the matrix that the analytical can be fused with the creative or inventive energies of the African-American experience and thus make *understanding* a highly charged state—in fact, more in line therefore with Branch's and my use of the word. This charged understanding prohibits the ascendant position to reason and, instead, unifies reason with play or rhetorical invention:

> An inventive, tropological, investigative model such as that proposed by *Blues, Ideology, and Afro-American Literature* entails not only awareness of the metaphorical nature of the blues matrix, but also a willingness on my own part to do more than merely hear, read, or see the blues. I must also play (with and on) them. Since the explanatory possibilities of a blues matrix—like analytical possibilities of a delimited set of forces in unified field theory—are hypothetically

> unbounded, the blues challenge investigative *understanding* to an unlimited play. (11)

I argue that Baker's sense of the model's being investigative clears space for us as teachers to experiment, explore, sound, and signify on the blues in such a way that we demonstrate understanding of the blues by playing on, off, by, and through the blues. Teachers may, therefore, be seen as performers, as are blues artists and blues audiences.

But teachers are not really themselves bluesmen, unless we take Baker at his word and do more than the usual pedagogical methods of teaching literature through auditory and visual means. How can we do more than this? Does the bluesteacher (my term) simply adopt a kind of blues ethic, suggested by the matrix, and become (sym)pathetically bluesy and hence a better teacher of the blues than the teacher who hands out copies of Robert Johnson's lyrics and treats them as poetry reflecting the black experience in the American South of the 1930s and 1940s?

The question gnaws at the heart of any teacher who wishes to liberate his or her spirit, and the spirits of his or her students, from a sense of abstraction and mere representation of the reality that shifts and fades and brightens behind even the most creative literary text. Baker never addresses pedagogical challenges directly in either the above-quoted work or in his *Modernism and the Harlem Renaissance,* but in the latter (and in his more recent *Black Studies, Rap, and the Academy*) seems to move ever closer to a methodology suggested by the theoretical approaches I have set forward in this study of subjective, dialogical, and colonial rhetorics:

> The blending, I want to suggest, of class and mass—poetic mastery discovered as a function of deformative folk sound—constitutes the essence of black discursive modernism. This blend is achieved within a fluid field. Indeed, if you have ever heard the blues righteously sung, you know that it sounds of and from fields burning under torpid Southern suns, or lands desolately drenched by too high rivers. The intended audience is black people themselves defined by the very blues tones and lyrics as sharers in a nation of common concern and culturally specific voice. (*Modernism* 93)

The folk sound is, in fact, the vernacular of the home, the field, family, and mother. It is the everyday language of the common man and woman and child, and in its capturing by the bluesman captures in turn the heart of its audience, whose language is heard through the voice, hands, and feet of the bluesman. The poetic mastery is, I argue, the rhetoric that allows for a certain elevation, intensification, focus, and feeling in this folk medium so that it becomes, indeed, "righteous" in the beholders' eyes and ears and bodies. This righteous rhetoric, I have argued, is dialogical precisely for its being grounded in the vernacular, rendering it accessible to the "mass" of the audience—and is also "colonial" because it speaks, as Baker asserts, of and to "a nation of common concern...."

While I object to Baker's reduction of the blues sound to a rural or country milieu, perhaps indicated too strongly here by his centering the discourse on the vernacular, I find more seriously disconcerting to a teacher *not* of African-American ancestry the implication that this phenomenon has a specifically intended audience, and that to move past this intention is to risk *uncommon* concerns and *acultural* voices. In short, a white teacher must misread, misteach, and de-signify the blues by virtue of his or her distance from the well of the blues.

The debate of color and criticism (I am conflating the latter term into the pedagogical enterprise, since our pedagogy inevitably requires the teacher to transmit, albeit sometimes in degraded form, the work of the critic) is the subject of Michael Awkward's "Negotiations of Power: White Critics, Black Texts, and the Self-Referential Impulse," in which Awkward discusses the range of responses among African-American literary critics to the question of the formative white discourse of literary criticism, and its uses by both white and black critics in discussing African-American texts. Awkward takes a position of relative skepticism, asserting that misinformed, or even "malicious," white analysis of the African-American texts continues to be published and deserves criticism on that basis. Awkward is valuable to the current discussion for the way he represents the current debate among African-American critics over their own project of not only working *on* texts but working *for* texts; he exposes to this reader the difficult work of knowing that one cannot simply "be" a critic but must, in the name of a "common concern," fight tooth and nail for the cultural value, the racial-linguistic construct, that art represents (50*ff*.).

Given that hard rhetorical positionality, it is no wonder that, if we turn to a white critic, the work may seem trivial or ignorant by comparison. And thus "misleading" or "malicious." Yet Awkward acknowledges, even if skeptically, that the interplay of white critic and black text will continue to occur and produce mixed results—a punning reference, my own, to the blues of today, which only exists for so many of us in a mixed color of black artist and white audience, and does not exist for any *particular* commercial, racial, or class matter—but, instead, exists for its powers to move the individual and make him and her join in a collective response to the blues, of joy, laughter, sorrow, and enough rhythm to get any hall, house, or back porch shaking.

The way may exist, therefore, for a teacher to look into the blues for a way to teach it, to see its power and beauty as not withheld from some and given to others—but existing in such a way that the individual can feel it and respond with authentic language, thought, and feeling, and in such a way that the subjective response of the student is not, in fact, sufficient, but can be "scaffolded" into a higher practice by which racial and cultural matters can be discerned and discussed. As a brief example, listening to J. B. Lenoir's "Down in Mississippi" is followed by subjective responses ranging from "He sounds scared" to "He feels like a rabbit" to "I don't know what he's talking about" to "The drums are weird"; the teacher's first response might be to show that Lenoir as an African-American artist may have been "signifying" on the nature of living black in Mississippi. Student responses are themselves, roughly speaking, audience versions of signifying, and teachers can begin to "prod" students further away from their first work and closer to more serious work in reading the culture and artist that gave rise to the work.

"Scaffolding" is an educator's term for the ways in which teachers facilitate a student's move from social knowledge to scientific knowledge, or what are called, respectively, by Lev Vygotsky spontaneous and scientific concepts. (Vygotsky is a linguist and philosopher of critical value to contemporary education theory's attention to the social patterns and development of speech and collaborative skills.) Spontaneous concepts are those that exist in community settings—roughly akin to our understanding of the vernacular, the street, the literacy that exists in our homes and backyards and playgrounds and streetcorners. Scientific concepts are those that exist in our schools—roughly equivalent to our academic or critical literacies, our discourses we learn in the academic disciplines, our modes of inquiry guided by scientific principles. What Vygotsky and many contemporary educators wish to see in our schools is a combining of these two concepts into one, in which the student's "natural" or social abilities are brought into conjunction with scientific principles as espoused by the academic disciplines (whether they use the term "scientific" or not is beside the point) so that the learning process is cross-contextual (i.e. the student desires what the school knows and the school desires what the student knows). The "scaffold" is a metaphor not unlike Baker's metaphorical use of the matrix in that it pictures a structure that is not a permanent one but skeletal, constructed for the purpose of allowing another to be built within it, at which time the scaffold is withdrawn or taken down, erased.

According to Carol Lee, scaffolding can have an explicit use in classrooms that are working with African-American texts. Texts that use signifying as black interpretive response need scaffolding by teachers so that these texts are fully understood by any student reader. Lee defines scaffolding in this context:

> The learner, having demonstrated an independent level of problem solving within the realm of a spontaneous concept, would then be placed in a social context with a more expert teacher, who through prodding, modeling, and questioning would bring the novice closer to a more adult, a more scientific, representation of the task at hand. The learning context was considered social in that the learner does not acquire scientific concepts by herself in isolation. (96)

Lee is advocating a teacher role that scaffolds the linguistic phenomenon of signifying from an oral "moment" or "act" into a considered, analyzed, textual feature of great importance to a full understanding of African-American literary texts. Lee calls these "moves" in "prodding" students through constitutive, relational, connective, and disconfirming questions (101). These questions focus attention and thought upon student talk, itself generated by discussions about literary texts. Their ultimate aim is to join social and scientific concepts, thus to join personal with cultural knowing to create a community of learners whose skills and knowledge productively signify each other.

How can this pedagogical method keep the blues alive in a classroom? Does Lee's sense of signifying-as-scaffold follow Baker's blues-as-matrix into teaching (by) the blues? The answer to my second question is Yes, following the reasons I have suggested for answering my first question: the blues can be felt and understood in any pedagogical context sensitive enough to know the blues *as they can come to us* through ear, eye, hands, body, and feet. The proposal that follows is based on the rhetorical theories discussed in this study, and on the master tropes of Gates and Baker and Floyd, the teaching practice of Branch, and the education theory proposed by Lee. It is presented in the form of a narrative, ethnographically stitched from the writer's experiences, observations, and understandings as they exist in a field of vision bounded on all sides by the music of language and the language of music.

I would want my class to be something like the Delta Blues Festival I attended a few of years ago in Greenville, Mississippi. I had driven down from Oxford and gone through Clarksdale and Cleveland and found my way into a long line of cars stretching south out of Greenville. A mile or two south we turned east into a dirt road that went straight into the cotton fields. It was September and the air was heavy and hot, reminding me of deep summer in Buffalo when the temperature would barely drop at night and you would wake up and your sheets were still damp and the sun up and that mist in the air. In Buffalo we would go to the beaches on Lake Erie or down to the Niagara River or out into the hills past Springville. For relief in the Delta there seemed to be the riverside and the Wal-Marts outside every town, and cold drinks wherever you could find them.

In this cotton field there were big bare patches set out for parking. I joined a long line that snaked through matted-down grass to an open dirt lot, parked and started walking in the direction of a hurricane fence that had been put up overnight, it looked like, and went through holding my backpack on my shoulder and my folding chair—the little lady at Wal-Mart had called it a deer seat—in one hand, saying hi to the men standing around the gates and pulling my baseball cap down low against the shimmering glare of the sun.

The festival looked like about an acre or two of cleared cotton field, grown-up grass, powerlines coming in on an old telephone wire, a few rows of portable toilets, and two stages. The stages were all I wanted at first. Somebody was already playing—a gospel group from Jackson—and I was drawn to the sound even though I could feel I was moving too fast, too straight in this big wide open space that had no real orientation to it except parking in the rear.

The big stage was farthest away from the parking, and I worked my way through lawn chairs, blankets, stools, coolers, to about forty feet from the front of the stage, where a white duo from Greenville were about to start up playing old rock'n'roll on a piano and drums. I opened up the chair and rocked its legs into the soft dirt, sat down with a sigh and dropped my backpack between my feet. I turned and said hello to the group of five people to my right who looked set up for the whole day and night with a cooler the size of a small couch, big hats, chairs, fans, binoculars, easy friendliness and a settled-in local feeling that I envied.

The crowd was coming in slowly, filling in the spaces around me. I felt the kind of thirst you feel when you know you can't fix it: deep and dusty. The two-liter bottle of Sprite in my backpack was already warm and fizzed in my mouth to almost nothing before I could swallow it. I had a bag of pretzels and a package of gum for what I anticipated to be four or five hours of music. I tried to settle back against my chair and felt the sweat trickle down my back and settle into the waistband of my jeans. The rock'n'rollers had been replaced by a couple of festival organizers who droned on—the group beside me was talking about who was there and who wasn't there, where they were sitting, who they were with, and what they were doing. They seemed intent on clearing up any uncertainty about what this festival was about—it wasn't the music, not yet, it was the people, as if you have just moved to a new town and want to know who lives there and it turns out that you know them all.

But the music then began in earnest. A favorite of mine, Big Jack Johnson, also called The Oil Man, had come on *to no acclaim whatsoever.* The stage was maybe forty feet square, scaffold and backdrop, wires, speakers, boxes, crates and amplifiers. . His group of young players, the Blues Upsetters, started up a harshly amped but smooth funky bottom for Johnson's slide playing on a Gibson Flying V, to which the audience had very little to say. I looked around and wondered why Johnson seemed to be playing to an empty field. Maybe it was too early, maybe it was too hot, not enough bodies to get a thick response going—I didn't know, but I loved the sound of the band and Johnson's husky voice. His slideplaying was raucous and all the more fun for the inattentiveness of the crowd—I assumed that this was only the start of what the crowd expected and was saving itself for somebody else.

Johnson and his young band exited to desultory applause. I tried to watch the group next to me to see why Johnson wasn't reaching them—maybe he was and I didn't know the signs—but they kept on drinking and talking about everybody and work and town and smiled and nodded to me once more and went on with the business of the day, which was talk, visiting, and the kind of looking around that wasn't casual but definitely *interested*.

I had no one in particular to look to except my group of five, the performers up on stage, and a kind of mass of black and white bodies that were filling in every dirt space on the ground as the afternoon wore on. I spent a long time watching the ones who went back and forth to their seats: I could see city dwellers, probably Memphis or New Orleans, in too-good clothes and expensive straw hats and church clothes, younger people with long hair, jeans, caps, tie-dyed shirts, and pale skin, older blacks who were coming in and out of the crowd with food and drinks, chicken and beer and ribs like a well-oiled delivery system. I could see the field was nearly ringed with booths and stands, and as one soul singer from Jackson tried her best to get a response going from the women down front I asked my group beside me to look after my things.

They had started to frown at a group of white high school kids who were standing in a ragged, swirling circle throwing beer at each other and jumping up and down in time to some other music. The man closest to me caught my eye after I had turned from watching the kids and said, "Assholes." I nodded and then shook my head—a couple of contradictory signifiers he seemed to accept looking into my eyes with a squint, a Greenville company cap with a crushed, mesh crown sitting back on his head. I told him I was going to look around, gave the high school kids a look that, where I came from, was called "stink eye" and threaded my way around sun umbrellas, a baby's crib, legs, arms. and a row of old black men who had carried in a bench to sit on.

In an arc working off one end of the stage were booths of handicrafts, souvenirs, and food. Farther back were the toilets and the chair rental. At the end of the arc was a small stage, its back facing the big one. It was more like a garage than a stage; some of the acts from the big stage would go here afterwards to turn it down and talk. The old-time rock'n'rollers were setting up and I trusted my luck and left, turned around and went back around the booths, past the pig's feet and chicken and ribs, soft drinks and beer, sculptures in wood and ceramic and beads, painting of African figures and hangings of bright beads and fabric, an African Christ and African children, and a booth with clothing—dashikis and brightly-colored embroidered satin shirts—wallets and purses bound and beaded in leather and cloth, and the souvenirs for the ones like me who had a thousand miles to go home through and the thought of just a tee shirt to get you there.

The sun had fallen into a three o'clock bombardment of the field, and I thought, wiping the sweat from my eyes, that this is what Otis Rush had gotten out of when he went north to Chicago and that West-side club where he took on Buddy Guy one night after playing upstairs on his windowsill for weeks. Muddy Waters got away, too, and a few million others, but they often sang of this place. When I got back to my chair I had my tee shirt bundled up in one hand and stuffed it into my backpack, took out my bag of pretzels and settled back, pushing my cap even lower on my head to keep the sun out of my eyes. My neighbor group was quiet, motionless now as they seemed to soak in the heat. My acquaintance said nothing to me but stretched out his arm toward me like a crane rotating over a construction site, a can of beer in his hand. I took it, thanked him, he nodded and said nothing. The others in his group looked briefly toward me but were still silent in the sun and heat. Only the harp player on stage was making a sound.

Willie Foster was old and thin, walked up quietly to the microphone, spoke briefly and played unaccompanied harp that felt to me like the sound of the air itself, sweet, warm, and slow. I liked his playing and it went into me and for a little while I could feel that he had done this for years and years and this was only another day for him, and the sound of his harp was just the way he went about living and about making people feel what he felt. I thought of Rice Miller once because his harp was quiet and watery, jaunty in places but soulfully stretched and caressed in others. He didn't have Miller's voice, but a deeper voice, not irascible and puckish like Miller's, but flat and sad, introspective, a dignity in the voice that was not projected into the crowd but more around the harp itself, as if he felt the harp was the reedy sound of another voice he was talking back to.

The cotton field simmered, and the harp was a hundred miles away from Johnson's raucous electricity, but I thought I had gotten a glimpse of the community that they both played for and from within—a community of listeners and players who sat out here in this sun and humidity and performed this ritual of speaking and listening, moving and dancing, and stillness.

When another soul singer who had a group of horns along with the usual guitars and drums started to whip up some hot lyrics about what men and women can and cannot do, I dug out my camera and snapped pictures in all directions and tucked it away quickly. I decided that she would take me out of the festival before the sun came all the way down. She had the audience laughing. The three women in my neighboring group were taking it all down and turning it on the two men, who started to laugh and curse. My acquaintance had shifted forward in his chair, hung his arms down between his legs and was laughing at the ground as the words came off the stage, through his women friends, and down on him. The high school kids had been squeezed out and, but for me, it felt local and suddenly loose and settled again, but this time funny and upbeat, and the sweat I could see on everyone's shirts and faces didn't matter, didn't bother.

It was time for me to leave, a long drive back on strange roads, another one to Memphis the next morning. I buttoned up my backpack, looked around me once more and waited for the woman to finish before standing up. I caught the eye of my neighbor—he had sat back in his chair and was mopping his face with a red handkerchief—and said, "I gotta go." He lifted his head just a fraction so that his eye caught mine and the sun at the same moment. He smiled a little. "Take care now," he said, and lifted his left arm the way you do when you are pledging on a Bible, the palm outward and vertical. I repeated the gesture toward him, pulled up my chair, and headed back for the gate.

I drove back through Greenville and headed due east, driving through Itta Bena, where B.B. King was born, and into Greenwood, where Robert Johnson probably died, and Carroll County, one I thought might be named after some ancestor of mine; I watched the hills come up under the car as the sun set behind me. I snapped pictures through the windshield and looked north toward Avalon, where John Hurt had lived, felt the breeze cool a little when I crossed the interstate and turned north for Oxford. I found the Mississippi-Tennessee football game on the radio, turned on my headlights and wondered where this big road had come from with six lanes and nobody on it but me.

The next morning I was driving to the Memphis airport asking myself if I had made the right choice going down to Greenville when I could have stayed in Oxford and heard R. L. Burnside at a club just off the town square that night. Burnside is one of the older bluesmen of the hill country of Mississippi, a stylistic descendant of Fred McDowell, reminding others of John Lee Hooker in the way he hypnotizes blues rhythms with a slide and a horizontal axis to the melody that drones like cicadas in August. I could have sat in that club and been treated to a fine performance, but driving through Byhalia, thinking of Faulkner's death in this town, thinking too of missing Burnside and taking in the festival, I knew that I had chosen what I thought was the better place for the blues. The better place was where I would be happier.

That was the blues for me—where I would be happier, where I would feel at *home*. The formula caught in my mind like some attractive *non sequiturs* can. They don't quite make sense until you fumble around with them for awhile. The blues for me came on best when I felt really good because of something that had *everything* to do with me but that I could not myself express. This was the way that Otis Rush had reached me only a week earlier in Chicago. That living, singing tone of his guitar, so like a woman's vibrato, was a sound I heard in my own mind at times, but could never express in sound—maybe it was my own mother's singing voice from so long ago. And there it was, immersing the audience at the club, flowing out of Rush's Mesa Boogie amp like electric water or blue air. The feeling was extraordinarily pleasurable, a release from my inside world and at the very same moment a created, intense identification with it.

Otis Rush would always have to be in a club. That was the right place for him for me. Burnside would be right for other blues audiences in that club in Oxford. That day I drove down through the Delta to Greenville was part of the blues "complex" I have discussed, the immersion in a blues element that is only part music. Sitting outdoors in that humid heat didn't make anything better or worse, necessarily, but it couched the blues on the stage in a natural forum, this place not unlike the places where the field hollers were all the music that workers had, and which according to some like Roger Abrahams laid a lyrical and rhythmic foundation for the blues to come.

Driving to Memphis, alone in the car with thoughts of how to recapture this apparent sense of the blues with students to come, I was aware then and still am that the subjective response is the source of love—and hence also a source of truth or beauty—for what we call art. I don't know if I can privilege this response above the others I have discussed in this book—a more considered sense of rhetoric, or performance, of cultural or political statement—but it seems to arrive first and thus has a power of its own. It draws attention to itself and to its source, this subjective response. Walking through an art gallery, I am ready for something, I am not sure what, and my eyes pass from frame to frame waiting for that something. When I feel it, I stop and work on the piece. The affective quality of a work of art is eventually subsumed by, or indistinguishable from, our understanding of it. Our understanding—as Branch and Baker suggest—is an intuitive as well as a logical knowing. But first, for me, comes that aesthetic response of "I like the colors" or "What a beautiful face" or, in the case of the blues, "Great left hand on the piano" or "I love the way she *hoots*."

Much earlier I called these matters of taste (i.e. personal preferences that simply reflect a visceral encounter with the blues). Matters of taste inform many of our arguments about the blues, and much of our pleasure with the blues is talking endlessly about these details of our aesthetic response. I have argued, however, that these matters of taste are not enough. I remind myself here of Cleanth Brooks and Robert Penn Warren's dismissal of what they called the "threshold of interest," the real but rather shallow level of appreciation students have of a text that does not include, but may only precede, analysis or deeper understanding.

Brooks and Warren were ultimately aiming at a New Critical reading of the text as a balanced symmetry of countervalences, ambiguous tensions, which when resolved formed a lovely urn of meaning. They erased the subjective—and all that the subjective implies for its situatedness—in favor of a unitary reading. Fair enough—it is still what many teachers strive for in their literature classrooms. Controversy, agreement, resolution.

I find the concept of the threshold a useful one, not in the condescending manner that Brooks and Warren did, but in its ability to winnow any undifferentiated body of work down to a righteously chosen few works. As I did with my nine readings, so my students may do with those nine—or any other nine or fifty performances.

To paraphrase Baker, Floyd, and Lee, we allow ourselves to signify on the blues, to invent without conscious invention, our own responsive blues. This responsive blues, for me, is that sense of intense pleasure, a release of identity into the music, a feeling of *"There* it is!" when Muddy Waters delays his vocal for just that heartbeat that makes me lean a little forward for it, like a churchgoer waiting for the rhetorical second shoe to fall.

Sometimes there isn't even that degree of awareness; it's more an unreflective "into the music" that resists picking apart even to the extent of saying what it is about the music that reaches you. It's just the overall impact, the groove, the sound, the Chess sound, the Malaco sound, the Houston sound. Sometimes it is this resistance to analysis or reflection that, indeed, gives the music its soul feeling, a unity that wraps it all up tight so that you don't start carving it up, Western-style.

But that direction of unreflective feeling is in the opposite direction from the place I want my students to go, although like back roads they can go back to the place where the groove hit them. There are always ways back with the blues because its simplicity is a strength that can always be felt in the dark or after a long journey outward. The direction I want my students to go is from the aesthetic response, the soul feeling the music, through or over the "threshold of interest" so that there is some preliminary work in discussing what it is about this or that blues that interests them, and onward down the road to considerations of rhetoric and American and African-American cultural contexts and performances.

The road metaphor butts up against the front wall of the classroom pretty quickly, and there is no cure for it in most classrooms but bringing the music into the classroom by boom box or cassette player or the many videos that are available today showing the blues being played by old and new greats, unknowns and music teachers, in clubs, concert halls, street corners, and television studios. I have found the video route to be less enabling than I would have thought, given my general claim to the importance of performance details. The details are there, but they are in overwhelming numbers for students, whom I have found closing their eyes to hear just the music. The videos have been useful later, as the scope of the student's vision or perception enlarges beyond just that initial encounter with blues music.

I sometimes feel like a pied piper leading children into the blues in a somewhat self-interested, subversive manner, away from canonical pursuits and into personal ones. But I have found just as often that students have such a natural facility with music-listening (not often the blues, but other genres that are just as rewardingly "deep") that the teacher's role is not so leader-like as it is guide-like; the difference may be subtle, but I believe it is important. I don't want to push the blues, I don't want to sell it, but I want to *offer* it, and the role of guide allows this act to be, I believe, ethically sound both to the blues and its culture.

Introducing the issue of the ethical becomes an important bridge between subjective response and rhetorical analysis of the blues and blues performance. Questions like these reflect our interest in subjective rhetoric, but stress the *amplification* (Quintilian 8.4) of the listener's experience with the blues from a felt experience to one that is analyzed with precision and critical thought:

> What are the feelings of the blues?
> What are the voices of the blues?
> What are the identities of the blues?
> Who is the audience?
> How are you the audience?
> What do you hear? Like? Dislike? Wish to understand?

These questions can lead discussions to considerations of the bluesmakers, who are *not yet* in these discussions "rhetoricians" but just *musicmakers*. Their ethical presence will vary widely of course, but will allow students to see that these makers—as Larry Neal sees them—are real men and women who were working at a craft and art in real places and real times. They were making people laugh and dance, get together and make noise.

A discussion of *ethos*—the individual and his or her character as it carries the music to an audience—leads, as Neal leads us, to the sense of the collective or community voice, and stepping backward, we see larger concentric circles of culture and race. The journey through these regions moves outward and inevitably takes on the identity of a rhetorical analysis as the music falls back or into the center (and to be returned to again and again, like the thirsty man to his well).

This rhetorical analysis can be carried out in several ways. One way is to consider the rhetorical perspectives discussed earlier—subjective dialogical, and colonial—*consecutively*. The teacher asks questions such as these:

> Who did this blues talk to?
> How did it talk?
> What got talked back to this blues?
> Was the talkback a blues too?
> What kind of language is this, anyway?
> Is this black or white or brown or grey?

What distinguishes a Bakhtinian rhetoric from the postcolonial to follow is its relative innocence. We are still in the aesthetic experience in that sense, but are analyzing the blues as a statement between groups and individuals who wish to communicate to each other because of prior arrangements. What arises from these discussions is a general sense that the blues matters as a production of labor, art, craft, community, culture and race, items that can be discussed, again, either consecutively or without explicit distinction.

To continue down the blues road, and meeting challenges consecutively, the postcolonial perspective is taken. Questions to be asked here are,

> Who has power in the blues?
> Where did it come from and where did it go?
> Is this power differential along race, class, and gender lines?
> What language does the colonized speak in the blues?
> Does the blues solve a problem for the colonized or colonizers?
> How is the blues a symbol of postcolonial black America?
> Or is it a part of an earlier age?

Postcolonial theory suggests to students that literary works of art are spoken in such a way as to deform and signify upon the language and values and culture of the colonizing force. Thus, the blues is not so much dialogical as it is *subversive* of master rhetorical forms. The blues can speak of the white world and the black world in a language that is purely neither.

African-American culture is seen in these discussions as an island of colonization within the larger archipelago of an American multiculture, surrounded by dominating white structures that render it inferior in much the same way as imperial England did by inventorying the cultures of Africa and the Far East. This notion allows us to see other cultural products of minority cultures in the way we see the blues—as hybrid forms that speak back to and, simultaneously, *for* the conquerors. It is no wonder, then, if we adopt this postcolonial perspective, that there is a white audience for the blues. But the way we interpret the motives of this audience remain many. For example, we can in classroom discussions place ourselves very easily in that position, and ask ourselves the reasons for our attention, or even love, of the blues. In this study's first chapter I suggested that guilt is one factor, that Orientalism is another, subjectivity is another.

> What factor does race play in our cultural heritage?
> As individuals, does the color of art matter? Why?

A white audience for the blues suggests to many a universality of message, transcending race or culture. This, too, can be discussed in classrooms—and extended to any literary work or performative text. And, as Jane Tompkins argues, the reverse of universality—particularity or locality—can be seen as perhaps the highest value of the blues or other cultural work: it exhibits a unique character, a difference, that is its own reason for being.

Working consecutively through our theoretical instruments, we can come to the last cluster—African-American theory and criticism—formulated here by Gates and Baker, worked into larger musical discussions by Samuel Floyd, and made an explicit pedagogical tool by Carol Lee. Parameters of response to the literary text, or call, is "bested" or encompassed, deformed, remarked upon, or *signified*. While audiences may see this most obviously in improvisational genres like jazz, and to a lesser extent the blues, this rhetoric is better seen as the trope that moves through the tradition in order to invigorate, evolve, and display it. In microcosm a full-tone bend by Albert King in response to a halftone by B.B, (and in turn a short sharp wrist-driven vibrato by B.B.), black rhetoric in macrocosm becomes the process by which, against all odds, black linguistic art acknowledges (while it deconstructs) white or Western linguistic standards *including those it has set itself.*

In classrooms questions like

> What is black music?
> What is black language?

What are black values as found in this music or art?

can open up discussions about the importance of seeing ways with words as extending past the assumed Plain Western mode that is, according to Baker, "preeminently bourgeois, and optically white" (*Harlem* 6). Baker wants us to hear with the ears of Caliban, so that Western modes are acknowledged, as Baker acknowledges Shakespeare, while hearing an intentional difference, Caliban "in control, metamorphosing a linguistics of mastery with masterful sound" (69).

This sense of mastery can lead classrooms back to traditional discussions of poetic greatness, romantic affiliations with the individual artist, their relation to tradition, and so on. In effect, the canon and its strengths and weaknesses are re-opened for African-American cultural debates. Classrooms can explode this sense of linguistic formalism by a reinvestigation of just how many languages are involved in the making of the blues: melody, rhythm, tone, pitch, words, gesture. Each has a grammar and syntax and style that can be opened for discussion so that students see the rhetorical *consciousness* of the bluesman, his or her crafted statements to their audiences. Blues becomes a rhetoric of thought and feeling, not just an unreflective gesture of "primitive" power.

This road through several rhetorics is, I suggest, a passage through consecutive ways of looking at the blues. This method may strike some as too linear or programmatic. I have found it useful in separating the individual from his or her object of study so that larger relations between arts and cultures may be perceived. But these varying perspectives on the blues can just as well be combined, re-ordered, re-balanced according to the context in which the blues is being studied. The blues, I have been arguing, is not only a text, it is an act, and therefore can always be understood in terms of the company it keeps, or is made to keep.

Earlier I suggested that a romantic view sees the blues as a lonely act of self-reflection—in short, no company required. Others, like Keil, see the blues as particularly social in its move to the urban centers, and sees figures like Muddy Waters as lightning rods for African-American communalism. But in the classroom environment (and I hope this is not the classroom of the eulogy) the blues coexists with American literature. It is as literature that the blues is studied in university English departments, and it is those departments that I am primarily addressing in this study. The company it keeps, then, is typically the poetry of the American twentieth and twenty-first centuries, or cut more finely, African-American poetry of the twentieth and twenty-first centuries. Occasionally, one will see a course in the lyric, and to have a stanza or two of Robert Johnson must strike the teacher and student as particularly daring or subversive, this turn into the popular sphere—as it did for some of us who taught Dylan in the 1960s or Springsteen in the 1980s. We nodded toward the vastly popular song lyric as if we were condescending to do so.

The blues can be condescended to very easily if put up against the canonized poetry of the twentieth century. The condescension, if benevolent, merely serves to repeat an old Big House gesture of the master toward his workers. On the surface it seems that to bring the blues lyric into discussions alongside those of McKay, Hughes, Lorde (to say nothing of Williams, Frost, and Stevens) is an honoring—or at the very least an acknowledgment of the blues lyric's *desire to sound*. On the other hand, the deck is so stacked in favor of the textual primacy of the poem that the lyric, stripped of its other languages, its complex of grammars and syntaxes, will feel and sound, by comparison, like a dried husk of corn.

I have returned to the dilemma described in the opening pages of this chapter: how to make the blues alive in its most eligible academic context—the department that studies living language and its cultural and aesthetic products—and make it resonate with its own beauty and power as part of a larger calling, to understand the blues as an American and African-American rhetoric. Some might say, if the way is not clear, "Leave it alone—those who need it will find it on their own," but this strikes me as capitulating a teacher's ethic to strive for a full access for his or her students to their cultural history and products, and secondly, to deny the value-making that goes on in every thinking, feeling individual as he or she encounters the rhetorical and the aesthetic.

Teach favorites, yes—and then (or *first*) teach the others. Admit to the privileging—and open it for discussion. Admit to subjectivities inside even the most masterful of professors, admit to excellence and quality, choosing and rhetoricizing those choices into argument for this canon or that. Admit to the colors of language, to the color of our skin, admit to the hierarchies of our learning, to the prejudice of our own teachers, our blindness, our narrow and accidental educations.

Admit that what we teach is a canon in itself, every syllabus an absurd canon of reductive, oppressive power. Admit that you don't like Frost and never did, yet you teach him every year. Admit that blues is off the subject, admit it is dirty and low down, elementary, unschooled, and now more than ever irrelevant. Admit you think the blues is for old men.

Listen to Bessie Smith, Cannon's Jug Stompers, Blind Willie Johnson, Tampa Red, Leroy Carr, Lonnie Johnson, Blind Lemon Jefferson, Ida Cox, Geeshie Wiley, Memphis Slim, Lightnin' Hopkins, Charles Brown, Blind Boy Fuller, Gary Davis, Sleepy John Estes, Magic Sam, Big Walter Horton, Albert Collins, Bukka White, Big Mama Thornton, Junior Parker, Snooks Eaglin, Robert Cray, Luther Tucker, Luther Allison, Sunnyland Slim, Roosevelt Sykes, Yank Rachell, Jessie Mae Hemphill, Etta James, Robert Cray, Freddie King and the blues bands at the local bar who do "Stormy Monday," "Have You Ever Loved a Woman," "Everyday I Have the Blues," and "Sweet Home Chicago" with enough energy and love to make you almost forget that the blues is nobody's to choose.

Ralph Ellison defines the rhetoric of the blues in such a way that might stand for the project of any teacher, but also for the project that a teacher sees as her task in the larger context of a social complexity today that begs for a multiplicity of soundings, signifying, and understandings that are not abstracted conclusions but are the inventions and products of "a sense of excitement and surprise of men living in the world—of enslaved and politically weak men successfully imposing their values upon a powerful society through song and dance" ("Blues People" 256).

The teacher who can feel this excitement and surprise about blues, or about literature, is already on the way to the front of the club where you are going to be allowed to sit in, to perform your way with the blues while the band takes it easy behind you and tries to make it sound good, even though your timing is off, you forget the words, somebody's talking down front, it's late and people have to go. The blues is behind you and you play on, with, through, by, and for the blues, you bend it up to you or down to you, you get down and shake it, and pretty soon it dances.

Works Cited

Abrahams, Roger. *Singing the Master: The Emergence of African American Culture in the Plantation South.* New York: Pantheon Books, 1992.
Amuta, Chidi. "Fanon, Cabral and Ngugi on National Liberation." *The Theory of African Literature.* NJ: Zed Books, 1989. Rpt. in Ashcroft, Griffiths and Tiffin. 158–163.
Aristotle. *On Rhetoric.* George Kennedy, trans. New York: Oxford UP, 1991.
Ashcroft, Bill, Gareth Griffiths, and Helen Tiffin, eds. *The Post-Colonial Studies Reader.* New York: Routledge, 1995.
Awkward, Michael. "Negotiations of Power: White Critics, Black Texts, and the Self-Referential Impulse." *Negotiating Difference: Race, Gender, and the Politics of Positionality.* Chicago: U of Chicago P, 1995. 59–91.
Baker, Houston, Jr. *Black Studies, Rap, and the Academy.* Chicago: U of Chicago P, 1993.
—. *Blues, Ideology, and Afro-American Literature: A Vernacular Theory.* Chicago: U of Chicago P, 1984.
—. *Modernism and the Harlem Renaissance.* Chicago: U of Chicago P, 1987.
Bakhtin, Mikhail. *Rabelais and His World.* 1965. Trans. H. Iswolsky. Bloomington: Indiana UP, 1984.
—. "Discourse in the Novel." 1935. *The Dialogic Imagination.* Trans. M. Holquist and C. Emerson. Austin: U of Texas P, 1981. 259–421.
—. "The Problem of Speech Genres." 1952–1953. *Speech Genres and Other Late Essays.* Trans. V.W McGee. Austin: U of Texas P, 1986.
Barlow, William. *Looking Up at Down: The Emergence of Blues Culture.* Philadelphia: Temple UP, 1989.
Berlin, James. *Rhetoric and Reality: Writing Instruction in American Colleges, 1900–1985.* Carbondale: Southern Illinois UP, 1987.
Bhabha, Homi. "Of Mimicry and Man: The Ambivalence of Colonial Discourse." *October* 28 (Spring 1984): 125–33.
Bleich, David. *Readings and Feelings: An Introduction to Subjective Criticism.* Urbana: National Council of Teachers of English, 1975.
Brathwaite, Edward. "Jazz and the West Indian Novel." Ashcroft, Griffiths, and Tiffin, 327–31.

Brooks, Cleanth, and Robert Penn Warren. "Letter to the Teacher." *Understanding Fiction*. Englewood Cliffs: Prentice-Hall 1959. xi-xx.
Broonzy, Bill, and Yannick Bruynoghe. *Big Bill Blues*. New York: Oak Publications, 1964.
Broonzy, Bill, Memphis Slim, and John Lee Williamson. *Blues in the Mississippi Night*. Salem: Rykodisc, 1990. RCD 90155.
Brown, Sterling. *The Collected Poems of Sterling Brown*. Ed. Michael Harper. New York: Harper and Row, 1980.
Burke, Kenneth. 1938. *Counter-Statement*. 2nd ed. Berkeley: U of California P, 1968.
—. *A Grammar of Motives*. 1945. Berkeley: U of California P, 1969.
—. *A Rhetoric of Motives*. 1950. Berkeley: U of California P, 1969.
Calt, Stephen. *I'd Rather Be the Devil: Skip James and the Blues*. New York: Da Capo Press, 1994.
Calt, Stephen, and Gayle Wardlow. *King of the Delta Blues: The Life and Music of Charlie Patton*. Newton NJ: Rock Chapel Press, 1988.
Campbell, George. *The Philosophy of Rhetoric*. 1776. Carbondale: Southern Illinois UP, 1963.
Charters, Samuel. *The Country Blues*. New York: Rinehart, 1959.
—. *The Bluesmen*. 1967. Rep. with *Sweet as the Showers of Rain* as *The Bluesmakers*. New York: Da Capo Press, 1991.
Cicero. *Cicero on Oratory and Orators*. J. S. Watson, trans. Carbondale: Southern Illinois UP, 1970.
Conley, Thomas M. *Rhetoric in the European Tradition*. Chicago:U of Chicago P, 1990.
Davis, Angela. *Blues Legacies and Black Feminism*. New York: Pantheon, 1998.
Davis, Francis. *The History of the Blues: The Roots, the Music, the People*. New York: Hyperion, 1995.
Drozdowski, Ted. "Blues at the Crossroads." *Pulse!* 206 (August 2001): 50–54.
—. "The Rush Is On." *Pulse!* 127 (June 1994):, 55–56, 67–68.
Ducille, Ann. "Blues Notes on Black Sexuality: Sex and the Texts of Jessie Fauset and Nella Larsen." *Journal of the History of Sexuality* 3.3 (January 1993): 418-44.
Eagleton, Terry. *Literary Theory: An Introduction*. Minneapolis: U of Minnesota P, 1983.
Early, Gerald, ed. *Speech and Power: The African-American Essay and Its Cultural Content from Polemics to Pulpit*. Vol. 2. New York: The Ecco Press, 1993.
Ellison, Ralph. "Blues People." *Shadow and Act*. 1964. New York: Vintage, 1995. 247–58.
—. *Invisible Man*. 1952. New York: Vintage, 1990.

—. "Richard Wright's Blues." *Shadow and Act.* 1964. New York: Vintage, 1995. 77–94.
"Eric's First Online Chat." July 24, 2000. AOL Live. Chat Transcript. http://eric-clapton.co.uk/interviewsandarticles/aoltranscript.htm (13 December 2005).
Evans, David. *Big Road Blues: Tradition and Creativity in the Folk Blues.* 1982. New York: Da Capo Press, 1987.
Fahey, John. *Charley Patton.* London: Studio Vista, 1971.
Fanon, Franz. "On National Culture" and "The Pitfalls of National Consciousness." Ashcroft, Griffiths, and Tiffin, 153–57.
Fee, Margery. From "Why C. K. Stead Didn't Like Keri Hulme's *The Bone People:* Who Can Write as Other?" *Australian and New Zealand Studies in Canada* 1 (1989). Rpt. in Ashcroft, Griffiths, and Tiffin, 242–45.
Ferris, William. *Blues from the Delta.* 1978. New York: Da Capo Press, 1984.
Fish, Stanley. "Rhetoric." *Doing What Comes Naturally: Change, Rhetoric, and the Practice of Theory in Literary and Legal Studies.* Durham: Duke UP, 1989. 471–502.
Floyd, Samuel. *The Power of Black Music: Interpreting Its History from Africa to the United States.* New York: Oxford UP, 1995.
Foucault, Michel. "The Order of Discourse." *Untying the Text: A Post-Structuralist Reader.* Ed. Robert Young. Boston: Routledge & Kegan Paul, 1981. 48–78.
Garon, Paul, and Beth Garon. *Woman With Guitar: Memphis Minnie's Blues.* New York: Da Capo Press, 1994.
Gates, Henry Louis, Jr. *The Signifying Monkey: A Theory of African-American Literary Criticism.* New York: Oxford UP, 1988.
Gillett, Charlie. *The Sound of the City.* Rev. ed. New York: Pantheon, 1983.
Glover, Tony, Scott Dirks, and Ward Gaines. *Blues with a Feeling: The Little Walter Story.* New York: Routledge, 2002.
Grazian, David. *Blue Chicago: The Search for Authenticity in Urban Blues Clubs.* Chicago: U of Chicago P, 2003.
Greenberg, Alan. *Love in Vain.* New York: Da Capo Press, 1994.
Griffiths, Gareth. "The Myth of Authenticity." *Describing Empire.* Ed. Chris Tiffin and Alan Lawson. London: Routledge, 1994. Rpt. in Ashcroft, Griffiths, and Tiffin, 237–41.
Groom, Bob. *The Blues Revival.* London: Studio Vista, 1971.
Guralnick, Peter. "Eric Clapton at the Passion Threshold." *Musician* 136 (February 1990): 44–56.
Hart, Mary, et al. *The Blues: A Bibliographical Guide.* New York: Garland Press, 1989.
Holland, Norman. *5 Readers Reading.* New Haven: Yale UP, 1975.
Huddleston, Rodney. *Introduction to the Grammar of English.* Cambridge: Cambridge UP, 1984.

Hughes, Langston. *Selected Poems*. 1959. New York: Vintage, 1987.
Humphrey. Mark. "Holy Blues: The Gospel Tradition." *Nothing But the Blues*. Ed. Lawrence Cohn. New York: Abbeville Press, 1993. 107–50.
Iser, Wolfgang. *The Act of Reading: A Theory of Aesthetic Response*. Baltimore: Johns Hopkins UP, 1978.
Jones, LeRoi. *Blues People: The Negro Experience in White America and the Music That Developed From It*. New York: William Morrow, 1963.
Keats, John. "Ode to a Nightingale." *The Complete Poems of John Keats*. New York: The Modern Library, 1994.
Keil, Charles. *Urban Blues*. 1966. Chicago: U of Chicago P, 1991.
Kincaid, Jamaica. *A Small Place*. New York: Farrar, Straus and Giroux, 1988.
Lee, Carol. *Signifying As a Scaffold for Literary Interpretation: The Pedagogical Implications of an African American Discourse Genre*. Urbana IL: National Council of Teachers of English, 1993.
Lester, Cheryl. "Racial Awareness and Arrested Development: *The Sound and the Fury* and the Great Migration." *The Cambridge Companion to William Faulkner*. Ed. Philip M. Weinstein. New York: Cambridge UP, 1995. 123–45.
Lieb, Sandra. *Mother of the Blues: A Study of Ma Rainey*. Amherst: U of Massachusetts P, 1981.
Lipscomb, Mance. *I Say Me for a Parable: The Oral Autobiography of Mance Lipscomb, Texas Bluesman*. 1993. New York: Da Capo Press, 1994.
Lomax, Alan. *The Land Where Blues Began*. New York: Pantheon, 1993.
Morris, Pam, ed. *The Bakhtin Reader: Selected Writings of Bakhtin, Medvedev, Voloshinov*. London: Edward Arnold, 1994.
Muddy Waters, Maintenance Shop Blues. Yazoo Video. 1992.
Murray, Albert. *The Blue Devils of Nada: A Contemporary American Approach to Aesthetic Statement*. New York: Pantheon, 1996.
—. *Stomping the Blues*. 1976. New York: Vintage, 1982.
—. *Train Whistle Guitar*. 1974. New York: Vintage, 1998.
Murray, Charles Shaar. *Crosstown Traffic: Jimi Hendrix and Post-War Pop*. London: Faber and Faber, 1989.
Neal, Larry. "The Ethos of the Blues." *The Black Scholar* (Summer 1972). Rpt. in Early, 55–62.
Obrecht, Jas. "Buddy Guy." *Blues Guitar: The Men Who Made the Music*. 2nd ed. Ed. Jas Obrecht. San Francisco: Miller Freeman, 1993.
Oliver, Paul. *The Meaning of the Blues*. 1960. 2nd ed. Rep. as *Blues Fell This Morning*. New York: Cambridge UP, 1990.
—. *Conversations with the Blues*. New York: Horizon Press, 1965.
—. *Screening the Blues: Aspects of the Blues Tradition*. New York: Da Capo Press, 1968.

Olson Gary A., and Lynn Worsham. "Staging the Politics of Difference: Homi Bhabha's Critical Literacy." *Race, Rhetoric, and the Postcolonial.* Ed. Gary A. Olson and Lynn Worsham. Albany: State U of New York P, 1999. 3–42.
O'Neal, Jim. "I Once Was Lost, But Now I'm Found: The Blues Revival of the 1960s." *Nothing But the Blues.* Ed. Lawrence Cohn. New York: Abbeville Press, 1993. 347–87.
Oster, Harry. *Living Country Blues.* Detroit: Folklore Associates, 1969.
Palmer, Robert. *Deep Blues.* New York: Penguin, 1981.
—. "Baby Blues." *Guitar World.* 16.12 (December 1994): 119–21.
Pearson, Barry Lee. *Sounds So Good to Me: The Bluesman's Story.* Philadelphia: U of Pennsylvania P, 1984.
Plato. *Phaedrus.* Walter Hamilton, trans. New York: Penguin, 1973.
Quintilian. *The Orator's Education. Trans. Donald Russell.* Cambridge: Harvard UP, 2001.
Rabinowitz, Peter J. *Before Reading: Narrative Conventions and the Politics of Interpretation.* Ithaca: Cornell UP, 1987.
Rooney, James. *Bossmen: Bill Monroe and Muddy Waters.* New York: The Dial Press, 1971.
Rosenblatt, Louise. *Literature as Exploration.* 1937. New York: Noble and Noble, 1968.
Royster, Jacqueline Jones. *Traces of a Stream: Literacy and Social Change among African American Women.* Pittsburgh: U of Pittsburgh P, 2000.
Sackheim, Eric. *The Blues Line.* New York: The Ecco Press, 1993.
Said, Edward. *Orientalism.* New York: Random House, 1978.
Santelli, Robert. *The Big Book of Blues.* New York: Penguin, 1993.
Sawyer, Charles. *The Arrival of B.B. King: the Authorized Biography.* New York: Doubleday, 1980.
Son House and Bukka White. Yazoo Video. 1991.
Spencer, Jon Michael. *Blues and Evil.* Knoxville: U of Tennessee P, 1993.
Steiner, George. *Real Presences.* Chicago: U of Chicago P, 1989.
Suleri, Sara. "The Rhetoric of English India." *The Rhetoric of English India.* Chicago: U of Chicago P, 1992. Rpt. in Ashcroft, Griffiths, and Tiffin, 111–13.
Titon, Jeff Todd. *Early Downhome Blues: A Musical and Cultural Analysis.* Urbana: U of Illinois P, 1977.
Tompkins, Jane. *Sensational Designs: The Cultural Work of American Fiction, 1790–1860.* New York: Oxford UP, 1985.
Underwood, Tut. "Billy Branch and Blues in the Schools." *Living Blues* 26.2 (March/April 1995): 66–71.
Vickers, Brian. *In Defence of Rhetoric.* New York: Oxford UP, 1988.
Vygotsky, Lev. *Thought and Language.* Rev. ed. Trans. Alex Kozulin. Cambridge: The MIT Press, 1986.

Weaver, Richard. "Language Is Sermonic." *Language Is Sermonic: Richard Weaver on the Nature of Rhetoric.* Ed. Richard Johannesen, Rennard Strickland, and Ralph T. Eubanks. Baton Rouge: Louisiana State UP, 1970.

—. "The *Phaedrus* and the Nature of Rhetoric." *The Ethics of Rhetoric.* Chicago: Regnery, 1953. 3–26.

Wellek, René, and Austin Warren. *Theory of Literature.* Rev. ed. New York: Harcourt Brace Jovanovich, 1970.

Wright, Richard. *Savage Holiday.* 1954. Chatham NJ: Chatham Booksellers, 1975.

Young, Robert, ed. *Untying the Text: A Post-Structuralist Reader.* Boston: Routledge & Kegan Paul, 1981.

Index

African-American culture, xiii, xx, xxi, xxiii, 24, 60, 66, 96, 106, 145, 146, 147, 161
American culture, xxi, xxii, 13, 38, 65, 66, 141
Amuta, Chidi, 96, 97, 167
appropriation, 14
Aristotle, xxiv, 11, 61, 167
Asch, Moses, 15
audience, 115
authenticity, 106, 169
Awkward, Michael, 149, 150, 167

Baker, Houston, xxv, 26, 68, 84, 87, 88, 107, 139, 142, 146-49, 151, 152, 158, 159, 162, 163, 167
Bakhtin, Mikhail, xxiv, 27, 51-65, 77, 79, 86, 93, 94, 97, 116, 117, 121, 134, 136, 167, 170; *heteroglossia*, 51
Baraka, Amiri. *See* LeRoi Jones.
Beatles, xii, xiv, xv, 102, 145
Below, Fred, 98, 100, 101, 111, 126
Bhabha, Homi, xxiv, 63-66, 74, 75, 78, 132, 167, 170
Bleich, David, 46, 47, 167
Bloomfield, Mike, 103
Branch, Billy, 143-47, 152, 158, 171
Broonzy, Big Bill, 32, 35, 64, 113, 168
Brown, James, 13, 92
Brown, Sterling, 14, 15, 36, 37, 52, 139, 165, 168

Burke, Kenneth, xxii, xxiv, 5, 44, 61, 62, 88, 106, 168; *A Rhetoric of Motives*, 168; *Counter-Statement*, 5, 44, 62, 168

Calt, Stephen, xiv, 21, 32, 33, 34, 35, 75-86, 168
Calt, Stephen and Gayle Wardlow, 33, 76, 77, 79
Campbell, George, 124, 168
Carr, Leroy, xv, 39, 165
Carver, George Washington, 97, 101
Charters, Samuel, xxiv, 14-20, 22, 23, 24, 28, 29, 30, 31, 33, 35, 67, 80, 81, 86, 89, 101, 168
Chess Records, xiv, 94, 108, 111, 123, 159
Cicero, xvi, xxiv, 59, 115, 118, 119, 120, 121, 128, 168
Clapton, Eric, vii, xii, 32, 65, 103, 105, 106, 108, 109, 130-136, 169
Collins, Albert, 37, 165
Coltrane, John, xiv, xxii, 102, 109
Copeland, Shemekia, 38, 91
Costello, Elvis, xiv
Count Basie, xii, 134
culture. *See* African-American culture, American culture

dance, xx
Davis, Angela, xiii, 26, 35, 168

Davis, Miles, xiii, xxii, 7, 11, 26, 35, 47, 89, 94, 105, 165, 168
Delta Blues Festival, 62, 152
dialogics, 167
discourse, 167, 169, 170
Drozdowski, Ted, xviii, 39, 168
Dylan, Bob, xii, xxv, 36, 115, 164

Ellison, Ralph, xxi, xxiv, 19-23, 26, 36, 37, 86, 107, 115, 142, 165, 168
eloquence, 3
Estes, Sleepy John, 64, 165
ethics, 172
Evans, David, xvi, xxiv, 27, 30, 31, 38, 43, 45, 57, 67, 80, 96, 100, 111, 140, 142, 169; *Big Road Blues*, xvi, 27, 30, 43, 169

Fanon, Franz, xxiv, 95, 96, 97, 167, 169
Fee, Margery, xxiv, 105, 106, 169
feelings, 49, 94, 98, 100, 167, 169
Ferris, William, xxiv, 26, 28, 29, 31, 38, 169; *Blues from the Delta*, 26, 28, 38, 169
Fish, Stanley, xv, 46, 169
Fitzgerald, F. Scott, xii, xiii, 4, 141
Floyd, Samuel, xxv, 43, 55, 95, 98, 105, 152, 159, 162, 169
Foster, Willie, 155
Foucault, Michel, 9, 169
Fuller, Blind Boy, 52, 165

Garon, Paul, 31
Garon, Paul and Beth, 32, 34, 87
Gates, Henry Louis, Jr., xxv, 26, 43, 52, 58, 100, 101, 107, 142, 147, 152, 162, 169
Glover, Tony, 98, 169
Goodman, Benny, xii
Grazian, David, 26

Griffiths, Gareth, xxiv, 67, 167, 169, 171
Guitar Slim, xix, 57
Guralnick, Peter, 31, 65, 169
Guy, Buddy, 44, 45, 62, 97, 107, 108, 125, 135, 155, 170

Harlem Renaissance, 36, 147, 148, 167
Hendrix, Jimi, vii, 38, 77, 102-9, 130, 170
Holland, Norman, xxiv, 46, 169
Hughes, Langston, xxii, 15, 36, 37, 89, 139, 164, 169
Hurston, Zora Neale, xxii, 52, 139
hybridity, 65, 66, 75, 97, 107

ideology, 147, 167
Iser, Wolfgang, xxiv, 46, 47, 78, 170

James, Skip, vii, 32, 55, 57, 80-87, 91, 168
jazz, 89, 167
Jefferson, Blind Lemon, 73, 165
Johnson, Big Jack, 57, 58, 153
Johnson, Blind Willie, 37, 92, 127, 165
Johnson, Robert, xiv, xviii, 32, 49, 53, 60, 61, 65, 73, 74, 86, 88, 101, 102, 111, 128, 129, 148, 156, 164
Jones, LeRoi, xviii, xxiv, 21, 67, 99; *Blues People*, xviii, 19, 21, 22, 23, 24, 63, 99, 107, 165, 168, 170

Keil, Charles, xxiii, xxiv, 25, 26, 29, 30, 38, 67, 117, 163, 170
Kelly, Vance, 38
Kimbrough, Junior, 38, 55, 105, 133
Kincaid, Jamaica, 63, 170
King, Albert, xxiii, 30, 49, 104, 105, 108, 134, 162

Index

King, B. B., 116-22, 125, 131, 135
King, Freddie, 134, 136, 165

Lee, Carol, xxv, 35, 105, 110, 151, 152, 157, 159, 162, 168, 170, 171
Lenoir, J. B., vii, 14, 109-16, 150
Lipscomb, Mance, xxii, 35, 49, 53, 54, 170
literature, 41, 42, 43, 147, 167, 171, 172
Little Richard, 92, 102, 103, 127
Little Walter, vii, 37, 94-101, 104, 111, 126, 127, 144
Lomax, Alan, xxiv, 14, 15, 31, 64, 67, 127, 128, 170

Memphis Minnie, vii, xxii, 8, 32, 34, 49, 53, 61, 69, 87-95, 100, 169
Miller, Rice. *See* Williamson, Sonny Boy II, 96, 99, 131, 155
Monk, Thelonious, xxii
Muddy Waters, vii, xii, 17, 32, 39, 62, 90, 94, 95, 96, 97, 98, 101, 106-08, 111, 123-31, 134, 145, 155, 159, 163, 170, 171
Murray, Albert, xxiv, 26-29, 31, 38, 57, 58, 92, 93, 94, 110, 130-33, 143, 170; *Stomping the Blues*, 26, 170
Murray, Charles Shaar, xxiv, 77, 130

Neal, Larry, xxiv, 11, 12, 13, 29, 34, 49, 115, 116, 118, 129, 140, 160, 170, 171

Oliver, Paul, xxiv, 14, 15, 18-23, 28, 31, 32, 60, 114, 170
oratory, 118, 119, 168

Palmer, Robert, xiv, xxiv, 26, 29, 31, 98, 117, 126, 133, 135, 171; *Deep Blues*, xiv, 29, 30, 98, 126, 133, 171

Parker, Charlie, xxii, 102, 109, 165
Patton, Charlie, vii, xiv, xv, xx, 10, 14, 21, 31, 33, 39, 49, 57, 58, 60, 73-80, 86, 105, 110, 117, 124, 140, 168, 169
Plato: *Phaedrus*, xxii, 120, 171, 172
postcolonial studies, 62, 63, 66, 67, 161, 170

Quintilian, xxiv, 13, 48, 49, 115, 116, 121, 122, 130, 160, 171; *The Orator's Education*, 171

Rabinowitz, Peter, xxiv, 70, 171
race, xix, 72, 167, 170
rhetoric, iii, x-xxii, xxiv, xxv, 3-10, 13, 14, 16, 20, 22-24, 27-30, 33-35, 38, 41-46, 48-52, 55-59, 62, 63, 65-67, 70, 71, 73, 74, 76, 79, 80, 82-88, 92-94, 97, 100-4, 106, 107, 109, 112, 114-19, 121, 122, 124, 125, 126, 128, 130, 133, 134, 136, 137, 139, 141, 142, 144, 146, 149, 158-65, 167-72; classical, 48; *controversia*, 45; *ethos*, 115, 170; oral, xiii, xix, xxv, 30, 32, 35, 37, 41, 52, 53, 93, 132, 140, 142, 146, 151; Testimony, 124
rhetoric, definition of, xiii
rhetoricality, xv
Rock, 168
Rooney, James, 32, 127, 171
Rosenblatt, Louise, xxiv, 41, 42, 43, 46, 116, 171
Royster, Jacqueline Jones, 12, 171
Rush, Otis, xii, xvii-xix, xxiii, xxiv, 30, 40, 62, 68, 69, 93, 131-36, 141, 155, 157, 168

Sackheim, Eric, 31, 32, 52, 53, 171
Sawyer, Charles, 121, 171

scaffolding, 150, 170
Signifying, 100, 169, 170
Smith, Bessie, 12, 37, 39, 47, 73, 89, 125, 140, 165
Son House, xix, xx, xxv, 39, 57, 59, 69, 73, 74, 77, 82, 128, 171
Spencer, Jon, xxiv, 21
Steiner, George, 68, 171
subjective criticism, 50
Suleri, Sula, 117, 171

teaching, 137, 139, 141-43, 145, 147-49, 151, 153, 155, 157, 159, 161, 163, 165, 167, 170, 171
testimony, 124
tradition, 168, 169, 170

Vaughan, Stevie Ray, 44, 103, 105
vernacular, 167
Vygotsky, 150, 151, 171

Wardlow, Gayle, xiv, 33, 77, 168
Waters, Muddy. *See* Muddy Waters
Weaver, Richard, x, xxii, xxiv, 41, 42, 95, 172
Williamson, Sonny Boy II, 99, 131
Wright, Richard, 19, 169, 172

www.ingramcontent.com/pod-product-compliance
Lightning Source LLC
Chambersburg PA
CBHW032025230426
43671CB00005B/201